JN062025

歯型と絵で教える英語発音

発音をはじめて教える人へ

Teaching English Pronunciation to Learners in Japan: Recipes for using a jaw model and illustrations

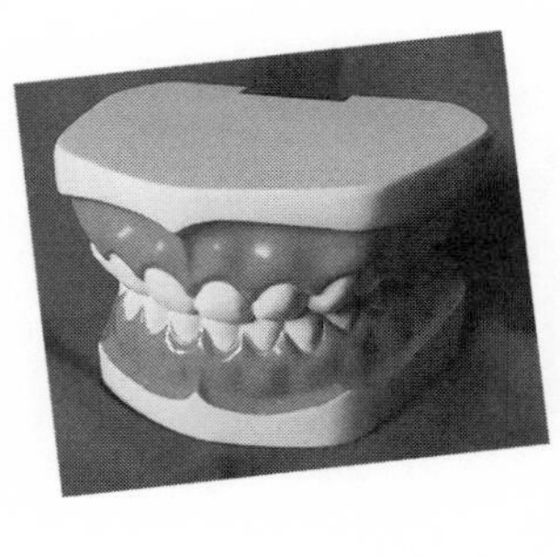

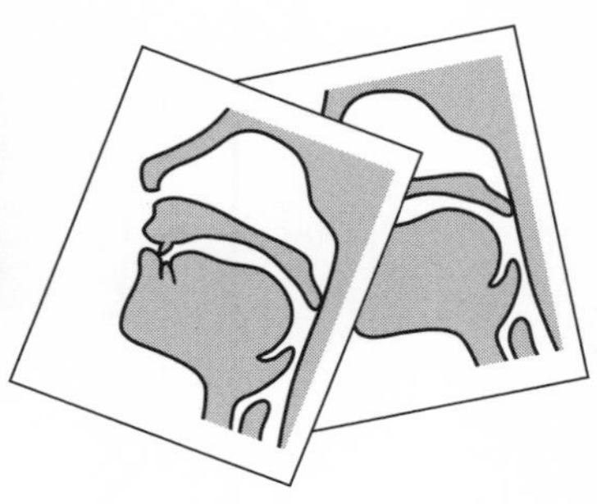

松坂ヒロシ
Matsusaka Hiroshi

開拓社

まえがき
Preface

R と L の発音の違いを学ぶのは簡単なのに，なぜ英語学習者たちはこのことで苦労しているのだろう—私は，この種のいくつかの疑問をずっと持ち続けてきました．このような単純な疑問が本書作成の基盤です．

Why do learners of English have such a hard time learning to pronounce /r/ and /l/ differently when it is so easy to learn to pronounce them?—I have had questions of this sort for years. My motivation to put together this book has come from simple questions like these.

発音学習は難しい，と思っている学習者は少なくありませんし，また，発音指導は時間がかかりすぎるので手をつけるのがこわい，と考えている指導者の方がたもいらっしゃいます．しかし，音声学の基本的知識を応用することによって発音学習をずっと楽なものに，そして楽しいものにさえすることができます．そこで，学習者を教える指導者の方がたに，音声学の分野の広がりのなかの，私が選んだ「使えるところ」をご紹介したいとの思いから，本を書くことにしました．当然，本書が扱うのは，英語のすべての音ではなく，多くの指導者が教えにくいと思っておられる音のみです．

Many learners think that learning pronunciation is difficult, and there are instructors of English who hesitate to begin to teach pronunciation because they think it would take too much time. Actually, pronunciation learning can be made far less difficult than people think—it can even be made a fun activity—by making use of a basic knowledge of phonetics. I thus decided to write a book to introduce to instructors of English some of the bits of English phonetics that I think can be put to good use for teaching pronunciation. Naturally, this book deals only with those sounds which many instructors think are difficult to teach, not with all the sounds of English.

本書は，現場での指導のアイディアを提供するためのものです．学術書ではありません．取り上げる音声事実はよく知られたものばかりです．事実を提示する際には，日本の英語学習者にとって理解しやすく，また役に立つような仕方で提示するよう努めました．音やその出し方の正確な描写はここでの私の目的ではありません．実際，掲載したイラストは，板書のご参考になるかと思い，手描きしました．生理音声学の教科書に掲載されるような図ではありません．他にも，学問的には厳密でない個所があると思います．本書の目的をご理解くださりお許しください．

This book is intended to present practical ideas, not academic discussion. The facts about English pronunciation taken up in this book are all well known. When I mention them, I try to do so in a way that makes them comprehensible and helpful to learners of English in Japan. Putting forward accurate descriptions of sounds and how they are articulated is not my purpose here. In fact, I have drawn the illustrations in this book by hand, in the hope that they may inspire instructors to draw illustrations on the board in the classroom themselves. They would not make it into textbooks of physiological phonetics. There may be other parts of this book that may be thought of as technically inaccurate, but I hope the reader will appreciate the aim of this book and forgive any inaccuracies.

本書は第 I 部と第 II 部に分かれています．第 I 部は，英語の発音指導をする以上これだけは押さえておいたほうがよいと私が考えている基本的項目をカバーしています．発音指導の経験の少ない指導者の方がたは，まずは第 I 部だけでもお読みください．第 II 部のほうは，より経験の多い指導者の方がたを意識して書きました．初級対象の発音指導には向かない内容があるかもしれませんが，発音の指導者はしばしばリスニングも教えなくてはなりませんから，細かい発音項目の知見を広げることは初級も含めさまざまのレベルの学習者のリスニング指導に役立つでしょう（初級ということばを私は単に「発音学習の初級」という意味で使っています）．

The book is divided into Part One and Part Two. Part One includes such basic items as I think all pronunciation instructors should know. Instructors without much experience are encouraged to read at least Part One for a start. Part Two is for more experienced instructors. You may find in Part Two discussion of details too advanced for beginning learners.

But instructors of pronunciation are often required to teach listening comprehension as well, and expanding knowledge about details of pronunciation will help them become better teachers of listening comprehension for learners at various levels, including the elementary level (using the word "elementary" here to refer to learners' pronunciation, not to their general English proficiency).

本書で扱うのは基本的には北米系の発音です．世界には多様な英語があるのだから，日本の学習者は日本的な英語発音をすればよいではないか，という立場もありますが，本書ではこの議論には踏み込まず，一定の規範に準拠した発音を重視することにしました．発音の規範についてさまざまの意見がありますが，ビデオ会議システムなどを使って人々が日常的に会話するようになり，音声認識テクノロジーの利用が広がっている今日，明瞭な発音が言語能力の重要な要素のひとつであることは，論を待たないと思います．

The pronunciation that I will be discussing in this book is basically North American-type pronunciation. There are TEFL experts who say that the world abounds in varieties of English and that there is thus nothing wrong with Japanese learners of English speaking English with a Japanese accent. Rather than going into a debate on this issue, I am attaching importance to teaching pronunciation in accordance with a certain phonetic norm. There are a wide range of opinions about the choice of the norm for pronunciation teaching, but one thing that I think is beyond dispute is that in this day and age, when people speak to each other, as a matter of everyday practice, by using devices like video teleconferencing systems, and also in view of the fact that use of speech recognition technology is widespread, clarity in pronunciation is one of the key factors of one's language proficiency.

説明には発音記号を使いましたが，発音記号を覚えて頂く必要はありません．学習者に覚えさせる必要もありません．発音記号は音の区別のために使うだけです．発音記号による表記をシンプルにしたかったので，強勢の記号は付しませんでした．発音記号は斜線（/ /）に挟んで提示します．言語学者たちの間には，斜線と角括弧（[ ]）をそれぞれ抽象概念としての音素と物理的な音との表示に使う慣習がありますが，本書の目的にかんがみ，巻末の付録をのぞいてこの区別はしないことにしました．[1)]

Phonetic symbols are used in this book, but you do not need to learn them. Nor do you need to make learners learn them. The symbols are used simply for the purpose of distinguishing between sounds in my discussion. Stress marks are not given, as I wanted to make the phonetic representations simple. Phonetic symbols are given between oblique strokes (/ /). There is a convention among linguists whereby strokes and square brackets ([ ]) are used to represent phonemes as abstractions and phones as actual sounds, respectively, but, in view of the purpose of this book, I have decided not to make this distinction, except in the appendix.[1)]

英語の説明のほうがよく理解できるという指導者もいらっしゃると思いますので，英語の説明を添えました．対訳ではありませんが，必要な情報は盛り込みました．

All parts of the book are presented in English as well for the benefit of some readers. The English is not necessarily a faithful translation, but it covers all the information that the book is intended to convey.

本書制作の出発点は，私が分担執筆した鈴木渉・西原哲雄編『小学校英語のためのスキルアップセミナー ― 理論と実践を往還する ―』（開拓社，2019）の第２章でした．理論や文献の紹介を目的とした第１章の「音声の理論」に対して，この第２章は「音声の実践」というタイトルの，発音指導のマニュアルです．この章を担当したときはスペースの制約のために内容を取捨選択しましたが，もっと余裕をもって同じ趣旨の本を執筆したいという私の希望を，開拓社の川田賢・出版部部長がかなえてくださいました．お礼のことばもありません．また，英文校閲をしてくださり私の英語を丁寧に直してくださった早稲田大学教授アントニー・P・ニューエル先生に深く感謝申し上げます．もしなおも残ってしまった英語の問題があれば，それらはすべて私の責任に帰するものです．

The preparation of this book goes back to the publication by Kaitakusha Publishing Co. in 2019 of a book on teaching English to elementary school pupils, to which I contributed Chapter 2. In contrast to its Chapter

1, whose purpose it was to introduce to the reader theoretical analyses and relevant literature in the field of phonetics, Chapter 2 was meant to be a manual for pronunciation teaching. Ever since finishing my work on it, I have wanted to write a full book on the same theme, for the amount of space in the chapter that I wrote obliged me to discard a great deal of material that I would otherwise have liked to include. I thank Mr. Kawata Masaru, Director, Editorial Department, Kaitakusha, for allowing me to fulfill this ambition. I would also like to express my appreciation to Professor Anthony P. Newell, Waseda University, who proofread and painstakingly corrected the English. If there are any residual problems with it, I of course hold myself responsible for all of them.

最後に，私はこれまで私が発音指導をさせて頂いた数多くの学習者の皆さんにお礼申し上げます．この方がたのおかげで，私は，学習者のかかえる多様な問題について広範な知識を得るに至りました．また，練習にはきちんと結果がついてくることにも気づかせて頂きました．基礎練習を徹底的にやった人は後で速く上達します．私が発音指導者として成長することができたとすれば，それは学習者の方がたのおかげです．ありがとうございました．

I wish to conclude these remarks by thanking the huge number of learners whom I had the pleasure of serving as a pronunciation coach. They helped me to acquire an extensive knowledge of the range of problems that learners face. They also made me realize that training pays off: Learners who do thorough training on the basics later improve quickly. If I can teach pronunciation any better now than I was able to at the beginning of my career, it is to all these learners that I owe my growth as a teacher.

松坂ヒロシ
Matsusaka Hiroshi

目 次
Contents

第 II 部 (Part Two)

本書において言及される小道具など
Teaching aids mentioned in this book

1. 歯型（第 1，2，6，8，9，13 章において言及）
(The jaw model (mentioned in Chapters 1, 2, 6, 8, 9, and 13))

本書では発音指導の道具としてしばしば歯磨き指導用の「顎模型」（図 0.1，図 0.2）に言及します．本書では「歯型」と呼ぶことにします．歯型は，特に子音の発音の指導に役立ちます．子音の発音を教える際には，舌が口のどの部分に触れるかを教えると学習者の理解が進みますが，歯型は舌の触れる場所を示すのに最適です．

A jaw model, as we shall call it in this book (Figure 0.1 and Figure 0.2), is commonly used in schools for toothbrush training, but it is also useful for

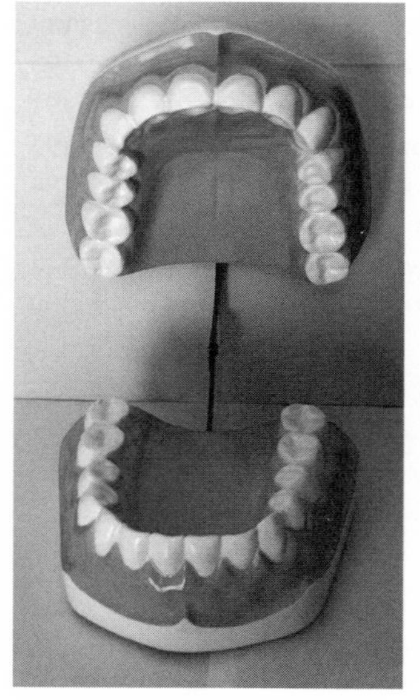

図 0.1　歯型（Jaw model）

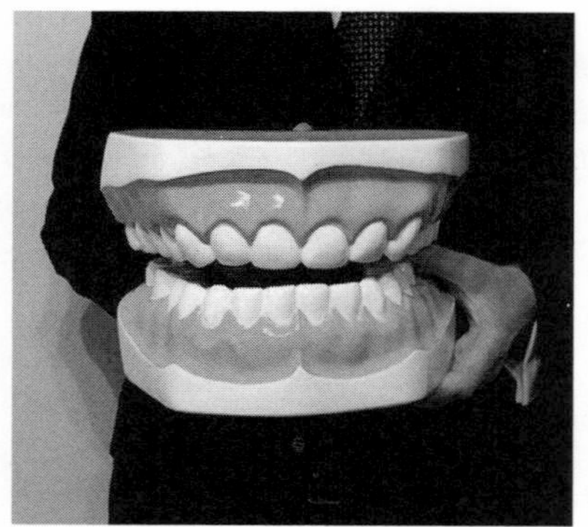

図 0.2　歯型を持ったところ
(Jaw model held by hand)

teaching sounds, especially consonants, as it is often the case that learners quickly learn how to articulate a consonant by learning what part(s) of the mouth the tongue should come into contact with when they say it.

2. 上の歯列弓の絵，またはその簡易版（第 1，2，5，6，13，15，17，18 章において言及）[1)]

(Illustration of the upper dental arch or a simplified version thereof (mentioned in Chapters 1, 2, 5, 6, 13, 15, 17, and 18)) [1)]

歯型がない場合は，上の歯列弓の絵（図 0.3）で代用できます．インターネットで「歯列弓」ということばで画像検索すると，いろいろの画像が得られます．学習者が歯列弓の意味を理解したあとでは，図 0.4 のような簡単な板書で事足りる場合もあります．図 0.4 の例では，舌先が触れる場所に印をつけました．

If a jaw model is unavailable, you can use an illustration of the upper dental arch (Figure 0.3) instead. You can obtain such illustrations on the Internet by putting words like “dental arch” or “dental arches” in the search box. If you are sure that learners have understood the meaning of the illustration, you can even draw a simplified illustration (Figure 0.4) on the board in class, for example, in lieu of a detailed one. Figure 0.4 is an example of the use of a mark to indicate where the tongue tip should be when saying a specific sound.

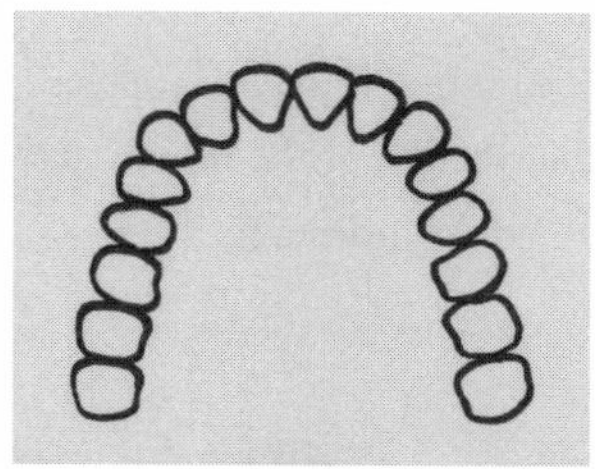

図 0.3　上の歯列弓の絵
(Upper dental arch)

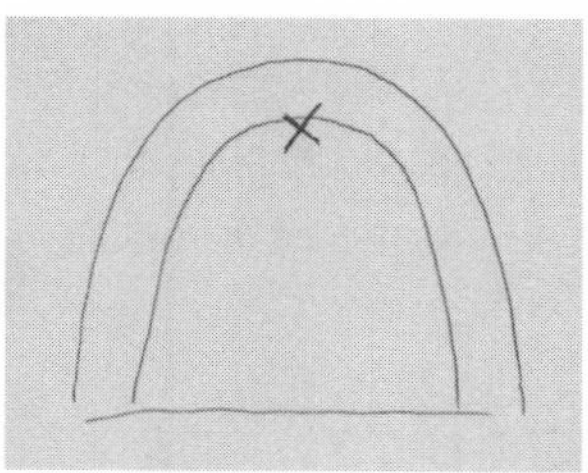

図 0.4　上の歯列弓を簡素化したイラスト
(Simplified illustration of the upper dental arch)

3. 口を横から見た断面図（第 1, 2, 4–7, 9, 11–14, 16, 18 章において言及）
(Median section of the mouth (mentioned in Chapters 1, 2, 4–7, 9, 11–14, 16, and 18))

この断面図（図 0.5）の使用は，発音指導上非常に有効な方法です．なめらかに描けるように日ごろから練習しておくとよいでしょう．学習者がこの図に慣れてくれば，図をさらに簡素化して，図 0.6 のようにその一部を描くだけにすることも可能です．

An illustration of a median section of the mouth (Figure 0.5) is extremely useful in teaching a range of different kinds of sounds. You should practice drawing it so that you can draw it with ease in the classroom. Once learners are accustomed to the illustration, you can focus on one part of the section and draw a simpler picture (Figure 0.6).

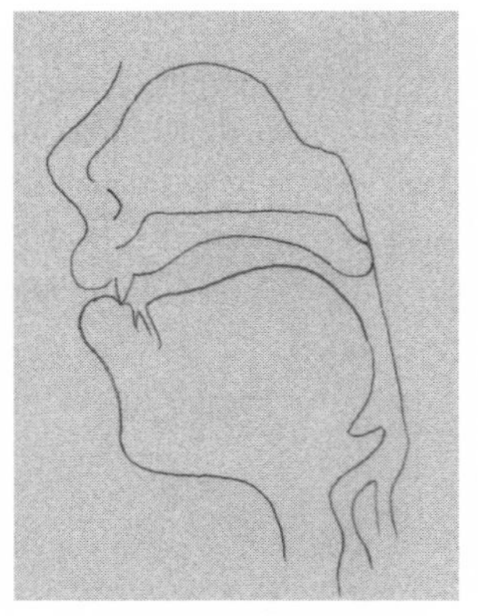

図 0.5　口の断面図
(Median section of the mouth)

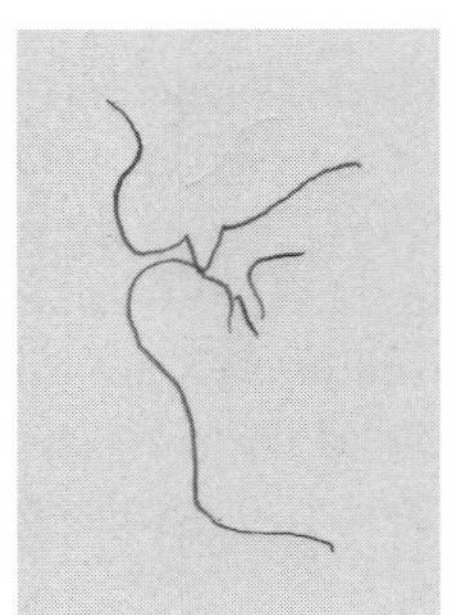

図 0.6　断面図の一部
(Median section of the mouth: partial illustration)

4. 発音のものさし（第 3，8，10 章において言及）
(Pronunciation scale (mentioned in Chapters 3, 8, and 10))

母音同士の関係をものさし上に示したものです（図 0.7）．英語の母音を教える際には，日本語の母音を基準にして，たとえば，英語のこの母音は日本語の X という母音とほぼ同じだとか，英語のこの母音は日本語の母音の Y と Z との間だとかいう説明をすると，学習者にとって英語の母音が把握しやすくなります．発音のものさしは，厚紙などで作っておいてもよいし，板書やパワーポイントで示しても結構です．

A simple scale (Figure 0.7) can show the relation between vowels. A good way to define a vowel for learners is to tell them that a specific English vowel is almost the same as the Japanese vowel X or it is between the Japanese vowels Y and Z, for example. You can (a) make a scale with cardboard and use that or (b) draw one on the board in the classroom or (c) show one in a PowerPoint slide.

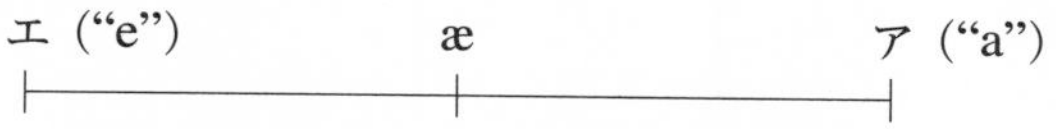

図 0.7　発音のものさしの例 (Example of a pronunciation scale)

発音のものさしは，母音を教えるときだけでなく，学習者の母音を評価するのにも使えます．学習者の出す音のおおよその位置をものさしの上で示し，もっとアに寄せるように，とか，もっとエに寄せるように，とかの指示を出すことができます．

The pronunciation scale is useful not only for teaching learners how vowels should be pronounced but also for assessing vowels produced by learners. Upon hearing a vowel produced by learners, the instructor can place it on the scale and, if learners should produce a vowel closer to either end of the scale, they can be told to do so.

ものさしを不必要に長くしないようご注意ください．ものさしが長すぎると，指導者はつい細かな差異を問題にして正確な母音を求めたくなりがちです．大事なことは，学習者が出す音がネイティブスピーカーの出す音とそっくりであるようにする，ということではありません．重要なのは，学習者が出す音が他の音とまぎらわしくないようにする，ということです．

One caveat that I would add is that you should avoid making the scale unnecessarily long, as a long scale may tempt the instructor to discuss fine differences and demand too much accuracy from learners when using the scale. The instructor should help learners produce vowels which would not be mistaken for other vowels rather than ask for vowels identical to those produced by native English speakers.

5. スプーン（第 1，4 章において言及）
（Spoon（mentioned in Chapters 1 and 4））

スプーンは /l/ の発音の指導に使えます．中央を低くした舌の形のイメージを学習者に説明するのに有効です．また，スプーンは学習者が上下の唇を近づけるのを防ぐのに使うことができます．すなわち，学習者は，/uː//ʊ/ の前の /h/ を発音するときに唇で不要なノイズを出しがちですが，スプーンによってこれを防ぐことができます．

A spoon may be used for teaching /l/. To help learners form an image of the shape of the tongue for the articulation of the sound, you can compare the shape of the tongue and that of a spoon and explain that the central part of the tongue should be low for articulating /l/. A spoon can also be used to prevent learners from making the upper and lower lips come too close to each other and creating noise. Learners tend to create unnecessary noise at the lips for saying /h/ when it is followed by /uː/ or /ʊ/, and a spoon may be useful for preventing this.

6. つまようじ（第 5 章において言及）
（Toothpick（mentioned in Chapter 5））

/s/ に対して /ʃ/ の発音の際の舌先の位置がやや後ろであることを示すために，つまようじで上の歯ぐきに触れることが有効である場合があります．

A toothpick may be used for teaching /ʃ/. As compared with /s/, /ʃ/ requires learners to hold the tongue tip some way toward the back. Having learners touch their upper teeth ridge with a toothpick may help them grasp the location of the teeth ridge and get a sense of where their tongue tip should be when they say /ʃ/.

7. 割り箸（第 2，5 章において言及）
（Chopstick (mentioned in Chapters 2 and 5)）

/θ/ /ð/ の発音の指導に使えます．舌先を上下の歯で軽くかむとこれらの子音が楽に発音できますが，このことを説明するのに割り箸が使えます（図 0.8）．また，前項で説明したつまようじの代わりに割り箸を使うこともできます．

A chopstick (or a pair of disposable chopsticks) may be used for teaching /θ/ and /ð/. It helps learners to lightly bite the tongue tip when they try to say these sounds, and a chopstick may be used to help them see how far toward the front the tongue tip should be for practicing these sounds (Figure 0.8). A chopstick may also be used in place of the toothpick mentioned in the previous paragraph.

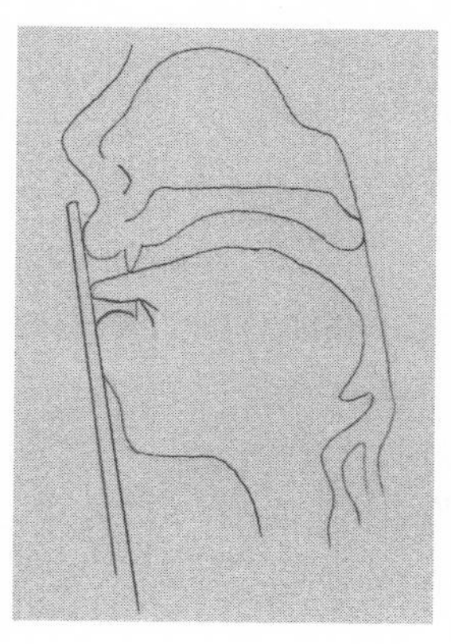

図 0.8　割り箸を使った /θ/ /ð/ の練習
(Use of a chopstick for practicing /θ/ and /ð/)

8. ホース（第 2 章において言及）
（Hosepipe (mentioned in Chapter 2)）

ホース（図 0.9）は，/θ/ と /s/ との違いを教える際に役立ちます．/θ/ と /s/ の周波数の高さの差を学習者に実感させるのに，ホースの一方から息を吹き込み，もう一方の端を指でつぶしてノイズを出すことができます．押さえ方によってするどい音やそうでない音を出すことができます．

A hosepipe (Figure 0.9) may be used for teaching the difference between /θ/ and /s/. For helping learners get the feel of the difference between /θ/ and /s/ in frequency, you can blow air into one end of the pipe and squeeze the other end with your fingers, creating high- and low-frequency noise.

図 0.9　ホース (Hosepipe)

9. 厚紙製の，口の開きを示すもの (第 8，9 章において言及)

(A board used for discussing the opening between the jaws (mentioned in Chapters 8 and 9))

アゴの開きが大きいか小さいかは英語の母音の発音の指導でしばしば重要なポイントとなります．開きを示すために厚紙で写真のようなものを作っておくと便利です (図 0.10，図 0.11)．下アゴ部分は別の板でできており，これがピンを軸にして動くようになっています．このような道具の代わりに，単にアゴの開きをホッチキスの絵のようなイラストで表すこともできます (図 0.12)．

The degree of the opening between the jaws is often an important topic in the discussion of the articulation of vowels. You may find a board made of cardboard like the one in the photographs (Figure 0.10 and Figure 0.11) very useful for showing learners how much the mouth should be open when saying a specific vowel. The photographs show a rectangular board, to which a separate piece of cardboard is attached to represent the lower jaw; the latter turns on a pin. If such a board is not available, you can show the opening of the mouth using a simple illustration that looks like a picture of a stapler (Figure 0.12).

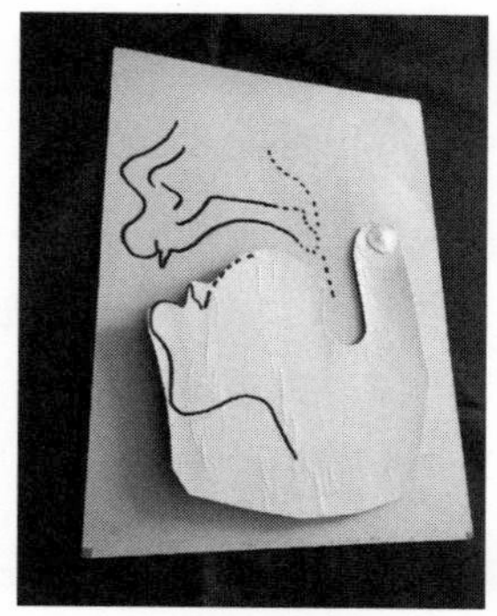

図 0.10 口の開きを示すボード (Board used to indicate the opening between the jaws)

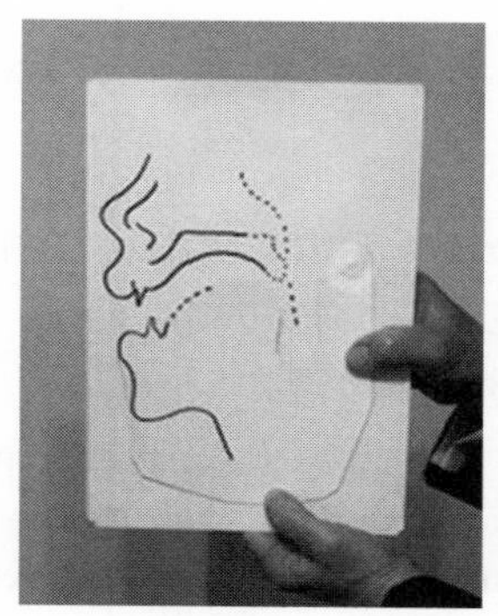

図 0.11 口の開きを示すボードを持って使っているところ (Board being used)

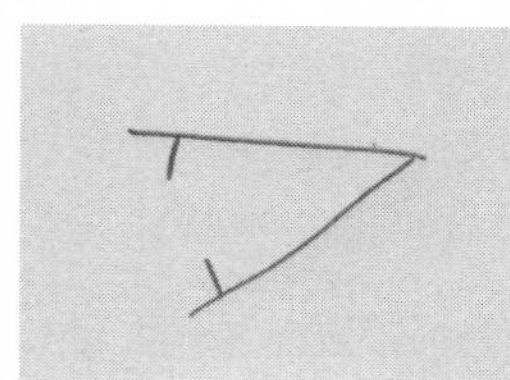

図 0.12 口の開きを示す絵 (Illustration showing the opening between the jaws)

10. 口の正面図（第 7，14 章において言及）

(Frontal illustration of the mouth (mentioned in Chapters 7 and 14))

口を正面から見た図（図 0.13）は，/w/ /nl/ /dl/ /tl/ の指導の際に役立ちます．

An illustration of a frontal view of the mouth (Figure 0.13) is useful for teaching /w/, /nl/, /dl/, and /tl/.

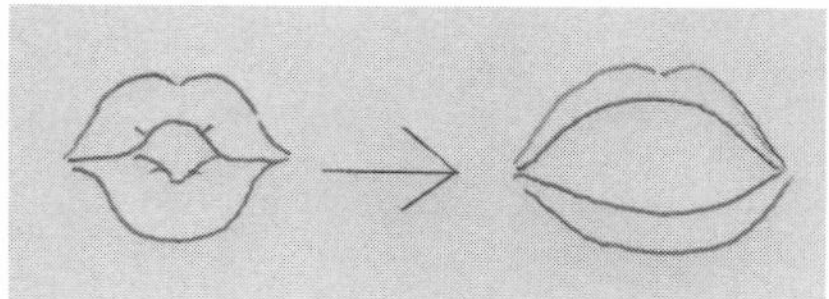

図 0.13 /w/ の発音の際の唇の動き (Movement of the lips in the articulation of /w/)

11. アクセント表示（第 19 章において言及）
(Representations of stress patterns (mentioned in Chapter 19))

アクセントを視覚的に表した図（図 0.14）．大きい四角が第一アクセント，中くらいの四角が第二アクセント，小さい四角がアクセントのないことを表します．

Stress patterns may be represented visually in a variety of ways. They are represented with squares in this book, a big one representing primary stress, a middle-sized one secondary stress, and a small square absence of stress (Figure 0.14).

□ □ □ □ □
in- -ter- -na- -tion- -al

図 0.14 アクセントの表示 (Representation of stress)

12. イントネーションの表示[2]（第 19 章において言及）
(Representations of intonation patterns (mentioned in Chapter 19))[2]

イントネーション，つまり声の上がり下がりを，楽譜のような形で表したもの（図 0.15）．上下の線は話し声の声域を表します．大きい丸が第一アクセントを，中くらいの丸が第二アクセントを，小さい点がアクセントのない拍をそれぞれ表します．

Intonation, namely ups and downs in pitch, is represented by what looks like a musical score, the line at the top and the line at the bottom indicating the speaking voice range (Figure 0.15). A big dot represents primary stress, a middle-sized one represents secondary stress, and a small one represents absence of stress.

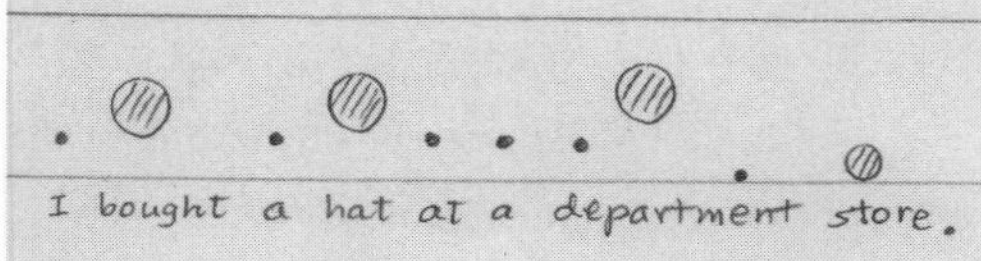

図 0.15 イントネーションの表示 (Representation of intonation)

第 I 部

Part One

第 1 章
R と L は教えやすい — /r/ /l/ の指導

たとえば right, light　　　　How to teach /r/ and /l/

1. /r/ の指導のポイント (How to teach /r/)

〈まずはここから (To begin with ...)〉

とても教えやすい項目です．まず /r/ から始めましょう．/r/ を教える際には，上の奥歯のすぐ内側の歯ぐきを左右同時になめるよう指導することが有効です．歯型を使い，両手の人差し指でその個所を示すとよいでしょう（図 1.1）．

This is a very easy item to teach. To teach /r/, tell learners to place the sides of their tongue against the upper teeth ridge at two spots at the same time: spots just inside the right and left back teeth. You can show the spots in question with your forefingers (Figure 1.1).

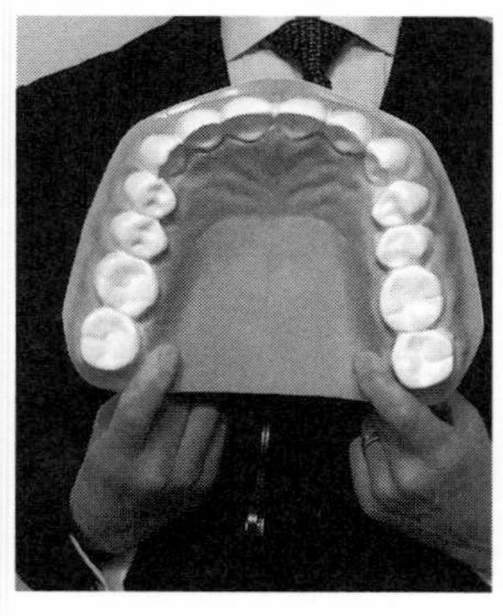

図 1.1　/r/ を言うときに舌が触れる場所；両手で示したところ (The spots on the teeth ridge that the tongue touches in the articulation of /r/—shown with both hands)

または，片手の指で同じ 2 個所を示すこともできます（図 1.2）．さらに，簡単な板書で示すこともできます（図 1.3）．印の場所を舌でなめるよう指示すればよいのです．

Or show the spots using your thumb and forefinger (Figure 1.2). Furthermore, you can convey the same information with a simple illustration like Figure 1.3 and tell learners to place the sides of their tongue against the upper teeth ridge at the two spots where the x marks are.

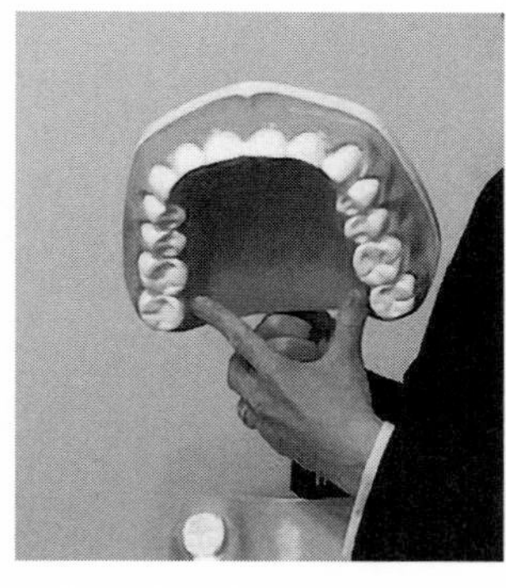

図 1.2　/r/ を言うときに舌が触れる場所；片手で示したところ（The spots on the teeth ridge that the tongue touches in the articulation of /r/ — shown with one hand）

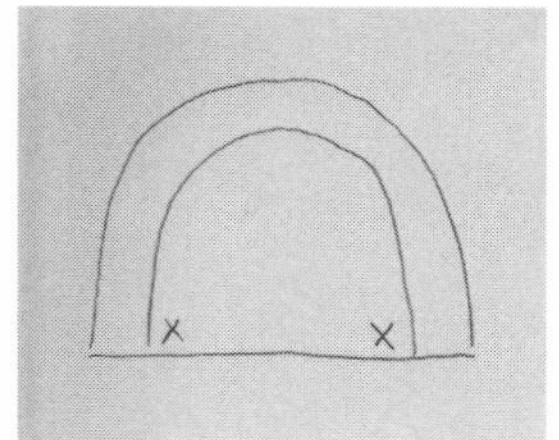

図 1.3　図 1.1，図 1.2 の情報を伝えるイラスト（Illustration conveying the same information as Figure 1.1 and Figure 1.2）

〈こんなときは（If you face a challenge ...)〉

学習者によっては /r/ の響きを十分出すことができず，単に「アー」のような音を出してしまいます．この場合は，(a) 口をもっと閉じ気味にすること，(b) 舌をもっと後ろに引くこと，の 2 点の注意を与えることで問題を解決できる可能性があります．

Some learners may fail to articulate /r/, and they may simply say something like "uh." In such a case, tell them (a) to close their mouth further and/or (b) to draw their tongue further toward the back.

2. /l/ の指導のポイント (How to teach /l/)

〈まずはここから (To begin with ...)〉

/l/ を教える際には，舌先で上の前歯のすぐ後ろ，または前歯のはえぎわをなめるよう指導することが有効です（図 1.4）．同じ情報を図 1.5，図 1.6 のような図を板書することによって説明することもできます．

Have learners lick a spot just behind the upper front teeth or a spot where the upper teeth ridge borders on the upper front teeth (see Figure 1.4). You can convey the same information by drawing pictures like Figure 1.5 and Figure 1.6 on the board in the classroom.

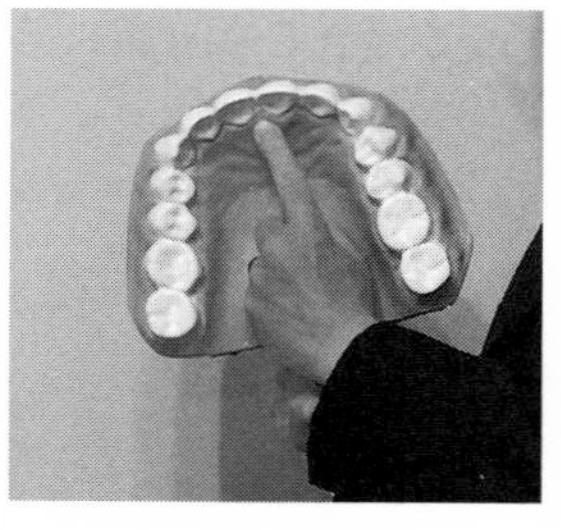

図 1.4 /l/ を言うときに舌が触れる場所 (The spot on the teeth ridge that the tongue touches in the articulation of /l/)

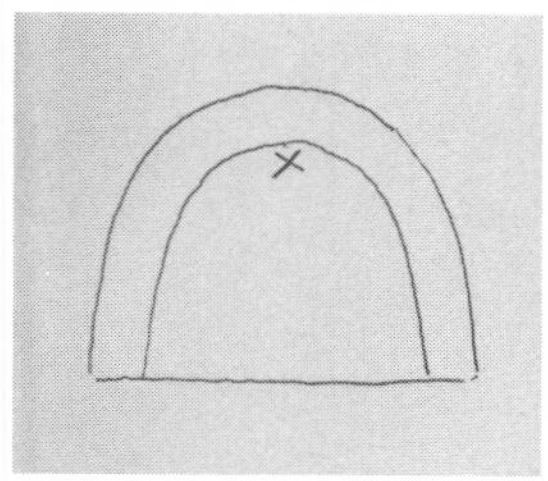

図 1.5 図 1.4 の情報を伝えるイラスト (Illustration conveying the same information as Figure 1.4)

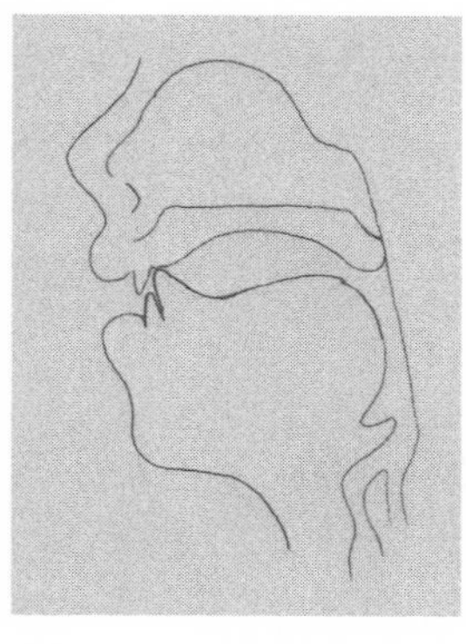

図 1.6　/l/ の発音：横から見たところ (Median section of the mouth: articulation of /l/)

〈こんなときは (If you face a challenge ...)〉

学習者によっては，舌が平らになってしまって，/l/ の響きが出ないこともあります（図 1.7）．この場合，舌先をもっととがらせるように指導したり，舌の中央を低くして舌がスプーンのような形（図 1.8）になるよう指導したりすると問題が解決することもあります．図 1.8 の写真のスプーンは先をややとがらせるために加工したものですが，普通のスプーンを使った説明でもポイントは伝わるでしょう．

Some learners may make their tongue flat and fail to articulate /l/ (Figure 1.7). In such a case, tell them to lower the center of their tongue so that the tongue assumes a spoon-like shape. The spoon in Figure 1.8 has been carved to make its tip narrower, but, if you explain using an ordinary spoon, most learners will still get the point.

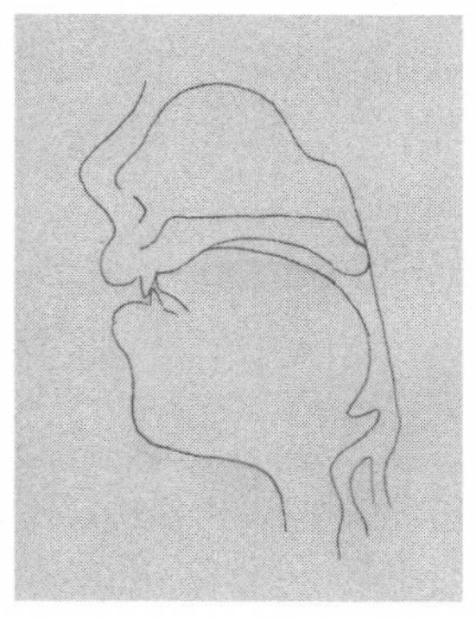

図 1.7　/l/ を言おうとしているところ：舌が平らになりすぎている (Median section of the mouth: articulation of /l/ attempted unsuccessfully with the tongue too flat)

図 1.8 スプーン：/l/ の舌の形の説明に役立つ
(Spoon: useful for showing the shape of the tongue for saying /l/)

もうひとつのよくある問題は，別の子音の前か単語の最後に来る /l/ を言う際（たとえば help や bell の場合），唇を丸くする，ということです．この問題の原因は，日本語のルとの連想です．ひとつの解決法は，学習者に対してこのような場所に現れる /l/ を言うときには口をやや開けて唇をリラックスせよと言うことです．

Another common problem is that learners often round their lips when saying /l/ if the sound precedes another consonant or is at the end of a word, as in *help* and *bell*. The cause of this problem is that they associate /l/ with the Japanese syllable "ru," which requires lip rounding. One possible solution to this is to tell learners to slightly open their mouth and relax their lips when saying /l/ in these phonetic environments.

3. /r/ と /l/ とラ行子音 (English /r/, English /l/, and Japanese /r/)

いま学習者の頭の中での /l/ とルとの結びつきについて述べましたが，一般に，学習者は，/r/ や /l/ を出そうとして，日本語のラ行子音のアタマの音を出しがちです．実際には，ラ行子音の場合，舌先は口の天井に触れるので，舌の形は /r/ のそれとは異なります．また，ラ行子音の場合，舌先が触れる位置は口の天井の奥のほう（図 1.9 参照）なので，舌の形は /l/ のそれとも異なります．

I have just mentioned the link between /l/ and "ru" in learners' minds. In general, learners, when attempting to articulate /r/ or /l/, are liable to produce the Japanese /r/, namely the consonant at the beginning of the Japanese syllables "ra," "ri," "ru," "re," and "ro." This Japanese consonant is different from the English /r/ in that, when the former is said, the tip of the tongue touches the roof of the mouth. The Japanese /r/ is different from /l/, too, in that the place of contact between the roof of the mouth and the tip of the tongue when the Japanese /r/ is said is toward the back (Figure 1.9), whereas /l/ requires the place of contact to be very close to the front teeth.

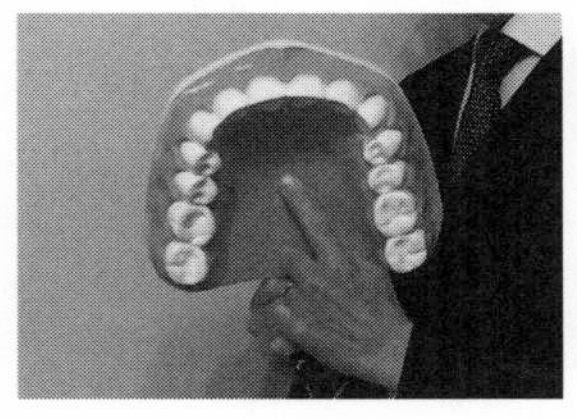

図 1.9　ラ行子音を言うときに舌が触れる場所 (The spot on the roof of the mouth that the tongue touches in the articulation of the Japanese /r/)

/r/ と /l/ の違いについて，学習者のうちには，「/r/ も /l/ もラ行子音とほとんど同じであり，ただ舌が口の天井に触れないか触れるかだけが両者の違い」(図 1.10) であると誤解している人がいます．

Some learners mistakenly think that both /r/ and /l/ are almost the same sound as the Japanese /r/ and that the only difference between the English /r/ and the English /l/ is that the tongue does not touch the roof of the mouth for /r/ but does for /l/ (Figure1.10).

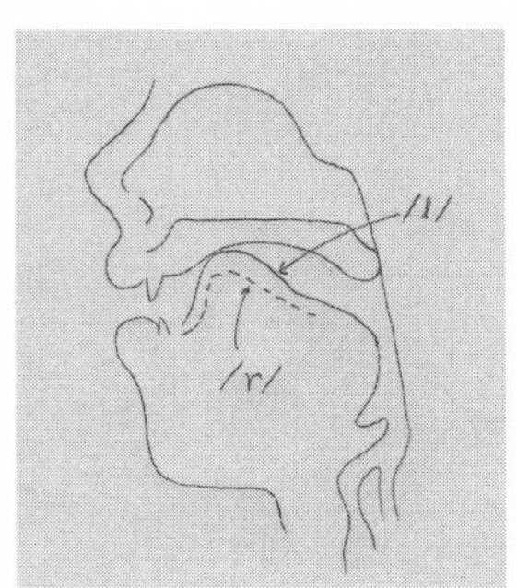

図 1.10　日本の一部の学習者の誤った認識のなかでの r/l の差 (/r/ and /l/ as perceived incorrectly by some learners)

これは舌が触れる位置のことを無視した認識です．この認識は改める必要があります．触れないか触れるかの差があるということは，「舌先」だけに着目した場合には正しいですが，触れるか触れないかの差が口の天井の同じ位置で生じているのではありません．/r/ と /l/ の指導に当たっては，舌がどこに触れるかをしっかり教えてください．

This perception is wrong because it does not take the place of contact into account. While it is true that the tip of the tongue touches the roof of the mouth for /l/ and not for /r/, it is wrong to assume that the difference between the two sounds in question concerns what happens at the same spot on the roof of the mouth. When you teach /r/ and /l/, you should make sure that learners understand what part of the roof of the mouth the tongue touches in the articulation of those sounds.

4. 練習のための言語材料 (Materials for practice)

下線部に注意して発音するよう指示してください.

Make learners pay attention to the underlined part(s) of each item.

単語

(1) right (2) rain (3) room (4) orange
(5) correct（正しい） (6) light（光，軽い） (7) lead（導く）
(8) late（遅い） (9) like (10) believe（信じる）

フレーズ

(1) red coat（赤いコート）
(2) heavy rain（激しい雨）
(3) long list（長いリスト）
(4) a lot of rain（たくさんの雨）

センテンス

(1) I remember it was raining on Monday.
（月曜は雨だったことを私は覚えている.）
(2) Linda likes lemonade.（リンダ＝女性の名＝はレモネードが好きだ.）
(3) The river is really long.（その川は本当に長い.）

会話

A: I think I'll have orange juice. How about you?
（オレンジジュースにしようかな．あなたは？）
B: I'll have lemonade.（レモネードにする.）

A:　You always have lemonade. You really like it, don't you?
　(いつもレモネードだね．本当に好きなんだね．)

B:　Yes, I do. I love it. But I like orange juice, too.
　(うん．大好き．でもオレンジジュースも好きですよ．)

下線のない箇所にも /l/ がありますが，下線部に特に集中して練習させてください．

There are instances of /l/ which are not underlined, but focus on the underlined /l/ and /r/.)

5．アクティビティー見本 (Idea for an activity)

「私を野球に連れてって」(Take me out to the ball game)

イラストを使って，学習者同士，または指導者と学習者で，会話を行ってください．例として，次のようなやりとりが考えられます．

Engage learners in a conversation with each other or with you. Possible exchanges are as follows.

A:　At Corner X, which way do you want to go?
　(X の角でどちらに行きたいですか？)

B:　I want to go to the right [go to the left; go straight].
　(右に［左に／まっすぐ］) 行きたいです．)

.....

A:　At corner Y, should you go straight?
　(Y の角であなたはまっすぐ行くべきですか？)

B:　No. I should turn right.
　(いえ，右に曲がるべきです．)

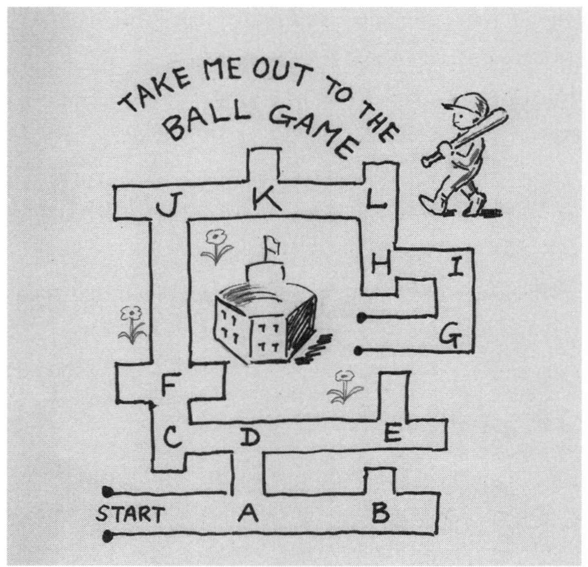

ここでの焦点は /r/ /l/ です．学習者の発音に問題があったら，次のように対応してください．（1）活動が終わってから，明示的に指導する．（2）活動の最中であれば，リキャストにより指導する（会話の流れをそこなわず，学習者の言葉を，誤りを正したうえで投げ返す；下の例参照）．

The focus here is on /r/ and /l/. If learners' pronunciation is problematical, do the following: (1) provide explicit instruction after the activity; (2) provide recasts (the instructor reformulates learners' utterances, with mistakes corrected, while maintaining the flow of the communication—see the example below) during the activity.

Learner: I should turn /laɪt/.

Instructor (*providing a recast*): Oh, you should turn /raɪt/. OK.

第2章

THは，ゆるい音として教える―/θ/ /ð/の指導

たとえば <u>th</u>ank，<u>th</u>is

How to teach /θ/ and /ð/

1. /θ/の指導のポイント (How to teach /θ/)

〈まずはここから (To begin with ...)〉

thank，think などの単語のアタマの音は，/θ/ という記号で表します．/θ/ を教える際には，舌先を上下の前歯の間に挟み，舌先をゆるくかんで息を出すように指導することが有効です．このことを板書で示したり（図 2.1），歯型を使って上の前歯に舌が当たっていることを示したりするとよいでしょう（図 2.2）．さらに，より簡単な板書で示すこともできます（図 2.3）．印の場所に舌を触れさせるよう指導すればよいのです．

The phonetic symbol for the consonant at the beginning of words like *thank* and *think* is /θ/. When teaching this sound, have learners lightly bite the tongue tip with their upper and lower front teeth and breathe out. You can show the tongue position by drawing an illustration on the board in the classroom (Figure 2.1) or by using a jaw model (Figure 2.2). Furthermore, you can convey the same information with a simpler illustration

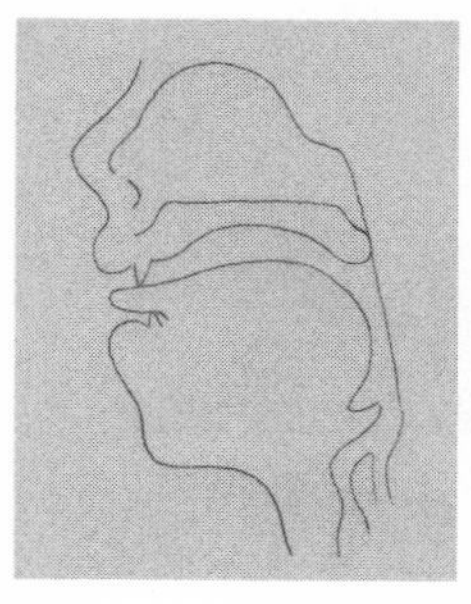

図 2.1 /θ/ の発音 (Articulation of /θ/)

like Figure 2.3 and tell learners to make the tongue touch the upper front teeth where the x mark is.

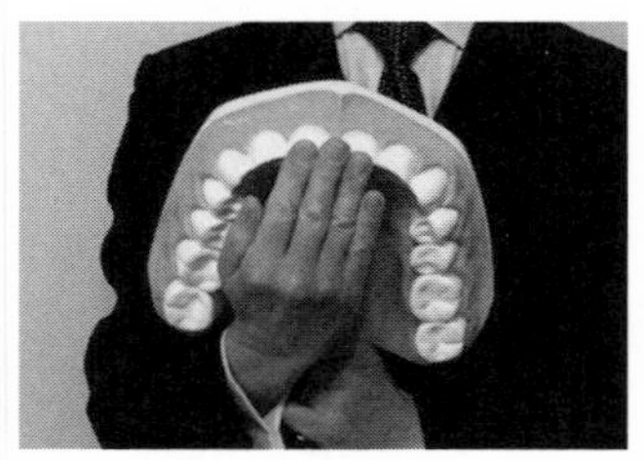

図 2.2 /θ/ の発音
(Articulation of /θ/)

図 2.3 図 2.2 の情報を伝えるイラスト
(Illustration conveying the same information as Figure 2.2)

/θ/ の指導で大事なことは，/s/ と /θ/ が異なることを学習者に感じてもらうことです．/s/ が周波数の高い，するどい音であるのに対し，/θ/ は周波数の低い，するどさのない，ゆるい音（私はこれを「間の抜けた音」と呼んでいます）です．私はこの事実を利用して，ホースを使って両方の音の響きを教えることがあります．ホースの一方の切り口から息を吹き込み，他の切り口を手でつぶすと（図 2.4），息はつぶれた切り口を通るときにノイズを作ります．切り口そのものをつぶすより，切り口から 1 センチほど離れた場所をつぶしたほうがよく聞こえるノイズが出ます（図 2.5）．押さえ方が強いとノイズはするどい音となり，押さえた手を多少ゆるめるとノイズはするどく

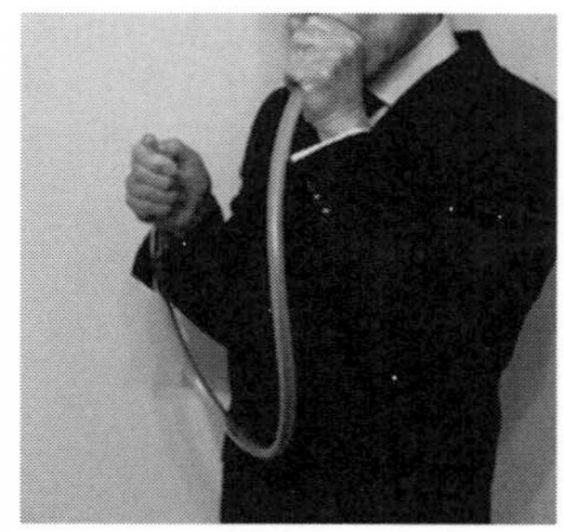

図 2.4 ホース (Hosepipe)

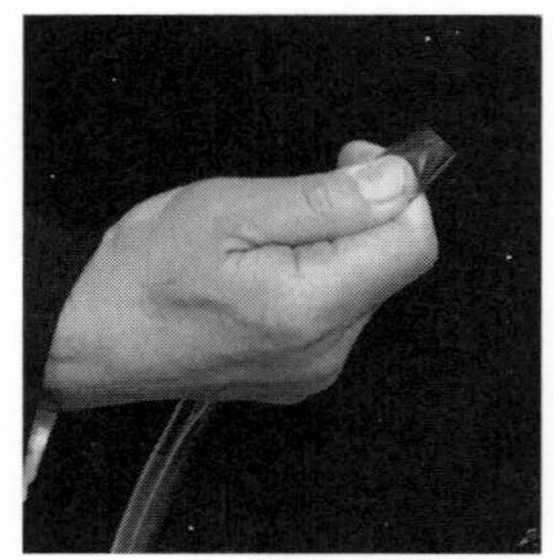

図 2.5 ホースの先のつぶし方
(How to squeeze the hosepipe)

ない「フー」というような音となります．するどい音とするどくない音との響きの違いを学習者に感じさせ，/s/ よりもするどくない音を出すように指導すれば，学習者は /s/ とは異なる /θ/ を出してくれる可能性があります．

One important point to remember when teaching /θ/ is that you should help learners get the feel of the difference between the quality of /θ/ and that of /s/: /θ/ and /s/ are a low- and a high-frequency sound, respectively. While /s/ is a sharp, hissing sound, /θ/ is a low-frequency sound which sounds flat, as if it lacked energy. I take advantage of the difference between these two sounds in frequency and teach them using a hosepipe. You can blow air into a pipe at one end of it while squeezing the other end with your hand, producing noise (Figure 2.4—it is best to squeeze the hosepipe about a centimeter away from its very end, as in Figure 2.5). If you squeeze the end hard, you can produce a sharp sound; if you loosen your grip, you will produce a less sharp sound which is like a whispered "hoo." After getting the feel of the difference between a sharp and a not-so-sharp sound, learners may be able to aim at the quality of /θ/ with more ease.

〈こんなときは (If you face a challenge ...)〉

学習者によっては，舌先をかんでいるつもりだと本人が言っていても，指導者の耳に /θ/ が聞こえないことがあります．この原因は，多くの場合，(a) かみかたが強すぎて息が外に出て行くのが妨げられているか，(b) 舌の形に問題があって /θ/ と同時に /s/ の音が出ているか，である可能性が高いです．このような学習者に対しては，舌先が確実に口の外まで出るように，舌先で指をなめたり（図 2.6），割り箸などをなめたり（図 2.7）するよう勧めることが有効である場合があります．

Some learners cannot produce /θ/ even though they claim they are biting their tongue tip. In many cases the cause of this problem is either (a) that the learners bite the tongue tip so hard that air is not pushed out of their mouth smoothly or (b) that the shape of their tongue is not right and they produce /s/ as well as /θ/. I tell such learners to stick out their tongue far enough to be able to lick their finger (Figure 2.6) or a chopstick (Figure 2.7) held against their lips.

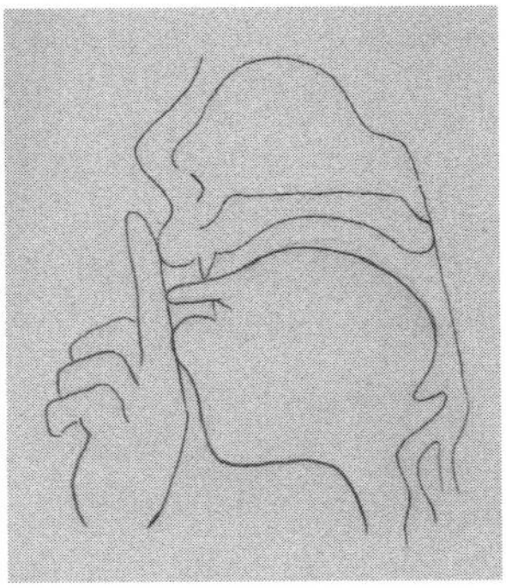

図 2.6　指をなめて /θ/ を練習
(Practicing /θ/ by licking a finger)

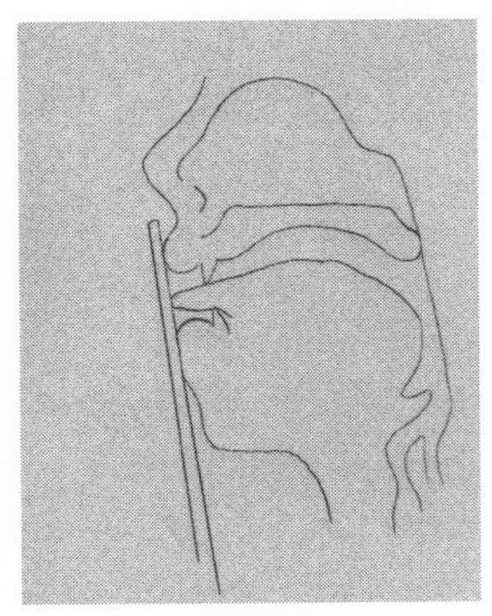

図 2.7　割り箸をなめて /θ/ を練習
(Practicing /θ/ by licking a chopstick)

舌先を軽くかむ指導法は日本で広く行われていますが，/θ/ の音は，(a) 舌先をかむだけでなく，(b) 舌先を上の前歯の先につけても（図 2.8），また，(c) 舌先を上の前歯の裏につけても（図 2.9），発音することができます．

Having learners lightly bite their tongue tip is a common way of teaching /θ/ in Japan. However, one can articulate /θ/ not only by (a) biting the tongue tip but also by (b) putting the tongue tip at the tip of the upper front teeth (Figure 2.8) or by (c) putting the tongue tip on the back of the upper front teeth (Figure 2.9).

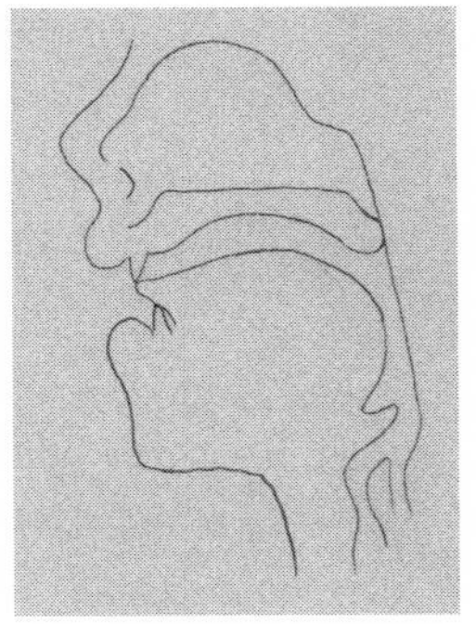

図 2.8　舌先が歯先に触れている
(The tongue tip on the tip of the upper front teeth)

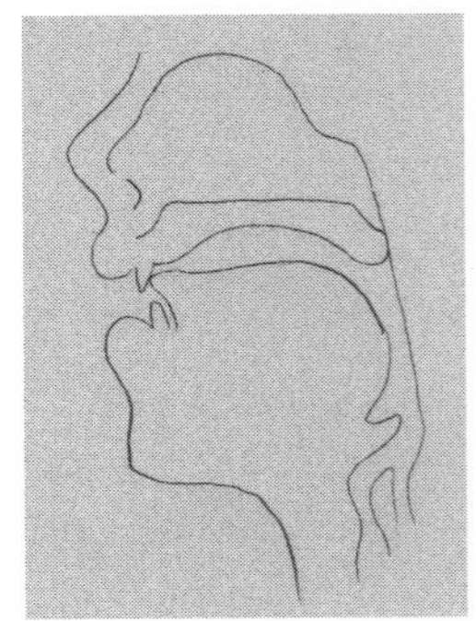

図 2.9　舌先が歯裏に触れている
(The tongue tip on the back of the upper front teeth)

上記（b）や（c）の方法のほうが（a）の方法よりも /θ/ を能率よく発音できると言えます．それは，（b）や（c）の方法のほうが舌の動きを小さくすることができるからです．しかし（b）や（c）には指導者の立場からすると欠点があります．学習者は，舌を歯先なり歯の裏なりに触れさせながら，同時に，舌の一部を歯ぐきに近づけてしまうことがあります（図 2.10）．こうすると，舌と歯ぐきとの間のすきまが狭くなり，/s/ の音が出てしまいます．

There is a sense in which (b) and (c) are more efficient ways of articulating /θ/ than (a), because the tongue makes smaller movements in (b) and (c). However, from the instructor's point of view, (b) and (c) have a demerit: When doing either of them, learners may unwittingly get their tongue close to the teeth ridge, allowing the narrow space between the tongue and the ridge to produce /s/ (Figure 2.10).

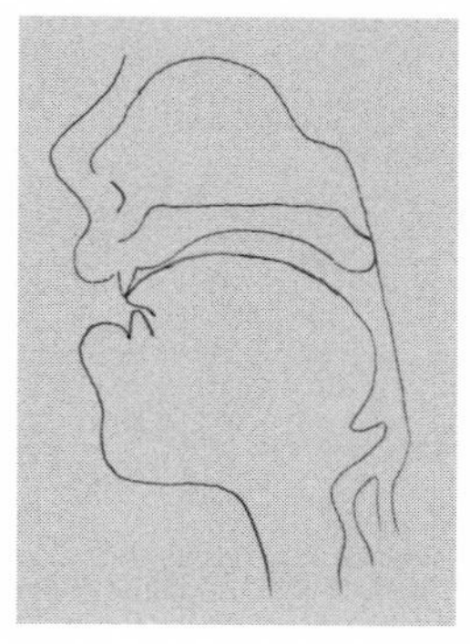

図 2.10　舌が平らになり /s/ の音が出る
(/s/ produced because the tongue is flat)

この問題を避けるため，私は図 2.1，図 2.2，図 2.3 に示した（a）の教え方で /θ/ を教えることにしています．（b）や（c）のほうが能率がよいと前述しましたが，私の経験では，（a）の方法で習った学習者も英語が速く話せるようになると自然に（b）や（c）の方法をとるようになって行くようです．そこで，確実に正しい音が出る（a）の方法で教え，あとは学習者が自然にもっと能率のよい方法を身につけるのを待つほうがよいと思います．

In order to avoid this potential problem I tell learners to do item (a) above when teaching /θ/. It is my observation that learners who have learned to do (a) will begin to do (b) or (c) when they have learned to speak fast. Thus, it is best in my opinion to teach (a) and just wait for learners to acquire more efficient ways of saying /θ/ later, without being taught.

2. /ð/ の指導のポイント (How to teach /ð/)

〈まずはここから (To begin with ...)〉

this（これ），that（あれ）などの単語のアタマの音は，/ð/ という記号で表します．/ð/ の音は，前のセクションで取り上げた /θ/ と，ある一点を除いて同じです．その一点とは，/θ/ と異なり，/ð/ は声を出して発音するということです．/θ/ のほうは，声を伴わない，無声音，いわばささやきの音です．[1)]

The phonetic symbol for the sound that appears at the beginning of words like *this* and *that* is /ð/. It is different from /θ/ in one respect only: Unlike /θ/, which is a voiceless, whispered sound,[1)] /ð/ is voiced.

〈こんなときは ... (If you face a challenge ...)〉

声を伴う音 /ð/ と声を伴わないささやきの音の /θ/ との区別が学習者にとって理解しにくい場合，のどに指を当てながら発音させる（図 2.11）とよいでしょう．声を伴う音 /ð/ を出しているとき，声帯のふるえを指で感ずることができます．声を伴わない音 /θ/ を出しているとき，ふるえは感じません．

If learners have difficulty understanding the difference between voiced and voiceless sounds, you may want to tell them to put some fingers on their throat (Figure 2.11). Learners can feel the vibration of the vocal cords on their fingers when saying /ð/, which is a voiced sound. They feel no vibration when saying the voiceless /θ/.

普通の声とささやき声の区別を知っていると，/ð/ や /θ/ 以外の音について学ぶ際にも役立ちます．なぜなら，声の有無以外には差がない，という音のペアがいろいろあり，ひとつのペアの片方の音をマスターするともう片方の音が学びやすくなるからです．

If learners are familiar with the distinction between an ordinary voice and a whisper, they can also learn about sounds other than /ð/ and /θ/ easily. There are various pairs of sounds in which the only difference between the two sounds is presence or absence of voice, and, if learners master one of the sounds in a pair, the other one will be easy to learn.

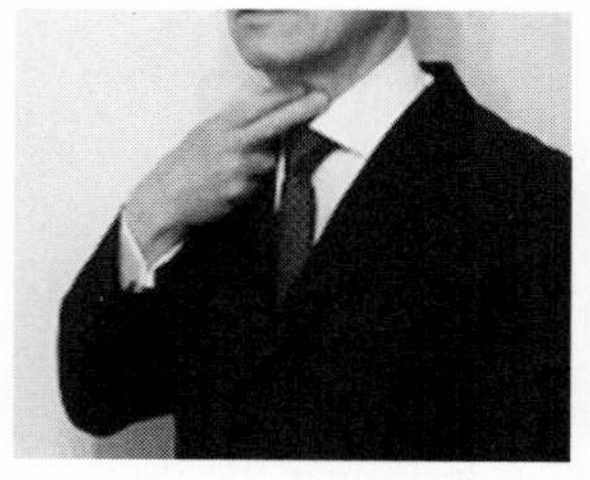

図 2.11　のどに指を当てて声が出ているかチェック（Putting fingers on the throat to check the production of voice）

/θ/ のところで，舌先を「ゆるくかむ」ということを述べました．これは大事なことです．きつくかむと息の流れが止まってしまいます．実際，学習者は，/ð/ の練習のときに舌を強くかみすぎて，歯と舌とで息をいったんせきとめてしまい，ダ，デ，ドのアタマの音に似た音を出すことがあります．[2)] このトラブルが起きたら，口をもっとリラックスさせてかみかたをゆるくするように指導する必要があります．

I said that, when saying /θ/, learners should bite their tongue tip *lightly*. This is an important caveat because, by biting the tongue tip *hard*, learners may stop the flow of air out of the mouth. In fact, learners may bite their tongue tip too hard when attempting to say /ð/, producing instead a sound like the sound at the beginning of the Japanese syllables "da," "de," and "do."[2)] When this problem arises, tell them to relax their mouth and make the bite looser.

3.　練習のための言語材料 (Materials for practice)

下線部に注意して発音するよう指示してください．

Make learners pay attention to the underlined part(s) of each item.

単語

(1) <u>th</u>ank（感謝する）　(2) <u>th</u>ink（考える）　(3) <u>th</u>ird　(4) too<u>th</u>（歯＝単数形）
(5) tee<u>th</u>（歯＝複数形）　(6) <u>th</u>is　(7) <u>th</u>ese　(8) <u>th</u>at
(9) <u>th</u>ose　(10) wi<u>th</u>

フレーズ

(1) thank you (2) thin paper (薄い紙)

(3) this book (4) stop and think (立ち止まって考える)

センテンス

(1) I think he is sick. (彼は病気だと私は思う.)

(2) They all like this cake. (彼らは皆このケーキが好きだ.)

(3) The book was this thick. (その本はこれくらいの厚みだった.)

会話

A: Are these notebooks yours? They were on that desk near the door.
(これらのノートはあなたのですか? ドア近くのあの机の上にあったんですけど.)

B: No. They're not mine. I think you should leave them there.
(いや, 私のではありません. そこに置いておいたほうがいいと思いますよ.)

A: OK. I'll put them back then. (分かりました. 戻しておきます.)

B: I'm sure somebody will come back to this classroom to pick them up.
(きっと誰かがこの教室に取りに戻って来ますよ.)

4. アクティビティー見本 (Idea for an activity)

「歌のレッスンのスケジュール」 (Singing lesson schedule)

声楽の先生が, 個人レッスンのスケジュールについて助手と話をしている, という想定で, 学習者同士, または指導者と学習者で, 声楽の先生や助手になったつもりで会話を行ってください. 例として, 次のようなやりとりが考えられます.

Assuming that a singing teacher and his/her assistant are talking about a schedule for private lessons, engage learners in a role-playing conversation with each other or with you. One possible exchange is as follows.

Singing teacher: When is Alice coming for a lesson?
(アリスはいつレッスンに来ますか?)

Assistant: She is coming at three o'clock on July twenty-third.
(彼女は 7 月 23 日 3 時に来ます.)

	3:00 p.m.	4:30 p.m.
July 3	Steve	Tom
July 13	Helen	Emily
July 23	Alice	Lucy
July 30	John	Ellen
July 31	Richard	Sue

ここでの焦点は /θ/ です．学習者の発音に問題があったら，次のように対応してください．(1) 活動が終わってから，明示的に指導する．(2) 活動の最中であれば，リキャスト (p. 10 参照) により指導する．

The focus here is on /θ/. If learners' pronunciation is problematical, do the following: (1) provide explicit instruction after the activity; (2) provide recasts (see p. 10) during the activity.

第 3 章

Apple の音はものさしを使って —/æ/ の指導

たとえば apple　How to teach /æ/

1. /æ/ の指導のポイント (How to teach /æ/)

〈まずはここから (To begin with ...)〉

apple (リンゴ), back (後ろ), hat (帽子) などに出て来る母音は /æ/ で表します.「Apple の音」などと名前をつけて教えている指導者もいらっしゃるようです. この音は, 日本語のエと日本語のアとの中間の音であると教えると分かりやすいと思います. この音を教えるときには, 図 3.1 のような発音のものさしを使うとよいでしょう.「本書において言及される小道具など」に書いた通り, 発音のものさしは黒板に簡単に書くことができます. 指導者が発音のものさしにそって指やポインターを動かしながら声を出し, アからエへ音をゆっくり変化させ, 逆にエからアへ変化させるとよいでしょう. 途中, /æ/ の地点を通るとき, いったん音の変化を止めて /æ/ を学習者に何秒か聞かせて音を覚えさせるとよいでしょう.

The vowel in words like *apple*, *back*, and *hat* is /æ/, which may be best explained to learners as a sound between the Japanese vowels "e" and "a." A pronunciation scale as in Figure 3.1 will be useful for teaching this sound. As I said in the section on teaching aids, a pronunciation scale is easy to draw on the board in class. When you teach /æ/, you can say "a" and gradually change it "e," moving a pointer or your finger along the scale. Then do it the other way, this time going from "e" to "a." When you pass the point for /æ/, spend a few seconds saying this sound to let learners hear it and remember it.

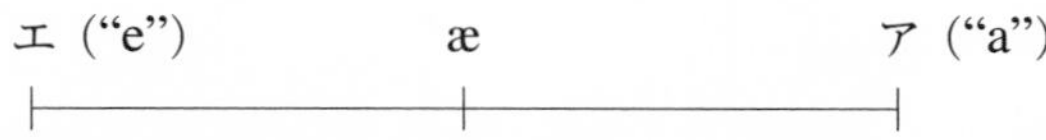

図 3.1　エからアに至る発音のものさし（Scale ranging between the Japanese “e” and “a” vowels）

/æ/ を教えるときに，「口でアと言いながら舌でエと言いなさい」とか，「口でエと言いながら舌でアと言いなさい」とかの指示が行われることがよくあるようです．いずれの指示も学習者が /æ/ に到達するのを助けるかもしれません．ただ，こうした指導は出発点としては効果的かもしれませんが，指導者は，学習者によく音に触れさせ，またよく練習をさせて，なるべく早く /æ/ がアでもエでもない独自の音であることを理解させるよう努めるべきです．

One way of teaching /æ/ that seems to be popular among some instructors is to tell learners that they should say the Japanese vowel “a” with their mouth except that they should say the Japanese vowel “e” with their tongue or to tell them that they should say “e” with their mouth except that they should say “a” with their tongue. These instructions may help learners to grasp what /æ/ is like. But, while comments of this sort may be effective in providing learners with a starting point, you should help them realize as soon as possible, through exposure and practice, that /æ/ is a sound of its own, not the same as “a” or “e.”

〈こんなときは (If you face a challenge ...)〉

上記の方法で学習者にうまく発音のしかたを伝えられない場合，「ナヤ」（納屋）という日本語を非常にゆっくり言うと，ナとヤとのちょうど境目のところにこの英語の /æ/ に近い音が現れやすいので (図 3.2) この事実を使って教えるのもひとつの方法です．学習者にできるだけゆっくり「ナヤ」と言ってもらって，ほどよい /æ/ が出た瞬間に「今のその音です」と評価を行えばよいわけです．ただ，学習者は，何かをゆっくり言うことに不慣れであることも多く，単にナとヤをそれぞれ伸ばして言い，ふたつの音の境目は速く言ってしまうことも考えられます．そのような場合，指導者は，何度も見本を示し，学習者が自分の発音を調節しながら指導者と同じことができるよう指導する必要があります.

If you have trouble teaching /æ/ in the way described above, you can make use of the Japanese word "naya" ("barn"). When you say this Japanese word, you will say a sound like /æ/ right at the boundary between "na" and "ya" (Figure 3.2). Make learners say "naya" slowly and tell them when a sound that may pass for /æ/ in your judgment has been produced. If learners are not used to saying something slowly, they may say "na" and "ya" slowly, prolonging the vowel in each syllable, but move from "na" to "ya" quickly. In such a case, you should repeatedly demonstrate the slow articulation of "naya" so that learners can learn to adjust their articulation and copy what you do.

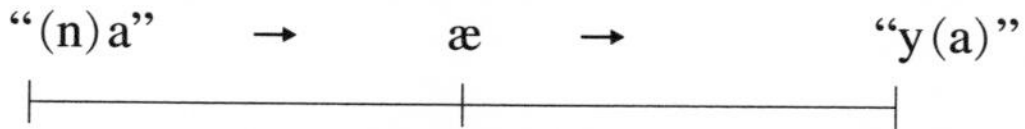

図 3.2　ナの終わりの音からヤのアタマの音に至る発音のものさし (Scale ranging from the end of Japanese "na" to the beginning of Japanese "ya")

/æ/ については，学習者が 2 種類の質問をする可能性があります.

There are two questions that learners may ask you regarding /æ/.

質問 1：ALT の先生はなぜ /æ/ でなく「エア」って言うのですか？

Question 1: Why does our ALT say "ea" instead of /æ/?

/æ/ の音を単純な /æ/ としてではなく「エア」のような響きの音で発音するネイティブスピーカーもいます．たとえば，half を /hæf/ でなく /heəf/ のように発音する人がいます.[1] 学習者がこのような発音を聞き，その点について質問をする可能性があります．学習者が気になるほどこの傾向の強いネイティブスピーカーの先生がいる場合，日本の指導者は，学習者に対して「そういう発音をするネイティブスピーカーもいます」とコメントし，/æ/ が出せればそれで完璧であることを伝えるべきでしょう.

There are some English speakers who say /eə/ for /æ/ (/heəf/ for *half*, for example).[1] Learners may have been exposed to this pronunciation and ask you a question about it. If they have an English-speaking instructor whose tendency to use /eə/ is strong enough to be readily noticed, you should mention that it is a sound prevalent among some English speakers and that, as far as this particular sound is concerned, learners' pronunciation is to be considered perfect if they can just say /æ/.

質問2：ALTの先生はなぜ「アー」って言うのですか？

Question 2: Why does our ALT say "ah" instead of /æ/?

いくつかの単語では，北米系の発音をする人が /æ/ を使うのにイギリス系の発音をする人が /ɑː/ を使います．たとえば，class, last, fast, laugh などの単語においてこの差が現れます．いま例に挙げた単語は，北米系の発音では /klæs/, /læst/, /fæst/, /læf/ ですが，イギリス系の発音では /klɑːs/, /lɑːst/, /fɑːst/, /lɑːf/ です．（/ɑ/ がどんな音かは第9章で詳しく説明しますが，とりあえずここでは，日本語のアとほぼ同じ音であるとご理解頂ければ十分です．）イギリス系の発音のネイティブスピーカーの先生がいる状況では，学習者からこの点について質問が出るかもしれません．

There are some words which speakers with North American-type pronunciation say with /æ/ but speakers with British-type pronunciation say with /ɑː/, such as *class, last, fast,* and *laugh* (/ɑ/ will be discussed in Chapter 9, but here it will be sufficient to mention that it is virtually the same as the Japanese "a" vowel). Learners who have an instructor with British-type pronunciation may ask a question about this sound.

以上2点のような質問が出た場合，指導者は，学習者の気づきを高く評価し，質問には丁寧に答えるべきです．このような点についての質問や回答は，英語にいくつものタイプの発音があることを学習者に実感させるよい機会です．ただ，同時に次のようなコメントをするのもよいと思います．

If questions are asked about issues such as the above, praise learners for being so perceptive and try to provide an informative response. Such an exchange between learner and instructor provides learners with a good opportunity for them to realize that there are many accents in English. You may wish to make the following comments at the same time.

(a) さまざまのタイプの発音はそれぞれひとつの体系をなす（つまり，ある体系の中のある音を使う話し手は，別の音についても同じ体系の中の音を使う）のであり，体系をくずさない限り多少の音の「ゆれ」はあり得ること．

Various types of pronunciation each form a system (in other words, speakers who use a certain sound from a certain system use other sounds from the same system). Speakers operate in accordance with a system, but there may be variation in the quality of the sounds that they produce within the framework of the system.

(b) 学習者が複数のタイプの発音をわざわざまぜることは賢明でないこと．

It is not advisable for learners to copy pronunciation from multiple sound systems.

2. 練習のための言語材料 (Materials for practice)

下線部に注意して発音するよう指示してください．/æ/ は二重下線の部分で使われます．

Make learners pay attention to the underlined part(s) of each item.

単語

(1) ran（走った＝過去形） (2) bat（バット） (3) fan（ファン；扇風機）
(4) hat (5) swam (swim の過去形) (6) run (走る＝現在形) (7) but
(8) fun（楽しみ） (9) hut（小屋） (10) swum（swim の過去分詞形）

フレーズ

(1) black cat（黒いネコ） (2) red hat（赤い帽子）
(3) listen to the band（バンドの音を聞く）
(4) take the bus back（バスに乗って戻る）

センテンス

(1) We ran up to the hut.（私たちは小屋まで走って上がった.）
(2) You must stand up.（立たなくてはなりません.）
(3) It's fun chatting with Dan.
（ダン＝男子の名＝とおしゃべりするのは楽しい.）

会話

A:　Do you hear a band playing?（バンドが演奏しているの，聞こえる？）

B:　Yes. Oh, look at that. It's a marching band. They're coming this way.
（うん．あ，あれ見て．マーチングバンドだ．こっちに来る．）

A:　Let's go stand over there and listen.（あそこに行って立って聞きましょう．）

B:　That's a good idea.（それがいい．）

3. アクティビティー見本 (Idea for an activity)

「違いは何？」(What's the difference?)

2枚の絵の間の違いをさがすゲームです．学習者同士，または指導者と学習者で会話を行ってください．例として，次のようなやりとりが考えられます．

Engage learners in a conversation with each other or with you and have them find differences between Picture A and Picture B. See the following for answers.

A:　What's the difference between Picture A and Picture B?
（Aの絵とBの絵との違いは何ですか？）

B:　In Picture A the woman is wearing a hat. In Picture B she isn't.
（Aの絵では女性が帽子をかぶっています．Bの絵ではかぶっていません．）

In Picture A the boy has an apple (in his hand). In Picture B he doesn't.
（Aの絵では男の子が（手に）リンゴを持っています．Bの絵では持っていません．）

In Picture A there is a map (of the park). In Picture B there is no map. There is a shop.
（Aの絵では（公園の）地図があります．Bの絵では地図はありません．お店があります．）

In Picture B the woman has a bag. In Picture A she doesn't.
（Bの絵では女性がバッグを持っています．Aの絵では持っていません．）

In Picture B there is a cat (in front of the bench). In Picture A there is no cat.

(B の絵では（ベンチの前に）ネコがいます．A の絵ではネコはいません．)

ここでの焦点は /æ/ です．学習者の発音に問題があったら，次のように対応してください．(1) 活動が終わってから，明示的に指導する．(2) 活動の最中であれば，リキャストにより指導する (p. 10 参照)．

The focus here is on /æ/. If learners' pronunciation is problematical, do the following: (1) provide explicit instruction after the activity; (2) provide recasts (see p. 10) during the activity.

第 4 章
フに聞こえる音 — /f/ /v/ /h/ の指導

たとえば fine, very, who　　　How to teach /f/, /v/, and /h/

1. /f/ の指導のポイント (How to teach /f/)

〈まずはここから (To begin with ...)〉

/f/ の音は，たとえば five, fine のアタマの音，enough の最後の音などとして使われます．この音を出すときには，図 4.1 のように，上の前歯を下唇の内側の，唾液でぬれているあたりに押し当てて，息を出すよう指導してください．前歯と唇とが触れる場所は外から見て分かりにくいので，指導者の口を見せるより図 4.1 を板書するほうが有効です．

/f/ appears at the beginning of words like *five* and *fine* and at the end of words like *enough*. To articulate this sound, learners should be told to press their upper front teeth on the inside of the lower lip, namely the wet part of it (as in Figure 4.1), and breathe out. As the point of contact between the upper teeth and the lip cannot be seen from the outside, drawing Figure 4.1 on the board in class is more effective for teaching /f/ than showing the instructor's mouth.

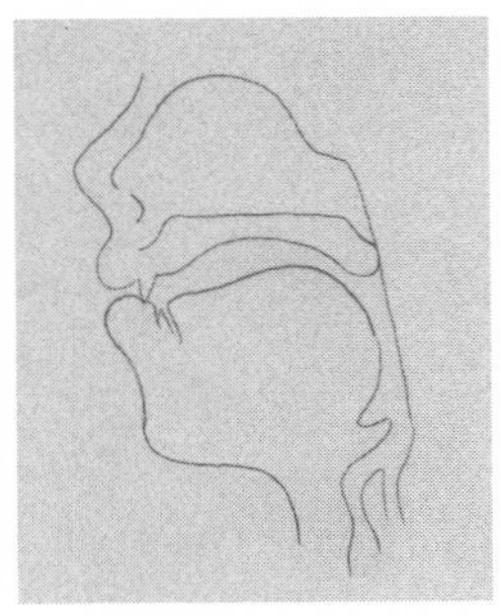

図 4.1　/f/ の発音 (Articulation of /f/)

〈こんなときは (If you face a challenge ...)〉

学習者が直面しがちなトラブルに 3 種類あります．まず，第一に，日本語のフの口の形（図 4.2）をする学習者がいます．このとき，学習者は唇だけを使い，歯を使っていません．このフの音は本章セクション 3 でも話題にする，ろうそくを吹き消すときの音です．これでは /f/ の音を出すことができません．図 4.1 のような絵を見せて，歯を使わなくてはならないことを教えてください．

There are three kinds of trouble that learners are likely to have when trying to say /f/. First, they may produce the consonant at the beginning of the Japanese syllable "fu" instead (Figure 4.2). This is a sound that is produced when one blows out a candle—a sound we shall come back to in Section 3 of this chapter. When learners do this, they are not using their teeth. Show them an illustration like Figure 4.1 and tell them that the use of the upper teeth is an important feature of /f/.

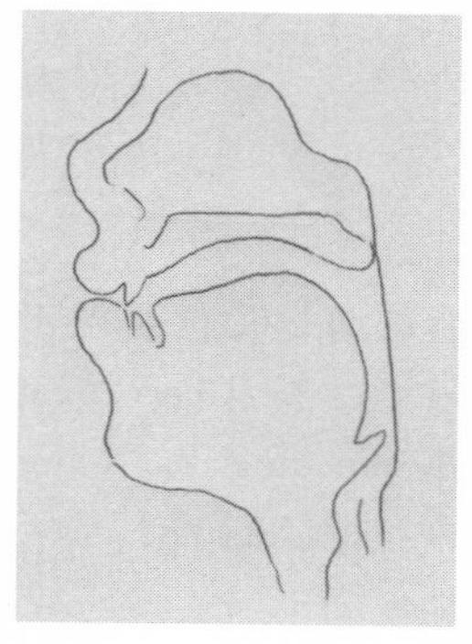

図 4.2　日本語のフを言うときの口 (Articulation of the consonant in the Japanese syllable "fu")

第二に，上の前歯を押し当てる場所に関する問題があります．学習者のうちには，前歯を唇の真上（図 4.3）または外のほう（図 4.4）に当てる人がいます．実は，この方法でも /f/ の音は出るのです．したがって，初級段階を卒業し，中級以上になっても，ずっとこの方法で /f/ の音を出し続ける学習者がいます．しかし，この方法には大きな欠点があります．それは，この方法をする際の口の動きが大きすぎて，直前の音から /f/ に移ったり，/f/ から直後の音に移ったりするときに，能率のよい口の動きができない，という欠点です．指導者は，このような方法で発音している学習者に気づいたら，図 4.1

のような口の形を指導すべきです.

Secondly, learners may put their upper front teeth on the top part of the lower lip (Figure 4.3) or the outside of the lower lip (Figure 4.4). Learners can actually produce /f/ in this way, too. Some learners thus keep articulating /f/ like this even after they reach an intermediate level in their progress in English. There is a problem with this way of saying /f/: The movement of the speech organs is considerable, making it difficult for learners to proceed efficiently from the previous sound to /f/ or from /f/ to the following sound. If you notice that learners are saying /f/ in this way, tell them to follow the way illustrated in Figure 4.1.

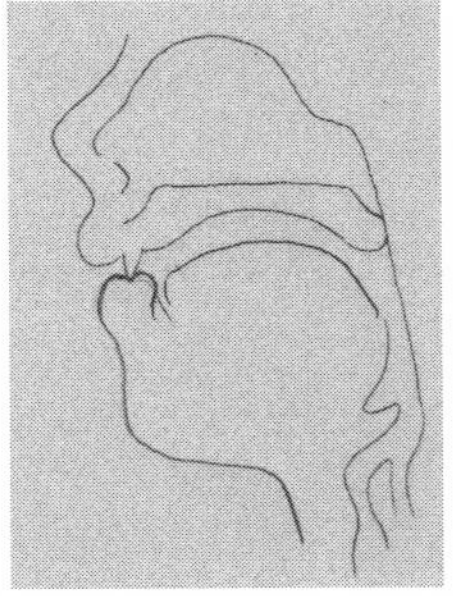

図 4.3 下唇の真上に歯が当たっている (Upper front teeth touching the top part of the lower lip)

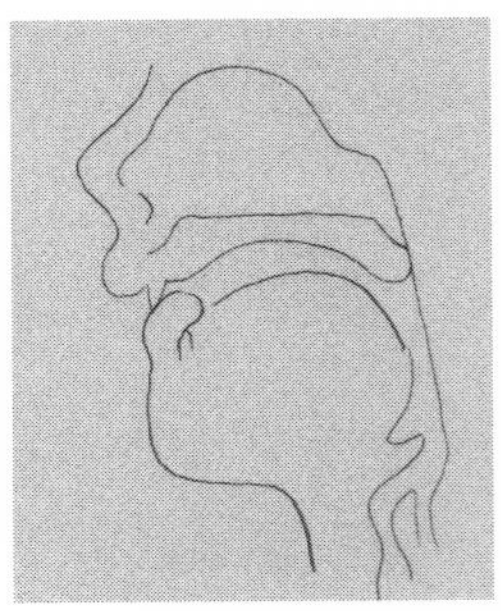

図 4.4 下唇の外側に前歯が当たっている (Upper front teeth touching the outer part of the lower lip)

第三に, 前歯が下唇に触れる形がたとえよくとも, 学習者の音がよく聞こえない場合があります. この原因は, 学習者が出す息の強さが足りないことです. このようなときには, 指導者は学習者に, 「息をたくさん出してください」と指導すべきです.

The third problem is that, even though learners put their upper front teeth on their lower lip properly, /f/ sometimes cannot be heard clearly. The cause of this problem is that learners do not breathe out with enough strength. If you notice this problem, tell learners to breathe out "a lot of air."

2. /v/ の指導のポイント (How to teach /v/)

〈まずはここから (To begin with ...)〉

/v/ は，たとえば very のアタマの音，have の最後の音として使われます．この音は，ある一点をのぞいて前のセクションで取り上げた /f/ と同じです．それは，/f/ が声を伴わないささやきの音であるのに対して，/v/ は声を伴う音だということです．口の形は /f/ の場合と同じです (図 4.5)．

/v/ appears in words like *very* and *have*. This sound is the same as /f/ except for one feature: Unlike /f/, which is voiceless, /v/ is a voiced sound. The shape of the speech organs is the same as in the case of /f/ (Figure 4.5).

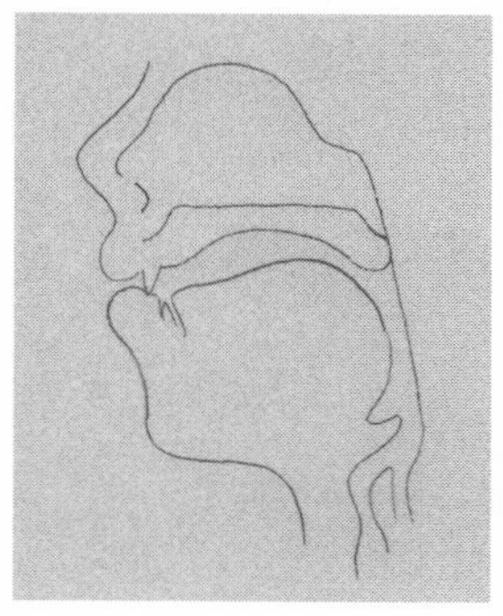

図 4.5　/v/ の発音 (Articulation of /v/)

声の有無が違うだけであとの点では同じであるふたつの音については，第 2 章セクション 2 に述べましたのでここでは繰り返しません．必要ならそのセクションに戻って，このようなふたつの音の関係について学習者に説明してください．

We already saw in Section 2 of Chapter 2 the way in which two sounds can be different in terms of voicing but not in other respects. Go back to that section if necessary and explain the relation between such sounds to learners.

〈こんなときは (If you face a challenge ...)〉

学習者が /v/ の音をうまく出せない場合，この人のかかえる問題は次の 2

種類のどちらかである可能性が高いと言えます．第一に，/v/ を /b/ の音で出してしまう場合があります．/b/ は，唇を閉じて（図 4.6），その唇を開きながら勢いよく息を外に出して作る音です．この音を出すとき，学習者は歯を使いませんので，歯を使うべき /v/ の音を出していないことになります．このような学習者に対しては，指導者は，図 4.5 に示したような正しい口の形を指導すべきです．

When learners cannot produce /v/, their problem is likely to be one of two kinds. First, learners may be producing /b/ instead of /v/. /b/ is a sound that one articulates by closing the lips (Figure 4.6) and then suddenly releasing air from the mouth as one opens the lips. When learners articulate /b/, they are not using their teeth, which means that they are not saying /v/. If this problem has arisen, tell learners to shape their speech organs correctly, as shown in Figure 4.5.

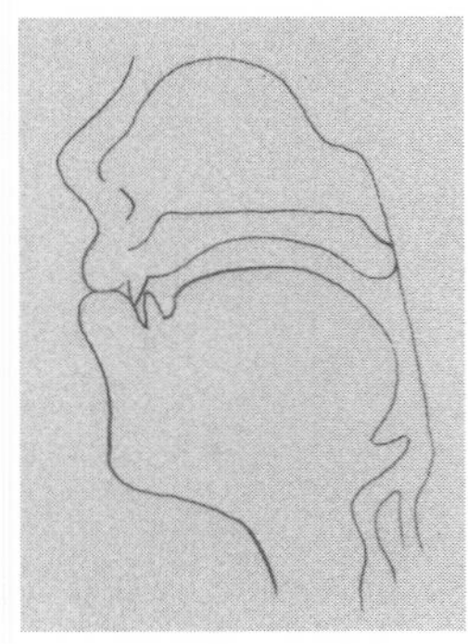

図 4.6　/b/ の発音 (Articulation of /b/)

第二に，前歯と下唇を触れさせているのにもかかわらず /v/ が出せず，/b/ に似た音を出してしまう学習者もいます．この場合，学習者は，息の出し方について誤っています．/b/ に似た音を出してしまう学習者は，前歯で下唇を強くかみすぎて，いったん息の流れを止めているのです．その上で口を開いて音を出そうとするので，息の流れは /b/ の場合と同じになってしまいます．正しい /v/ の場合，息は一度もせき止められません．

Secondly, some learners put their upper front teeth on the lower lip but still cannot articulate /v/ and produce a sound like /b/ instead. These learners are not using their breath correctly. They bite their lower lip with their front teeth tightly and thus stop the flow of air at one stage in the process of articulation before opening their mouth to let air out. When this happens, the flow of air created is precisely the same as that created in the production of /b/. If /v/ were articulated correctly, the flow of air would not be stopped.

/b/ に似た音を出してしまう学習者に対しては，ふたつのことを試してください．

第一に，前歯が図 4.5 のように下唇の内側の唾液でぬれているあたりについているかを確認してください．下唇を強くかみすぎる学習者の多くは，前歯をそのような場所に触れさせず，/f/ のところで述べた，下唇の真上（図 4.3）や，下唇の外側（図 4.4）に前歯を触れさせる形をしているものです．このような問題がないかをまずチェックし，問題があれば前歯が触れる位置を指導すべきです．

When you are faced with learners who produce a /b/-like sound instead of the correct /v/, try the following two things.

First, check to see whether they have their upper front teeth on the wet part of their lower lip, as in Figure 4.5. In all likelihood, learners who bite their lower lip too tightly do not have their front teeth on that part of their lower lip but have them either on the top of it (Figure 4.3) or on the outside (Figure 4.4). These are problems discussed in connection with /f/, but they apply to /v/ as well. If you recognize such a problem, you should tell learners to put their upper front teeth at the right place.

第二に，携帯電話や秒針のついた時計を使って時間を測りながら /v/ を練習することをお勧めします．すなわち，/v/ の音を，長く引っ張って—たとえば 5 秒続けて—出すよう指導します．/b/ のような音を出している学習者は，音を長く引っ張ることができません．音を引っ張ろうとして，むしろ，ブブブブのように /b/ の音を繰り返してしまいます．このブブブという音は学習者が前歯で下唇を強くかみすぎている証拠ですので，そのことを説明し，前歯と下唇の触れ方をもっと軽くして，息をたくさん使って /v/ を発音するよう指導してください．

Secondly, I recommend that you have learners time themselves with a mobile phone or a watch with a second hand when practicing /v/. Have them prolong the sound for, say, five seconds. Learners who produce a /b/-like sound for /v/ cannot draw it out and end up saying something like /bʊbʊbʊbʊ .../. If this happens, it indicates that learners are biting their lower lip too tightly. Explain this and tell them to press their upper front teeth on their lower lip more lightly and also to breathe out a lot of air as they try to say /v/.

3. /uː/ /ʊ/ の前の /h/ の指導のポイント

(How to teach /h/ followed by /uː/ or /ʊ/)

/h/ はこの章と第 18 章で取り上げます．ここでは，/uː/ または /ʊ/ が後ろに来たときの /h/ がポイントです．/h/ は学習者にとって出しやすい音ですが，/uː/ または /ʊ/ が後ろに来たときは例外です．学習者は，ろうそくを吹き消すときのように上下の唇を近づけてノイズを出しがちです（本章セクション 1 参照）．正しくは，/h/ はのどで出す音であり，唇からのノイズを伴う音ではありません．学習者に音のイメージをつかませるために，図 4.7 のようにスプーンを使うことができます．図のようにして学習者に who や hook を言わせると，彼らが唇でノイズを作るのを防ぐことができます．

/h/ is discussed in this chapter and Chapter 18. Here, the topic is /h/ followed by /uː/ or /ʊ/. /h/ is an easy consonant for learners to produce, except when it is followed by those vowels, as in *who* and *hook*. Learners tend to make the lips come close to each other, as if they were blowing out a candle—this is the same problem as the one I mentioned above in connection with the erroneous pronunciation of /f/—and produce an unnecessary noise when attempting to articulate /h/. Actually, /h/ is a sound articulated in the throat, and it should not be accompanied by any noise made at the lips. You can help learners get the acoustic image of /h/ by using a spoon, as in Figure 4.7, to prevent the upper and lower lips from coming too close to each other. Make them say *who* and *hook* that way, and they will not produce any noise at the lips.

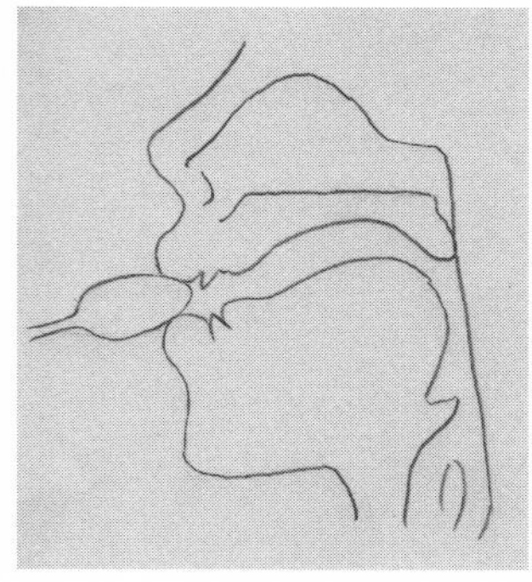

図 4.7　/uː/ /ʊ/ の前の /h/ の発音練習（Practicing the articulation of /h/ followed by /uː/ or /ʊ/）

4. 練習のための言語材料 (Materials for practice)

下線部に注意して発音するよう指示してください.

Make learners pay attention to the underlined part(s) of each item.

単語

(1) fine (2) food (3) tough (/tʌf/) (4) enough (/ɪnʌf/) (5) very (6) voice（声） (7) have (8) move (9) who (10) hood

フレーズ

(1) enough food（十分な食べ物）
(2) very best（まさに最高）
(3) save money（お金を節約する）
(4) fine hood（すばらしい頭巾）

センテンス

(1) Leaves will soon fall.（間もなく葉が落ちるでしょう.）
(2) I have a lot of food.（私はたくさん食べ物を持っています.）
(3) Who can do it first?（最初にできる人は誰ですか？）

会話

A: Have you seen this photo?（この写真を見たことがありますか？）
B: No, I haven't. Is this a photo of your family?（いいえ. ご家族の写真？）
A: Yes. It's from a very long time ago. More than fifty years ago. This

is my grandfather.
（そうです．ずっと昔の頃のものです．50 年以上昔．これがおじいさん．）

B: Very handsome. Who is sitting next to him?
（とてもハンサムですね．隣に座っているのは誰ですか？）

5. アクティビティー見本 (Idea for an activity)

「クリスマスの写真」(Christmas photo)

2020 年のクリスマスの記念写真に写っている人物の生まれた年と月にもとづき，写真撮影時に誰が何歳だったか当てるゲームです．学習者同士，または指導者と学習者で会話を行ってください．例として，次のようなやりとりが考えられます．

Here is a game in which players look at a picture taken at Christmas in 2020 and guess how old each of those photographed was when the picture was taken. Engage learners in a conversation with each other or with you. One possible exchange is as follows.

A: Who is the boy sitting on the floor?
（床に座っている男の子は誰ですか？）

B: Bob. He was born in August 2003. Can you figure out how old he was when the picture was taken?
（ボブです．彼は 2003 年 8 月に生まれました．写真が撮られたとき，彼は何歳だったか，分かりますか？）

A: Yes, I can. He was 17 years old.（分かります．17 歳でした．）

他の人の情報は以下の通りです．

Here is some information about the other people in the photograph.

The old man with a walking stick is Richard. He was born in October 1943.
（ステッキを持っている老人はリチャードです．彼は 1943 年 10 月に生まれました．）(Answer: 77)

The little girl is Cathy. She was born in June 2016.

（小さな女の子はキャシーです．彼女は 2016 年 6 月に生まれました.）(Answer: 4)

The woman right behind Cathy is her mother Laura. She was born in September 1993.

（キャシーのすぐ後ろの女性は彼女の母のローラです．彼女は 1993 年 9 月に生まれました.）(Answer: 27)

Right next to Laura is her husband, John. He was born in July 1986.

（ローラのとなりにいるのは夫のジョンです．彼は 1986 年 7 月に生まれました.）(Answer: 34)

The man standing close to the lamp is Brian. He was born in May 1956.

（スタンドに近いところで立っている男性はブライアンです．彼は 1956 年 5 月に生まれました.）(Answer: 64)

The woman next to Brian is Linda. She was born in September 1973.

（ブライアンのとなりの女性はリンダです．彼女は 1973 年 9 月に生まれました.）(Answer: 47)

The man standing next to the Christmas tree is Tom. He was born in February 1963.

（クリスマスツリーのとなりで立っている男性はトムです．彼は 1963 年 2 月に生まれました.）(Answer: 57)

ここでの焦点は /f/ /v/ /h/ です．学習者の発音に問題があったら，次のように対応してください．(1) 活動が終わってから，明示的に指導する．(2) 活動の最中であれば，リキャストにより指導する (p. 10 参照)．

The focus here is on /f/, /v/, and /h/. If learners' pronunciation is problematical, do the following: (1) provide explicit instruction after the activity; (2) provide recasts (see p. 10) during the activity.

第 5 章

シに聞こえる音—/s/ /ʃ/ の指導

たとえば see, she　How to teach /s/ and /ʃ/

1. /s/ /ʃ/ の指導のポイント (How to teach /s/ and /ʃ/)

〈まずはここから (To begin with ...)〉

/s/ の音は，たとえば same (同じ)，soon (すぐに) のアタマの音，nice の最後の音などとして使われます．この音は，日本語のサ，ス，セ，ソのアタマの音と同じです．この音を出すとき，舌は口の天井の図で示したところに触れています (図 5.1)．板書で示すのであれば図 5.2 のようなもので十分でしょう．しかし，その説明をしなくとも，日本の学習者のほとんどは，いま挙げた単語を楽に発音することができます．

/s/ appears at the beginning of *same* and *soon*, for example, and at the end of *nice*, for example. This sound is the same as the sound at the beginning of the Japanese syllables "sa," "su," "se," and "so." When this sound is articulated, the tongue is in contact with the parts of the roof of the mouth indicated by the shaded areas in Figure 5.1. If you want to draw an illustration on the board in class, something like Figure 5.2 should suffice. But, without seeing such illustrations, learners in Japan can say *same*, *soon*, and *nice* very easily.

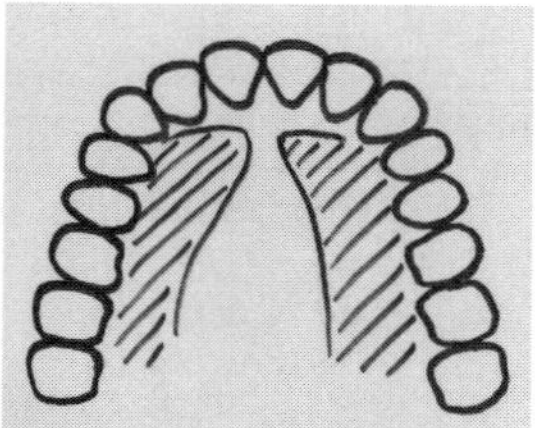

図 5.1 /s/ の際の舌の触れ方（Contact between the tongue and the roof of the mouth in the articulation of /s/）

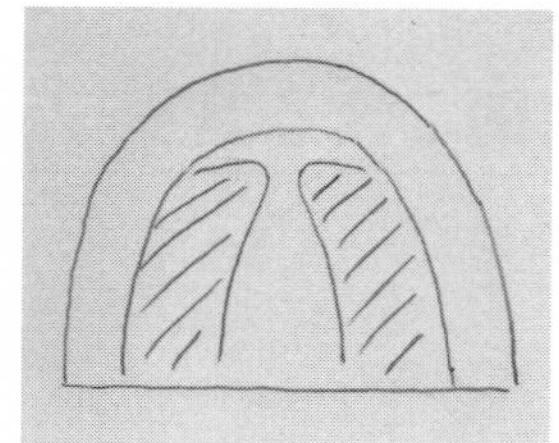

図 5.2 図 5.1 の簡略版（Simplified version of Figure 5.1）

/ʃ/ の音は，たとえば shell（貝），shoe（靴の片方）のアタマの音，wash の最後の音などとして使われます．この音を出すとき，舌は口の天井の図で示したところに触れています（図 5.3）．板書するのであれば図 5.4 のようなもので十分です．しかし，その説明をしなくとも，日本の学習者のほとんどは，いま挙げた単語を楽に発音することができます．

/ʃ/ appears at the beginning of *shell* and *shoe*, for example, and at the end of *wash*, for example. When this sound is articulated, the tongue is in contact with the parts of the roof of the mouth indicated by the shaded areas in Figure 5.3. For a simplified version of Figure 5.3 to be drawn on the board in class, see Figure 5.4. Learners in Japan are able to say those words with ease even without being explicitly given such information.

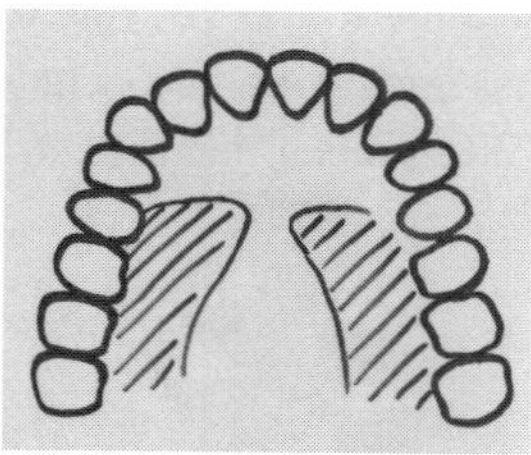

図 5.3 /ʃ/ の際の舌の触れ方（Contact between the tongue and the roof of the mouth in the articulation of /ʃ/）

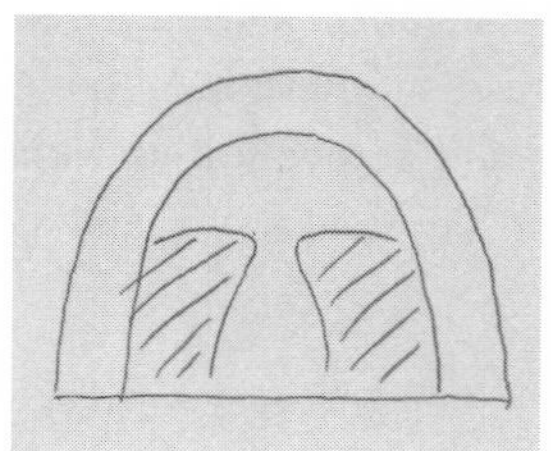

図 5.4 図 5.3 の簡略版（Simplified version of Figure 5.3）

〈こんなときは (If you face a challenge ...)〉

数は少ないのですが，一部の学習者は，上に挙げた same，soon，nice，shell，shoe，wash が言えても，see と she を区別したり sip と ship を区別したりすることができません．[1)] /s/ が苦手な学習者に対する最も簡単な教え方は，この音はスイ（「水泳」という日本語やなめらかさを表す「スイスイ」という擬態語などの最初の部分）のアタマの音に似ている，という説明をすることです．

> There are a small number of learners who cannot distinguish between *see* and *she* or between *sip* and *ship*, while they can say all the words cited above: *same, soon, nice, shell, shoe,* and *wash.*[1)] If they have a problem with /s/, the simplest way to teach it is to say that /s/ resembles the initial sound of "sui," a two-syllable sequence in Japanese (the first part of the Japanese word "suiei" = "swimming" or the first part of "suisui," a mimetic expression to refer to smooth movement, for example).

ただ，ここで，唇の丸みの問題が生じます．日本語を話す人がスィと言うとき，スの段階で少し唇を丸めるものです．しかし，英語の see，sip を言うときに唇を丸めると発音が不自然になります．そこで，学習者がスイと発音して /s/ の舌の形のイメージをつかめたら，「こんどは，(a) まず唇を始めからイの形に横に広げて，(b) それから，唇を使わず舌だけで同じものを言ってみましょう」と指導するとよいでしょう．

> Here arises an issue of lip rounding. Japanese speakers say "su" by rounding their lips, while the initial part of *see* and *sip* is not accompanied with lip rounding. After learners have tried saying "sui" and have obtained the image of the shape of the tongue for /s/, you should then tell them to say the same thing again by (a) first spreading their lips sideways, as if to say "i," and (b) then saying it with the tongue only, not with the lips.

また，逆に学習者が see や sip が言えても she や ship が言えない場合，/ʃ/ の最も簡単な教え方は，この音は日本語のシェのアタマの音と同じと考えてよい，と説明することです．たとえば，she については，シェィーというつもりで言うと近い音が出せるかもしれません．ただ，学習者がシェイーを出発点として she を言えるようになるためには，エという母音を言わないようにする必要があります．そこで，学習者が「シェイー」と発音して /ʃ/ のイメージがつかめたら，「こんどは，(a) まず唇を始めからイの形に横に広げて，(b) それから，唇を使わず舌だけで同じものを言ってみて，(c) 最後に余計な /e/ を入れないようにして /ʃiː/ と言いましょう」と指導するとよいでしょう．

If learners can say *see* and *sip* but not *she* or *ship*, the simplest way to teach /ʃ/ may be to say that this sound is the same as the initial sound of the Japanese syllable "she" (/ʃe/, a nonsense syllable). They may be able to say something close to the English word *she* if they try to say /ʃeiː/. But, of course, they need to quickly learn not to say the /e/ in /ʃeiː/. So, after learners have tried saying /ʃeiː/ and have obtained the image of the shape of the tongue for /ʃ/, you should then tell them to say the same thing again by (a) first spreading their lips sideways, as if to say "i," (b) then saying it using the tongue only, not the lips, and (c) finally saying /ʃiː/ without the superfluous /e/ part.

2. さらなる /s/ /ʃ/ の指導 (Further instruction on /s/ and /ʃ/)

日本語の音への言及によっても see (/siː/) と she (/ʃiː/) の区別，あるいは sip (/sɪp/) と ship (/ʃɪp/) の区別がうまく教えられないときは，舌の位置の説明が役に立つかもしれません．舌の位置という観点から二つの音を比べると，/s/ を言うときには舌先が前歯に近い位置にあり，/ʃ/ を言うときには舌先がそれよりも後ろにあると言えます．学習者に図 5.1 と図 5.3 とをよく見比べさせるとよいでしょう．また，図 5.5 を板書すれば，舌先の位置が異なることを学習者に理解させることができます．実線が /s/ を，点線が /ʃ/ を表します．

If you have tried referring to Japanese sounds and still have difficulty getting learners to distinguish between *see* (/siː/) and *she* (/ʃiː/) or between *sip* (/sɪp/) and *ship* (/ʃɪp/), you may want to mention the difference between /s/ and /ʃ/ in terms of tongue position. Tell learners that when they say /s/ the tip of their tongue should be closer to their upper front teeth than when they say /ʃ/. Have learners compare Figure 5.1 and Figure 5.3. Or draw an illustration like Figure 5.5, where the tongue position drawn with a solid line and that drawn with a dotted line represent /s/ and /ʃ/, respectively.

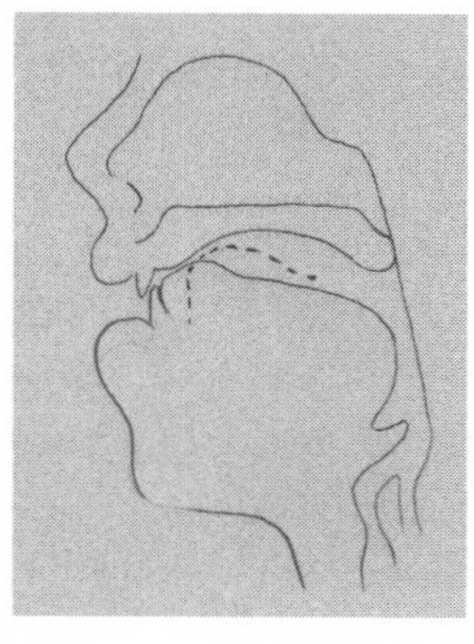

図 5.5　/s/ と /ʃ/ の発音の際の舌の位置（Tongue positions for the articulation of /s/ and /ʃ/）

まず，/s/ を言おうとして /ʃ/ を言ってしまう学習者に対しては，舌先をもっと前に寄せなさい，と指導することができます．最初に ship のアタマの音である /ʃ/ を言わせ，ゆっくりと—非常にゆっくりと—舌を前に動かしてもらい，舌先を thank のアタマの音である /θ/（第2章で取り上げました）の位置に向かって少しずつ移してもらうことです．その間，息を出し続けるように指示してください．そうすると，/θ/ に到達する前に一瞬，目指す /s/ の音を通過します．この方法で大事なことは，(a) /ʃ/ から /θ/ への移行は非常にゆっくりでなくてはならないこと，(b) 舌先が口の天井から大きく離れてしまうことなく，常に口の天井近くを移動すること，の2点です．

If learners try to say /s/ and end up saying /ʃ/, you can tell them to move their tongue forward. First, have them say /ʃ/, as in *ship*, and then have them slowly—very slowly—push the tongue forward and move the tongue tip little by little from the /ʃ/ position toward the position for /θ/ (as in *thank*, covered in Chapter 2), breathing air out throughout the process. Before they reach the /θ/ position, there will be a moment when the tongue assumes the position for /s/, the target sound. The key to this procedure is that (a) the transition from /ʃ/ toward /θ/ should be very slow and (b) learners should slide the tongue tip while keeping it close to the roof of the mouth and should not allow it to move away from there at any moment.

逆に /ʃ/ を言おうとして /s/ を言ってしまう学習者に対しては，舌先をもっと後ろに引きなさい，と指導することができます．つまようじか割り箸を上の前歯のすぐ後ろに当てて（図 5.6）歯ぐきの位置を学習者に確認させる，という方法がうまく行く場合もあります．/ʃ/ を言うときの舌先の位置は，それが箸やつまようじの先より前に出ないくらいの位置であるべきです．ただ，実際に /ʃ/ を言おうとするとつまようじなどが邪魔になりますので，/ʃ/ の発音はつまようじなどを抜いてから行ってください．

Conversely, if they try to say /ʃ/ and end up saying /s/, you can tell them to draw their tongue back. When you teach /ʃ/, you can have learners put one end of a chopstick or toothpick on their teeth ridge (Figure 5.6) and have them get the feel of where the teeth ridge is. When they say /ʃ/, the tongue tip should not be ahead of the spot where the tip of the chopstick or toothpick is. Learners should remove the chopstick or toothpick before actually practicing saying /ʃ/, however, because articulation of /ʃ/ would otherwise be made difficult.

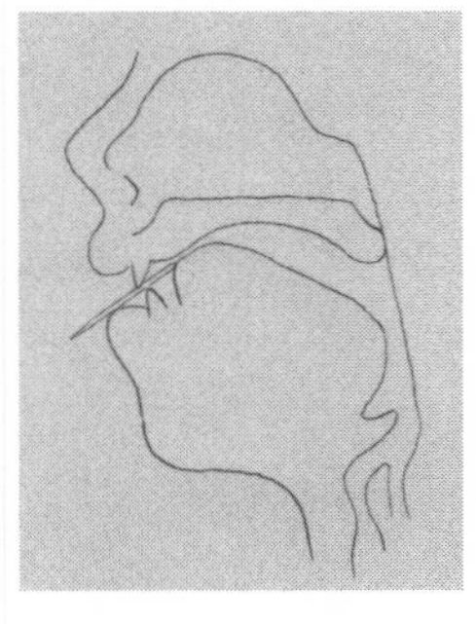

図 5.6 /ʃ/ のために舌を正しい位置に (Ensuring a tongue position for the articulation of /ʃ/)

/s/ と /ʃ/ の区別はほとんどの学習者にとっては難しくないものですので，指導者がこの章の内容を必要とする可能性は低いと思います．しかし，少数といえどもこれを苦手とする学習者がいることは事実で，トラブルは頑固であることが多いです．この問題への対応能力を備えておいてください．

The likelihood that you need to make use of the advice given in this chapter is low because the distinction between /s/ and /ʃ/ is easy for most learners to handle. But there are learners who find it difficult, and the problem is usually obstinate. Always be prepared to cope with this challenge.

3. 練習のための言語材料 (Materials for practice)

下線部に注意して発音するよう指示してください．一重下線は /s/，二重下線は /ʃ/ です．

Make learners pay attention to the underlined part(s) of each item.

単語

(1) see　(2) say　(3) sip（すする）　(4) soon
(5) soap　(6) she　(7) shape（形）　(8) ship
(9) shoe（靴＝単数なので片方）　(10) show

フレーズ

(1) a sheet of paper（紙 1 枚）
(2) see a show（ショーを見る）
(3) sail in a ship（船で航行する）

センテンス

(1) She was sick on Sunday.（彼女は日曜日病気だった．）
(2) The show will start soon.（ショーはすぐに始まります．）
(3) Have a seat and look at the question sheet.
（座って問題用紙を見てください．）

会話

A: Can you see the ship over there?（あそこの船が見えますか？）
B: Sure. I can see it.（はい．見えます．）
A: It arrived from Singapore yesterday.
（きのうシンガポールから着いたんです．）
B: It's a beautiful ship.（美しい船ですね．）

4. アクティビティー見本 (Idea for an activity)

「誰が何を好き？」(Who likes what?)

Sheila（シーラ，/ʃiːlə/ 女性名），Cecil（セシル，/sesɪl, -(ə)l/ 男性名），Celia（シーリア，/siːljə/ 女性名）の 3 人のいとこについて，学習者に次の文を聞かせ，表にチェックを入れさせてください．ここではチェックの入った表を提示します．

Have learners listen to the following sentences about three cousins, Sheila, Cecil, and Celia, and have learners put ticks in the table (here the ticks have been put in for you).

Sheila likes music. She enjoys playing the piano and playing the violin. She also likes cycling, tennis, and basketball.
（シーラは音楽が好きです．彼女はピアノとバイオリンを弾くのを楽しみます．彼女はまたサイクリング，テニス，バスケットボールが好きです．）
Cecil likes to swim and go out on his bicycle. He plays tennis, too.
（セシルは水泳と自転車での外出が好きです．テニスもやります．）
Celia goes swimming a lot. She plays tennis and basketball.
（シーリアはよく水泳をします．彼女はテニスとバスケットボールをします．）

	Sheila	Cecil	Celia
Swimming		✔	✔
Cycling	✔	✔	
Violin	✔		
Piano	✔		
Basketball	✔		✔
Tennis	✔	✔	✔

学習者同士，または指導者と学習者で会話を行ってください．例として，次のようなやりとりが考えられます．

Engage learners in a conversation with each other or with you. Possible exchanges are as follows.

A: Who likes swimming?（誰が水泳を好きなのですか？）

B: Cecil and Celia like swimming.（セシルとシーリアが水泳を好きです.）

A: Who likes tennis?（誰がテニスを好きなのですか？）

B: Sheila, Cecil, and Celia like tennis.
（シーラ，セシル，シーリアがテニスを好きです.）

ここでの焦点は /s/ /ʃ/ です．学習者の発音に問題があったら，次のように対応してください．(1) 活動が終わってから，明示的に指導する．(2) 活動の最中であれば，リキャストにより指導する（p. 10 参照）．

The focus here is on /s/ and /ʃ/. If learners' pronunciation is problematical, do the following: (1) provide explicit instruction after the activity; (2) provide recasts (see p. 10) during the activity.

第6章

N とンとは別の音 — /n/ の指導

たとえば <u>n</u>ice, ca<u>n</u>　How to teach /n/

1. /n/ の指導のポイント (How to teach /n/)

〈まずはここから (To begin with ...)〉

日本語にナ，ニ，ヌ，ネ，ノ，ンという文字がありますので，学習者は /n/ の発音を楽にできるだろうと指導者は考えるかもしれませんが，/n/ はきちんと指導する必要があります．以下にその理由を説明します．

Since there are the syllables "na," "ni," "nu," "ne," "no," and "n" in the Japanese sound system, you may think that learners can say /n/ easily. Actually, that is not the case. /n/ is one of those sounds that need to be carefully taught. The following paragraphs explain why.

/n/ の音は，たとえば nice，next のアタマの音，can，one の最後の音などとして使われます．この音を出すときには，図 6.1 のように，上の歯ぐきにそった馬蹄形の場所に舌のヘリが触れます．板書で説明するのであれば図 6.2 のようなもので十分でしょう．

/n/ appears at the beginning of words such as *nice* and *next* and at the end of words like *can* and *one*. To articulate this sound, one puts the tongue on the upper teeth ridge as in Figure 6.1 in a way in which a horseshoe-shaped area of contact is formed between the tongue and the teeth ridge. If you want to draw an illustration on the board in class, something like Figure 6.2 will suffice.

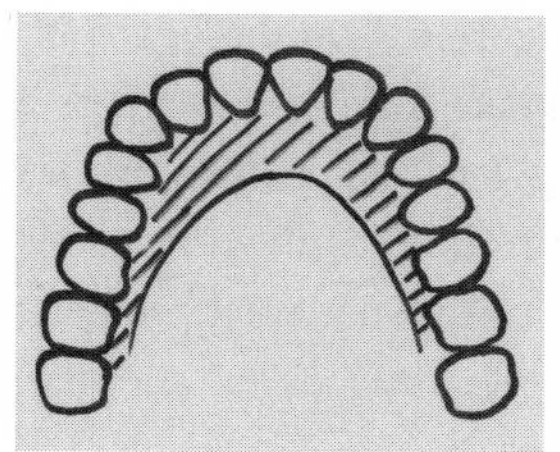

図 6.1　/n/ の発音（Articulation of /n/）

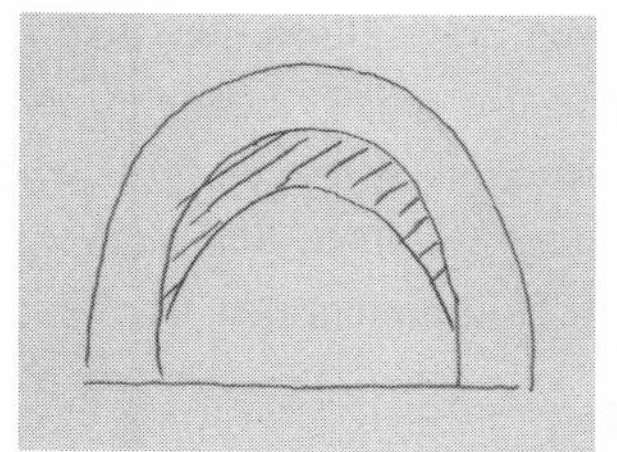

図 6.2　図 6.1 の簡略版（Simplified version of Figure 6.1）

これを横から見ると，図 6.3 のようになります．舌の先は上の前歯のすぐ後ろの歯ぐきにあります．

Figure 6.3 is an illustration of the median section of the mouth that shows how /n/ is articulated. Note that the tongue tip is on the upper teeth ridge, right behind the upper front teeth.

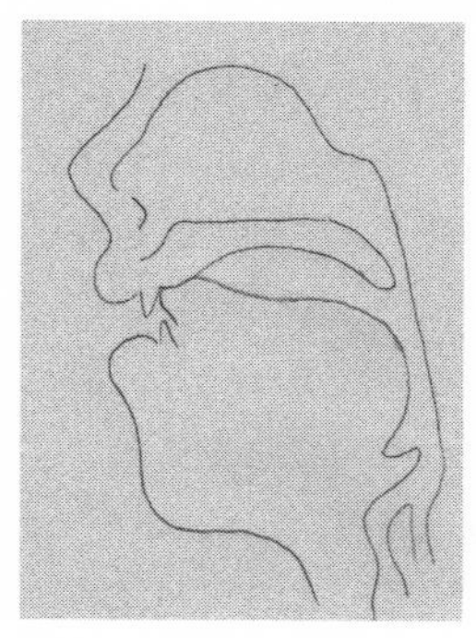

図 6.3　/n/ の発音（Articulation of /n/）

学習者は nice，next のアタマの音を言うとき，舌先を上の歯ぐきにつけることができます．ただ，図 6.2，図 6.3 の板書や図 6.4 に提示する歯型を使って舌先がつく位置を学習者に確認させることをお勧めします．後に説明する通り，学習者は，英語の /n/ を言うとき，常にこの位置に舌先をつけることができるとは限りません．学習者にとってこの問題を認識するのは大事なことです．

Learners can put the tongue tip properly on the upper teeth ridge when saying the initial sound in *nice* and *next*. Nevertheless, I recommend that you draw illustrations like Figure 6.2 and Figure 6.3 on the board in class or use a jaw model as in Figure 6.4 to make sure that learners know where their tongue tip is when saying /n/. As I will explain below, learners may not always be able to put the tongue tip there as they try to say /n/. It is important that learners should be aware of this potential problem.

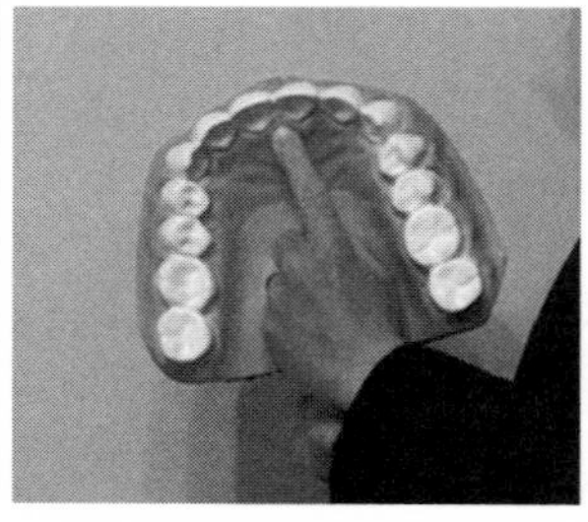

図 6.4 /n/ の発音の際の舌先の位置（Where the tongue tip should be for /n/）

〈こんなときは（If you face a challenge ...)〉

学習者は，nice の /n/，next の /n/ など，単語内で母音の前にある /n/ はうまく出すことができます．ところが，それ以外の場合，/n/ をうまく言えないことがあります．たとえば，学習者は，can，one などの語に出て来る /n/ の発音を苦手とします．具体的には，舌先を上の歯ぐきに触れさせないで /n/ を言おうとします．このことは図 6.5 を板書することで学習者に理解させることができます．(/n/ を言おうとして舌を口の天井の奥のほうに触れさせる学習者もいれば触れさせない学習者もいますが，このことを話題にする必要はありません．ここでの重要なポイントは舌先を触れさせないで /n/ を言おうとする学習者にそのことを認識させることです.）この問題は次のセクションで詳しく説明しますが，ここでは，とにかく，学習者が /n/ の音を図 6.1，図 6.2，図 6.3 に示すような方法で確実に出すよう，指導者は指導する必要があります．（もちろん，autumn のように，読まないことが決まっている n の文字をつづりに含む単語は別です.）

While learners are able to say /n/ right before a vowel in a word, as in *nice* and *next*, they may be unable to say the sound in other environments. For example, some learners find it difficult to say /n/ in *can* and *one*. These learners try to say /n/ in those words while keeping their tongue tip away from their upper teeth ridge. You can help them realize what they tend to do by drawing an illustration like Figure 6.5. (Some learners put the back of their tongue on the roof of their mouth; some don't. That is not an issue here. The important thing is to help learners realize that they are making the mistake of having their tongue tip *away* from the teeth ridge when trying to say the English /n/.) I will explain this problem in greater detail in the next section, but, for the time being, let me emphasize that you should make sure that learners articulate /n/ properly by doing what Figure 6.1, Figure 6.2, and Figure 6.3 indicate. (Of course, this does not apply to the silent letter "n" as in *autumn*.)

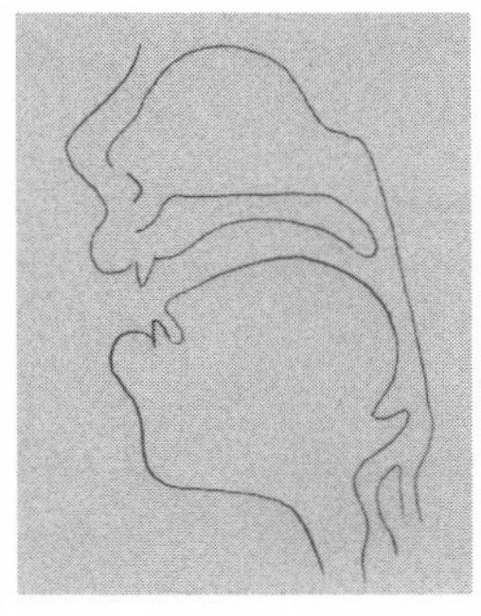

図 6.5　不完全な /n/：舌先が正しく触れていない．
(Incomplete /n/: no proper tongue-ridge contact)

2. /n/ は律義に発音すべし，と指導すること

(/n/ needs to be articulated—always)

前述した通り，特定の場所で /n/ がうまく言えない学習者は少なくなく，具体的には，この問題は次のような場合に起こります．まずは以下の (a) にだけでも対応してください．それ以外のトラブルについても (b) ～ (h) として一応紹介します．練習のポイントは，下に紹介するように，/n/ の音の直前に切れ目を入れてリピート練習することです．(この練習方法には第 20 章でも触れます．)

As I mentioned above, not a few learners have trouble saying /n/ in certain phonetic environments, outlined in (a)-(h) below. At least cope with the problem under (a). To overcome the problems mentioned here, have them do repetition practice with sentences or phrases that include /n/ and, when you have them do it, divide a phrase or sentence mid-word, immediately before /n/, as in the following examples. (This method of practice will be discussed again in Chapter 20.)

〈まずはここから (To begin with ...)〉

(a) /n/ が母音の直前に来る場合 (Cases where /n/ is followed by a vowel)

たとえば an apple, in England に見られるように, /n/ が母音 (apple のアタマの /æ/, England のアタマの /ɪ/) の直前に来る場合, /n/ を言おうとする学習者の舌先が正しく上の歯ぐきに触れず, 宙に浮いていることがあります. 正しくは, an apple の下線部でナに近い音, in England の下線部でニに近い音が聞こえるはずです. この問題に対応するためには, 次のようなリピート練習が有効です.

If /n/ is followed by a vowel, as in *an apple* and *in England*, learners may fail to have their tongue tip properly on the upper teeth ridge for /n/ and may instead have it up in the air in the mouth. What they should do is to say *an apple* in a way in which a sound like "na" is heard in the middle of the phrase and say *in England* so that a sound like "ni" is heard in the middle of the phrase. The following repetition practice will be useful to cope with this problem.

1. /æpl/ (apple)
2. /næpl/ (-n apple) (下線部のところでナに近い音が出るようにする)
3. /ənæpl/ (an apple) (下線部のところでナに近い音が出るようにする)

次に in England を例に取って説明しましょう.

1. /ɪŋglənd/ (England/)
2. /nɪŋglənd/ (-n England) (下線部のところでニに近い音が出るようにする)
3. /ɪnɪŋglənd/ (in England) (下線部のところでニに近い音が出るようにする)

ここで話題にしている, 単語の境目の /n/ は, 日本語のナ行の音を利用して教えることができますが, これは実は中途半端な指導で, 本当は, 語末の /n/ の指導を行うべきなのです. 語末の /n/ を常に正しく発音する学習者なら，別に日本語のナ行の音を言うという方便を使わなくとも，an apple や in England がすんなりと発音できます．そこで，以下に，語末の /n/ について述べます．

Learners can certainly pronounce the /n/ at a word boundary if they make use of the Japanese syllables "na," "ni," "nu," "ne," and "no," but, actually, teaching them to do this is only a half measure. You should really teach them to say word-final /n/ in all phonetic environments. Learners who always pronounce /n/ can say *an apple* and *in England* smoothly without resorting to the strategy of saying a Japanese syllable. So I would now like to turn to the discussion of word-final /n/ itself.

たとえば，Hello, everyone. と言うとき，-one の最後の /n/ を正しく言えない学習者がいます．/n/ のときに舌先が上の歯ぐきについているべきですが，多くの場合，学習者の舌先は口のなかで宙に浮いています．この問題をかかえる学習者には，-one をワヌのように，日本語のナ行の音をそえるつもりで言うことを試すよう提案してみてください．もちろん，ヌをはっきり言ってしまうと最後のウの母音が聞こえてしまいますので，最後の母音は出さないようにして，ヌのアタマの /n/ を言った瞬間に発音をやめるように指導するのです．手順としては，たとえば，学習者に（1）まずワヌと言ってみてもらう，（2）ヌの最後のウの音をできるだけ弱く言ってもらう，（3）最後のウを出さないようにして言ってもらう，という段階を追った方法が考えられます．語末の /n/ を征服した学習者は，下に列挙する（b）から（h）の学習が楽にできるはずです．

When saying *Hello, everyone*, for example, many learners fail to say /n/ at the end of *-one* correctly. They fail to make their tongue tip touch their teeth ridge, having their tongue tip up in the air in the mouth instead. To solve this problem, tell learners to first say "wanu," with a vowel after /n/. Of course, if they do say "wanu," the final vowel is heard too clearly. So you should then help them refrain from saying the vowel when /n/ has been said. For example, you can tell them to (1) first say "wanu," (2) then make the final vowel as weak as possible, and (3) finally say *one* without a vowel at the end. Learners who have mastered word-final /n/ should be able to handle cases (b)-(h) discussed below with ease.

〈こんなときは (If you face a challenge ...)〉

(a) 以外の場合における /n/ の発音のトラブルについても一応 (b) ～ (h) として列挙しておきます．初級の学習者についてはあまり必要度は高くないかもしれませんが，無理がなければ取り上げてください．すべての項目は，同じ問題です．/n/ を言うべきところで学習者の舌先が正しく上の歯ぐきに触れず，宙に浮いていることがあるのです．それぞれの項で提案するリピート練習方法が有効だと思います．

Here are cases, labeled (b) to (h), where /n/ occurs in environments other than (a). If you have beginning learners, you may not need to attach as much importance to these cases as you should to (a), but I am listing them in case learners are ready for learning about these other cases as well. All of the items are in fact about the same problem: Learners may fail to have their tongue tip properly on the upper teeth ridge and may instead have it up in the air in the mouth when they try to say /n/. The repetition practice suggested will be useful for coping with this problem.

(b) /n/ が /j/ の直前に来る場合 (Cases where /n/ is followed by /j/)

たとえば in your house に見られるように，/n/ が /j/ (your のアタマの /j/) の直前に来る場合です．in your の下線部でニュまたはニョに近い音が聞こえるはずです．

There are cases in which /n/ is followed by /j/, as in *in your house.* Learners should say this phrase in a way in which a sound like “nyu” or “nyo” is heard in the middle of the phrase.

リピート練習 (Repetition practice)

1. /jʊɚ haʊs/ (your house)
2. /n jʊɚ haʊs/ (-n your house)
   (下線部のところでニュまたはニョに近い音が出るようにする)
3. /ɪn jʊɚ haʊs/ (in your house)
   (下線部のところでニュまたはニョに近い音が出るようにする)

(c) /n/ が /w/ の直前に来る場合 (Cases where /n/ is followed by /w/)

たとえば in Washington に見られるように，/n/ が /w/（Washington のアタマの /w/）の直前に来る場合です．in Washington の下線部でヌワに近い音が聞こえるはずです．

There are cases in which /n/ is followed by /w/, as in *in Washington.* Learners should say this phrase in a way in which a sound like "nuwa" is heard in the middle of the phrase.

リピート練習（Repetition practice）

1. /wɑʃɪŋtən/（Washington）
2. /n wɑʃɪŋtən/（-n Washington）
（下線部のところでヌワに近い音が出るようにする）
3. /ɪn wɑʃɪŋtən/（in Washington）
（下線部のところでヌワに近い音が出るようにする）

(d)　/n/ が /h/ の直前に来る場合（Cases where /n/ is followed by /h/）

たとえば down here に見られるように，/n/ が /h/ の直前に来る場合です．down here の下線部でヌヒに近い音が聞こえるはずです．

There are cases in which /n/ is followed by /h/, as in *down here.* Learners should say this phrase in a way in which a sound like "nuhi" is heard in the middle of the phrase.

リピート練習（Repetition practice）

1. / hɪɚ/（here）
2. /n hɪɚ/（-n here）（下線部のところでヌヒ近い音が出るようにする）
3. /daʊn hɪɚ/（down here）
（下線部のところでヌヒに近い音が出るようにする）

(e)　/n/ が /s/ の直前に来る場合（Cases where /n/ is followed by /s/）

たとえば dance，on sale（特売で）に見られるように，/n/ が /s/ の直前に来る場合です．dance, on sale の下線部でンツに近い音が聞こえるはずです．

There are cases in which /n/ is followed by /s/, as in *dance* and *on sale.* Learners should say these items in a way in which a sound like /nts/ is heard in the middle of each phrase.

リピート練習（Repetition practice）

1. /ts/
2. /nts/
3. /dænts/（＝dance）（下線部のところでンツに近い音が出るようにする）

リピート練習（Repetition practice）

1. /seɪl/（＝sale）
2. /tseɪl/（下線部のところでツェに近い音が出るようにする）
3. /ntseɪl/（-n sale）（下線部のところでンツェに近い音が出るようにする）
4. /ɑntseɪl/（on sale）（下線部のところでンツェに近い音が出るようにする）

(f) /n/ が /ʃ/ の直前に来る場合（Cases where /n/ is followed by /ʃ/）

たとえば sunshine，ten sheep に見られるように，/n/ が /ʃ/ の直前に来る場合です．sunshine，ten sheep の下線部の /nʃ/ を /ntʃ/ と言うようにすることが有効です．

There are cases in which /n/ is followed by /ʃ/, as in *sunshine* and *ten sheep*. Learners should say these items in a way in which a sound like /ntʃ/ is heard where /nʃ/ occurs.

リピート練習（Repetition practice）

1. /ʃiːp/（＝sheep）
2. /tʃiːp/（下線部のところでチに近い音が出るようにする）
3. /ntʃiːp/（-n sheep）（下線部のところでンチに近い音が出るようにする）
4. /tentʃiːp/（＝ten sheep）（下線部のところでンチに近い音が出るようにする）

(g) /n/ が /f/ の直前に来る場合（Cases where /n/ is followed by /f/）

たとえば information，in France に見られるように，/n/ が /f/ の直前に来る場合です．information，in France の下線部から次の音に移るところでヌに近い音が聞こえるはずです．

There are cases in which /n/ is followed by /f/, as in *information* and *in France*. Learners should say these items in a way in which a sound like "nu" occurs right after /n/.

リピート練習 (Repetition practice)

1. /fɚmeɪʃən/ (-formation)
2. /nfɚmeɪʃən/ (-nformation)（下線部直後にヌに近い音が出るようにする）
3. /ɪnfɚmeɪʃən/ (information)（下線部直後にヌに近い音が出るようにする）

(h) /n/ が /r/ の直前に来る場合 (Cases where /n/ is followed by /r/)

たとえば Henry, in Rome に見られるように，/n/ が /r/ の直前に来る場合です．Henry，in Rome の下線部でヌリやヌロに近い音が聞こえるはずです．この項は，学習者が /r/ の発音をすでにマスターしたという前提に立っています．このことは，第 13 章セクション 3 で詳しく取り上げます．

There are cases in which /n/ is followed by /r/, as in *Henry* and *in Rome*. Learners should say *Henry* in a way in which a sound like "nuri" is heard in the middle of the name and say *in Rome* in a way in which a sound like "nuro" is heard in the middle of the phrase. What I am saying in this paragraph assumes that learners have already mastered /r/. See Section 3 of Chapter 13 for details.

リピート練習 (Repetition practice)

1. /ri/ (-ry)
2. /nri/ (-nry)（下線部のところでヌリに近い音が出るようにする）
3. /henri/ (Henry)（下線部のところでヌリに近い音が出るようにする）

リピート練習 (Repetition practice)

1. /roʊm/ (Rome)
2. /nroʊm/ (-n Rome)（下線部のところでヌロに近い音が出るようにする）
3. /ɪnroʊm/ (in Rome)（下線部のところでヌロに近い音が出るようにする）

3. 練習のための言語材料 (Materials for practice)

下線部に注意して発音するよう指示してください.

Make learners pay attention to the underlined part(s) of each item.

単語

(1) nice (2) one (3) pin (4) prince (王子) (5) information
(6) Henry (ヘンリー＝男子の名) (7) mansion (邸宅)
(8) unhappy (不幸せな，不満足な) (9) enrich (豊かにする)
(10) inward (内向きの)

フレーズ

(1) an apple (リンゴひとつ)
(2) in your house (あなたの家の中で)
(3) in his house (彼の家の中で)
(4) in Rome (ローマで)

センテンス

(1) There is only one. (ひとつしかない.)
(2) She lives in a big mansion. (彼女は大邸宅に住んでいる.)
(3) We sang ten songs. (私たちは 10 曲の歌を歌った.)

会話

A: Are you coming in your car? (あなたの車でいらっしゃるのですか？)
B: No. I'm coming in Henry's car. (いいえ．ヘンリーの車で来ます.)
A: I see. Can he find the way here? (そうですか．彼は道が分かりますか？)
B: I don't know. Can you call him and check?
(どうかな．彼に電話してチェックしてくれませんか？)

4. アクティビティー見本 (Idea for an activity)

「誰の自宅に何がある？」 (Who has what in the house?)

ふた通りの遊びかたがあります.

その1：ひとりのプレーヤーが，下に示す，チェックのついた表を持ちます．他のプレーヤーは同じ表のチェックのないものをそれぞれ持ちます（1枚をシェアしてもいいです）．他のプレーヤーは最初のプレーヤーに誰が何を自宅に持っているか質問し，表を完成して行きます．例として，次のようなやりとりが考えられます．

There are two ways to play this game.

(1) One of the players holds the table below, with ticks indicating who has what in the house. The other players each have a copy of the same table—but only with blank boxes. (Or they can share one such copy.) They ask the player questions to find out who has what in the house and try to put ticks in the right boxes in the blank table.

Possible exchanges are:

A: Does Victoria have a piano in her house?
（ビクトリアは彼女の家にピアノを持っていますか？）

B: Yes, she does.（はい，持っています.）

A: Does Jim have a microwave oven in his house?
（ジムは彼の家に電子レンジを持っていますか？）

B: No, he doesn't.（いいえ，持っていません.）

その2：ひとりのプレーヤーがひとりのキャラクターになりますが，どのキャラクターかは伏せます．このプレーヤーは他の人から自宅にあるものについての質問に答えます．他の人は最初のプレーヤーがどのキャラクターになっているのか，できるだけ早く当てようとします．例として，次のようなやりとりが考えられます．

(2) One player plays the part of one of the characters in the table but does not tell the others which character it is that he or she is playing. The other players ask him or her questions about what is in his or her house and try to find out which character is being played.

Possible exchanges are:

A: Do you have a piano in your house?
（あなたは家にピアノを持っていますか？）

B: Yes, I do.（はい，持っています.）

A: Do you have a dishwasher in your house?
（あなたは家に食洗機を持っていますか？）

B: No, I don't.（いいえ，持っていません.）

	Piano（ピアノ）	Fax machine（ファックス）	Dishwasher（食洗器）	Microwave oven（電子レンジ）
Victoria	✔	✔		
Jim	✔	✔	✔	
Alice			✔	✔
Bill	✔	✔		✔
Helen	✔			✔
John		✔		

ここでの焦点は in your house, in his house, in her house に出て来る /n/ です．学習者の発音に問題があったら，次のように対応してください．(1) 活動が終わってから，明示的に指導する．(2) 活動の最中であれば，リキャストにより指導する（p. 10 参照）.

The focus here is on /n/ in phrases such as *in your house, in his house,* and *in her house*. If learners' pronunciation is problematical, do the following: (1) provide explicit instruction after the activity; (2) provide recasts (see p. 10) during the activity.

第7章

すぼめた唇をどこまで開く—/w/ の指導

たとえば would, woman　　How to teach /w/

1. /w/ の指導のポイント (How to teach /w/)

〈まずはここから (To begin with ...)〉

/w/ の音は，たとえば walk，woman のアタマの音などとして使われます．question の最初（/kw-/ の部分）に出て来る音でもあります．この音を教えるときには，学習者に，唇をすぼめて狭い息の通り道を作らせ，その通り道を急に広げるよう指導してください．このことの説明には図 7.1 のような板書が役立ちます．

/w/ appears at the beginning of words like *walk* and *woman* and near the beginning of a word like *question* (in the /kw/ combination at the beginning of the word). To teach /w/, have learners round their lips and make a narrow opening between them for air to pass, and then have them suddenly enlarge the opening. An illustration like Figure 7.1 may help to explain this process.

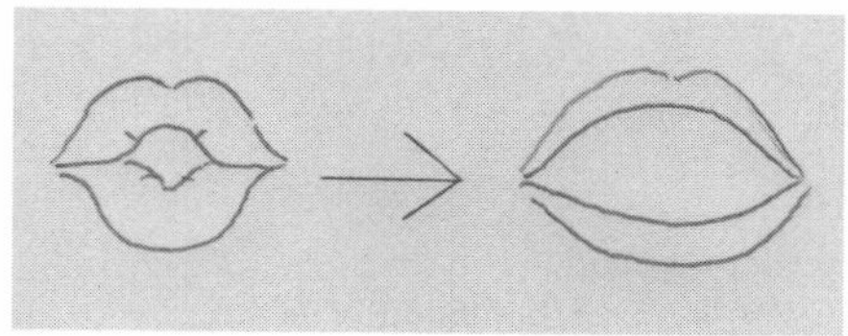

図 7.1　/w/ の際の唇の動き (Movement of the lips for the articulation of /w/)

〈こんなときは (If you face a challenge ...)〉

学習者のうちには，walk がうまく言えても question に出て来る /w/ を抜かして，この単語を「ケスチョン」のように言ってしまう人がいます．また，

/w/ を言ってはいるのですが弱くしか言わないために，この単語を「クエスチョン」(「クウェ」ではなく）のように言ってしまう人もいます．こうした問題を避けるためには，次のようなリピート練習をするとよいでしょう．

Some learners who can say *walk* correctly may nevertheless be unable to say *question*, pronouncing the word /kestʃən/ (without the /w/). Others may say /w/ only weakly and pronounce the word /kʊestʃən/. The following repetition practice may help learners solve these problems.

(1) /westʃən/ (question のアタマの /k/ を抜かして /w/ から言う．あたかも単語のつづりが westion であるかのように．) (Say *question* without the initial /k/, as if the word were spelled "westion.")

(2) question（上記の /westʃən/ のアタマに /k/ をつけて，単語を正しく言う．) (Put /k/ at the beginning of the above string of sounds and change it into *question*.)

上記 (2) の場合，/k/ の発音の瞬間には唇は丸まっているはずです．図 7.2 の板書によって，/k/ /w/ の関係を学習者に理解させることができます．

When learners do (2) above, their lips should be rounded at the time of the articulation of /k/. Figure 7.2 shows how lip rounding and the articulation of /k/ are simultaneously executed.

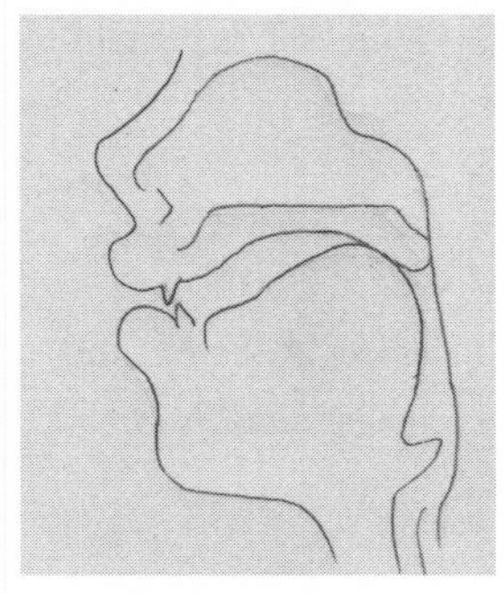

図 7.2 /kw/ の発音 (Articulation of /kw/)

2. /wʊ/ /wu:/ の指導のポイント (How to teach /wʊ/ and /wu:/)

〈まずはここから (To begin with ...)〉

/wʊ/ は woman，would のアタマに現れます．/wu:/ は wound （/wu:nd/「きず」）のアタマに現れます．唇を丸め，少しその丸みをゆるめ，ゆるめた結果が /ʊ/ または /u:/ となるよう指導してください．/wu:/ の頻度は低いですが /wʊ/ のほうは would，woman という頻度の高い重要語に出て来ますので，指導は /wʊ/ を重視して行ってください．/wʊ/ の唇の動きは図 7.3 のようになります．これを板書し，唇の丸みをゆるめた結果 /ʊ/ の唇の形となるよう指導してください．

/wʊ/ appears at the beginning of words like *woman* and *would*; /wu:/ appears at the beginning of *wound* (/wu:nd/). Have learners round their lips, then slightly loosen the rounding so that the resulting sound is /ʊ/ or /u:/. /wu:/ is an infrequent combination of sounds while /wʊ/ appears in high-frequency words such as *would* and *woman*, so focus more on /wʊ/ in class than on /wu:/. Figure 7.3 indicates how the lips are used for saying /wʊ/. You may want to draw this illustration on the board in class.

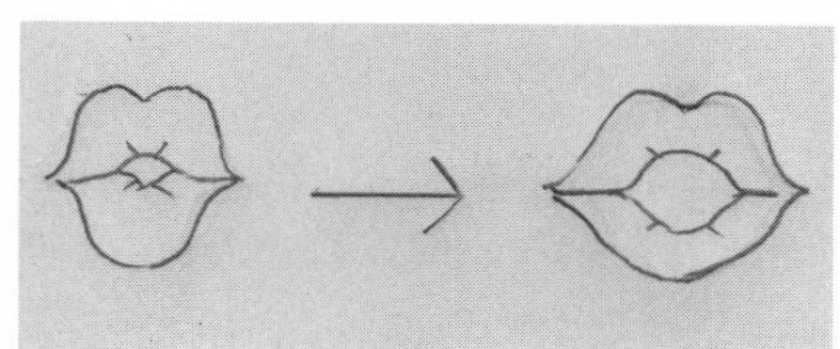

図 7.3　/wʊ/ の 発 音 (Articulation of /wʊ/)

日本の学習者にとって /wʊ/ と /wu:/ が難しい[1] のは，ワ行にウ段の音がないからです.[2] しかし，/wʊ/ の発音を教える際に，これを言うときの唇の動きに着目し，それに似た動きをしながら発音する日本語を使うことができます．私は，woman の発音を教えるときに「魚万」という架空の魚屋さんの屋号を使うことにしています．ウオマンのアタマのウオという部分を言うときの唇の動きは次のようになります．

The reason learners in Japan have trouble with /wʊ/ and /wu:/[1] is that there is no syllable in Japanese where the w-sound is followed by the "u" vowel.[2] When teaching /wʊ/, however, you can refer to a Japanese word where the lips move in the same way as they do when /wʊ/ is said: When I teach how to say *woman*, I bring up the fictitious name of a fictitious fish shop, "Uoman." When saying the first part of this name, the speaker moves the lips in the following way.

(1) 唇を丸めてウと言う．（英語の /w/ を言うときほどは丸みは強くありませんが，ある程度の丸みがあります．）(Round the lips—moderately, not so closely as when one says the English /w/ sound.)

(2) オに移る際に丸まった唇が急に開く．(Suddenly open the passage of air between the lips when moving to the "o" vowel.)

(3) オという母音を言う．(Say the "o" vowel.)

この唇の動きは /wʊ/ と言うときのそれに酷似していますので，ウオマンということばが woman の発音の指導に使えるのです．

The movement of the lips that occurs in the above process is much like the movement of the lips that occurs when the speaker says /wʊ/. That is why you can use the Japanese name "Uoman" for teaching the pronunciation of *woman*.

〈こんなときは (If you face a challenge ...)〉

would は言えても wound (/wu:nd/) が言えない，という学習者がいる可能性があります．/wʊ/ より /wu:/ のほうが確かに難しいです．というのは，/ʊ/ より /u:/ のほうが唇をより小さくすぼめて出す音ですので，/w/ のあとで唇の開きを大きくし，それでも開きを /u:/ の小ささにとどめる，ということができないのです．この問題に対応するためには，次の 2 点を学習者に伝えるとよいと思います．(a) /w/ のための唇の開きをできるだけ小さくすること，(b) /u:/ を言うとき，唇の開きを限界まで小さくする必要はないこと（限界まで小さくするべきだと誤解している学習者がいます)，の 2 点です．また，練習のために /wu:wu:wu: .../ と言わせるのも有効です．

There may be learners who can say *would* but not *wound* (/wu:nd/). Indeed, /wu:/ is more difficult to say than /wʊ/ for many learners. Since /u:/ requires closer lip rounding than /ʊ/, learners cannot easily make the opening between the lips larger after saying /w/ and still make the opening as small as /u:/. To solve this problem, you may want to tell learners (a) that they should make the opening for /w/ as small as possible and (b) that, for saying /u:/, they do not need to round their lips to the limit (some learners mistakenly think that they should). Also, you can tell them to say /wu:wu:wu: ... / for practice.

3. 練習のための言語材料 (Materials for practice)

下線部に注意して発音するよう指示してください．

Make learners pay attention to the underlined part(s) of each item.

単語

(1) week (2) website (3) wax（蝋） (4) would (5) woman
(6) wood (7) wound (/wu:nd/ 怪我) (8) question
(9) quiet（静かな） (10) request（要請）

フレーズ

(1) very windy（とても風が強い）
(2) for two weeks（2 週間）
(3) minor wound（軽傷）
(4) made of wood（木製）

センテンス

(1) It's too warm in this room.（この部屋は暖かすぎる.）
(2) Would you please come here?（こちらに来て頂けませんか？）
(3) A woman was wounded in the accident.（女性が事故で怪我をした.）

会話

A: Would you please help me?（お願いします.）
B: Sure. What can I do for you?（はい．どんなご用でしょうか？）
A: I have a question about the dress in the display window.
（ショーウィンドウにあるドレスについて質問があるのですが.）
B: All right. Would you like to sit down? I'll be with you in a minute.

（分かりました．お座り頂けますか？すぐに対応させて頂きますので．）

（*what* のアタマの音は /w/ でなくささやき声の /hw/ でもかまいません．The initial consonant of *what* may be /w/ or /hw/; the latter is a whispered version of /w/.）

4. アクティビティー見本 (Idea for an activity)

「大きな夢コンテスト」 (Big-dream contest)

大きな夢のコンテストです．学習者同士，または指導者と学習者で会話を行ってください．例として，次のようなやりとりが考えられます．金額は変えて結構です．学習者全員が夢を語ったあとで，最も大きな夢（または最も独創的な夢，または最もバカバカしい夢，など独自の基準で最高レベルの夢）を語った学習者を選んでください．

Engage learners in a conversation with each other or with you and get them to compete for having the biggest dream or some other great ambition. One possible exchange is as follows. You can change the amount of money in any way you wish. After having all the learners say what their dream is, choose the person who mentioned the biggest dream (or the most original dream or the silliest dream or any other sort of dream that is remarkable by a criterion of your choice).

A: If you had a million yen, what would you do?
（百万円あったら何をしますか？）

B: I would buy a car. (車を買います.)

ここでの焦点は /w/ です．学習者の発音に問題があったら，次のように対応してください．(1) 活動が終わってから，明示的に指導する．(2) 活動の最中であれば，リキャストにより指導する (p. 10 参照)．

The focus here is on /w/. If learners' pronunciation is problematical, do the following: (1) provide explicit instruction after the activity; (2) provide recasts (see p. 10) during the activity.

第 8 章
イに聞こえる音 — /iː/ /ɪ/ の指導

たとえば sheep，ship　　How to teach /iː/ and /ɪ/

1.　/iː/ /ɪ/ の指導のポイント (How to teach /iː/ and /ɪ/)

〈まずはここから (To begin with ...)〉

/iː/ の音は，たとえば sea（海），sheep（羊）の下線部の母音として使われます．日本語のイに非常に近い音ですので，ほとんどの学習者はこの音を出すのに苦労しません．一方，/ɪ/ の音は，学習者にとってさほど楽ではありません．この音は，たとえば sit（すわる），ship（船）の下線部の母音として使われます．この音は日本語のイと日本語のエとの中間の音と説明すれば理解されやすいと思います．ふたつの音を日本語の母音と比べて発音のものさしで示すと図 8.1 のようになります．これを板書するとよいでしょう．

/iː/ appears in words like *sea* and *sheep*. It is so close to the Japanese "i" vowel that few learners have trouble producing it. /ɪ/, on the other hand, is not easy for learners to articulate. It appears in words like *sit* and *ship*. Learners will understand what it is like if you explain that it is a sound halfway between the Japanese "i" and "e" vowels. You may want to draw an illustration like Figure 8.1 to compare /iː/ and /ɪ/ in relation to Japanese vowels.

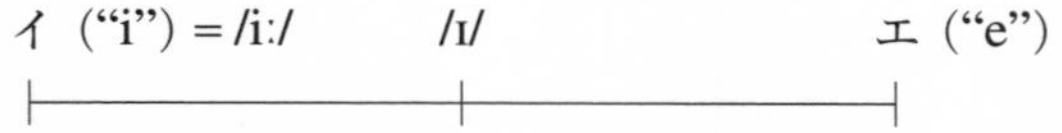

イ（"i"）= /iː/　　　/ɪ/　　　エ（"e"）

図 8.1　イからエに至る発音のものさし (Scale ranging between the Japanese "i" and "e" vowels)

/iː/ と /ɪ/ との差を，アゴの開きという切り口で説明することもできます．/iː/ を言うときには，日本語のイを言うときとほぼ同じで，アゴの開きは小さくなります（図 8.2）．この状態から，アゴを少しゆるめてアゴを開き気味にすると，/ɪ/ を言うのに適当な開きとなります（図 8.3）．同じ情報を，アゴの開きを示すボードでも伝えることができます（図 8.4，図 8.5）．ここにお示しする歯型やボードの開き具合の差は実際よりも大げさですが，学習者の頭の中にイメージを作るのには必要であるというのが私の経験です．もちろん，歯型やボードを使った指導の過程で，学習者に出してほしい音を指導者が聞かせ続ける必要があります．

You can explain the difference between /iː/ and /ɪ/ in terms of the degree of the opening between the jaws. Just as in the case of the Japanese "i" vowel, the opening between the jaws when one says /iː/ is small (Figure 8.2). When learners have learned to say /iː/, tell them to make the opening between the jaws slightly larger, and they will now be saying /ɪ/ (Figure 8.3). This information may also be conveyed with a board with a picture of the jaws drawn on it (Figure 8.4 and Figure 8.5). In the photographs, the jaw model and the board show the difference between the two vowels in the degree of the opening between the jaws as being greater than it really is, but it is my experience that the exaggeration is necessary for helping learners to get the feel of the difference. Of course, you should let learners hear the correct sounds as you use the jaw model or the board.

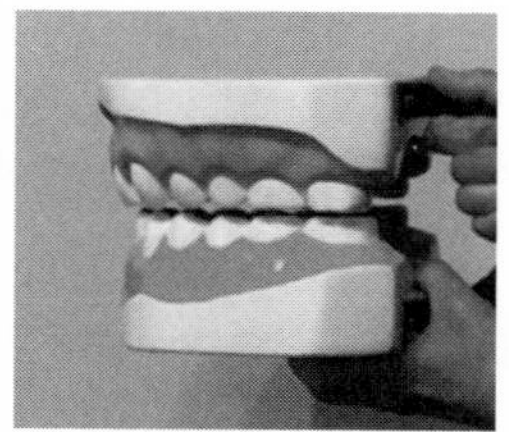

図 8.2 /iː/ の発音の際のアゴの開き (Opening between the jaws in the articulation of /iː/)

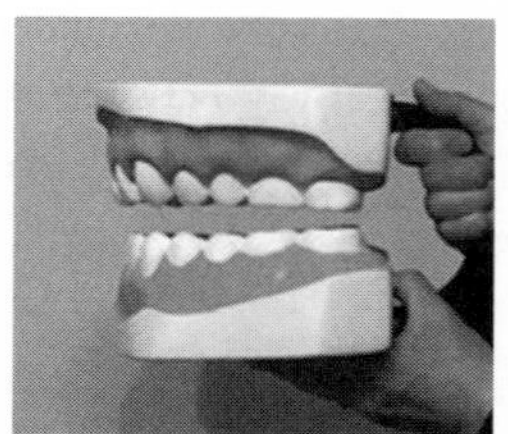

図 8.3 /ɪ/ の発音の際のアゴの開き (Opening between the jaws in the articulation of /ɪ/)

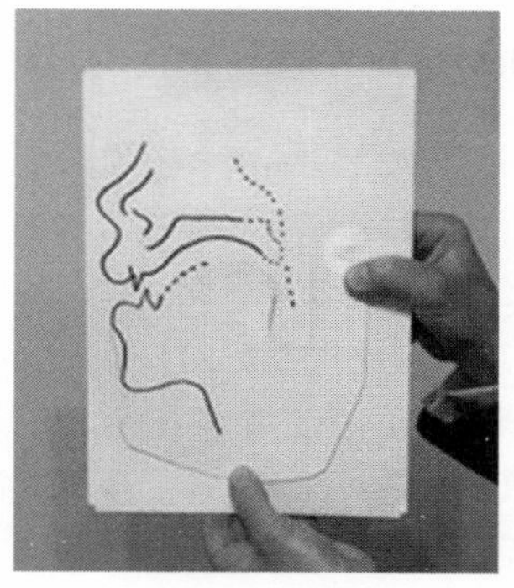

図 8.4　/iː/ の発音の際のアゴの開き（Opening between the jaws in the articulation of /iː/）

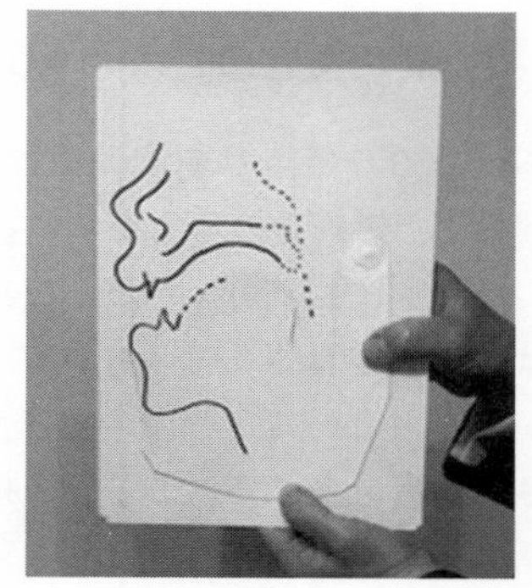

図 8.5　/ɪ/ の発音の際のアゴの開き（Opening between the jaws in the articulation of /ɪ/）

〈こんなときは（If you face a challenge ...)〉

学習者のなかには，/iː/ と /ɪ/ とを発音すべきときに，ふたつの音を長さだけで差をつける人が少なくありません．このような学習者は，/iː/ は /ɪ/ の2倍の長さだという誤解をしています．ひとつの原因は，外来語において /iː/ は伸ばす音として扱われ（たとえば「ピース」，「シート」），/ɪ/ は伸ばさない音として扱われる（たとえば「ピン」，「ミス」）ことかもしれません．また，/iː/ に /ː/ という長音符がついており，しかもそのテンの数が2個であることも誤解の原因かもしれません．私は，むしろ，これらふたつの音を教えるとき，しばしば，「今は長さを同じにして発音練習してみましょう」と指示します．次にその理由を説明します．

Some learners differentiate /iː/ and /ɪ/ only by making the former sound longer. They mistakenly think that /iː/ is twice as long as /ɪ/. One cause of this misunderstanding may be that /iː/ in loan words is treated as a long vowel, as in "piisu" ("peace") and "shiito" ("seat") and /ɪ/ is treated as a short vowel, as in "pin" ("pin") and "misu" ("mistake"). Another cause may be that the phonetic symbol /iː/ has a length mark made up of two dots. When I teach these sounds, I say to learners "Forget about the length of the vowels for the time being and spend exactly the same amount of time saying them." The following paragraph explains why.

2. /iː/ /ɪ/ の長さの問題 (The issue of the length of /iː/ and /ɪ/)

ふたつの音の指導をするときに長さに着目しないほうがよい理由を 3 点挙げます. これらの理由を学習者に説明する必要は生じないかもしれませんが, 指導者として知っておくことはよいことだと思います. 第一に, 長さの差は 2 対 1 では全くなく, 同じ音声環境で比べれば片方が少し長くなる傾向がある, といった程度の差だからです. 第二に, 学習者が /iː/ と /ɪ/ との長さに焦点を当ててしまうと, 肝心の音の質に意識が向かなくなる可能性があります. 第三に, 英語の音は文脈によって長さが変わるので, 同じ音でもさまざまの長さになります. たとえば, These mittens are too big. (/ðiːz mɪtənz ɑɚ tuː bɪg/「これらのミトン＝ふたまた手袋＝は大きすぎる」) において, /ɪ/ が 2 回出てきますが, 2 回目の /ɪ/ (文末の big に出て来る) は最初の /ɪ/ (mittens の mit- に出て来る) よりずっと長くなりますし, these の /iː/ より長い可能性すらあります. つまり, 音の長さを文脈から切り離して比べることは, 少なくとも発音指導上は, あまり生産的ではありません.

I can give three reasons why it is best not to focus on the issue of the length as you teach these vowels. You may not need to explain these reasons to learners, but you as the instructor should know them. First, the lengths of /iː/ and /ɪ/ are not 2 to 1. Compared in the same phonetic environment, /iː/ is only slightly longer than /ɪ/. Second, learners may fail to focus on the quality of the sounds in question if you allow them to focus on the length. Third, the length of a sound in English varies depending on the context, the same sound varying in length considerably. For example, in the sentence *These mittens are too big* (/ðiːz mɪtənz ɑɚ tuː bɪg/), where /ɪ/ appears twice, the second /ɪ/ (in *big*) is much longer than the first /ɪ/ (in *mittens*), and may even be longer than /iː/ in *these*. In other words, comparing the lengths of vowels out of context is not very productive, at least from the point of view of pronunciation teaching.

3. 練習のための言語材料 (Materials for practice)

下線部に注意して発音するよう指示してください. 一重下線は /iː/, 二重下線は /ɪ/ です.

Make learners pay attention to the underlined part(s) of each item.

単語

(1) peak（山頂）　(2) feet　(3) sheep　(4) heat
(5) least（最も少ない）　(6) pick（つまみ取る）　(7) fit（健康な）
(8) ship　(9) hit　(10) list（リスト）

フレーズ

(1) six feet（6 フィート）
(2) sit in the seat（席に座る）
(3) pick up the pieces（断片を拾う）
(4) Tim's team（ティム＝男子の名＝のチーム）

センテンス

I need to fix the window.（窓を直さなくてはならない.）
Please sit over here.（こちらにお座りください.）
The meeting is finished.（会議が終わっている.）

会話

A: I missed you at the meeting yesterday.
（きのうの会合にあなたがいなくて残念でした.）
B: I'm sorry. I was feeling sick all day yesterday.
（申し訳ない. きのう一日中気分が悪くて.）
A: Oh, no. Are you feeling all right now?
（それはいけない. いまは気分はいいの？）
B: Yes, thank you. I feel fine.（はい. ありがとう. 気分はいいです.）

5. アクティビティー見本 (Idea for an activity)

「土ぼこり」(Cloud of dust)

「土ぼこり」ゲームです. 土ぼこりの中に隠れているものを学習者に探させるべく, 学習者同士, または指導者と学習者で会話を行ってください. 例として, 次のようなやりとりが考えられます.

Engage learners in a conversation with each other or with you and have them say what they can see in the cloud. See the following for answers.

A: What do you see in the cloud of dust?
(土ぼこりの中に何が見えますか？)

B: I see a ship (or: sheep/bridge/fish/hippo(potamus)/chicken/leaf/pig).
(船（または羊，橋，魚，カバ，ニワトリ，木の葉，ブタ）が見えます.)

ここでの焦点は /iː/ /ɪ/ です．学習者の発音に問題があったら，次のように対応してください．(1) 活動が終わってから，明示的に指導する．(2) 活動の最中であれば，リキャストにより指導する (p. 10 参照).

The focus here is on /iː/ and /ɪ/. If learners' pronunciation is problematical, do the following: (1) provide explicit instruction after the activity; (2) provide recasts (see p. 10) during the activity.

第9章
アに聞こえる音—/ɚː/ /ɑɚ/ の指導

たとえば hurt, heart How to teach /ɚː/ and /ɑɚ/

1. /ɚː/ の指導のポイント (How to teach /ɚː/)

〈まずはここから (To begin with ...)〉

/ɚː/ の音は，bird，hurt，learn などに出て来ます．第1章で取り上げた /r/ の音をそのまま母音として使った音である，と説明すると学習者に理解してもらいやすいと思います．第1章でご覧に入れた /r/ の教え方の写真を再びご覧に入れます（図 9.1）．上の奥歯のすぐ内側の歯ぐき，すなわち指で示した場所を，左右同時になめて声を出し，これが /ɚː/ の音であると説明すれば十分です．

/ɚː/ appears in words like *bird*, *hurt*, and *learn*. Learners will understand the nature of this sound if you tell them that it is actually /r/ (discussed in Chapter 1) used as a vowel. Review how to teach /r/ by studying Figure 9.1, which is the same figure as Figure 1.1, given in Chapter 1 to illustrate how to teach /r/. Have learners articulate /ɚː/ by placing the sides of the tongue against the upper teeth ridge at the two spots shown with fingers in the photograph.

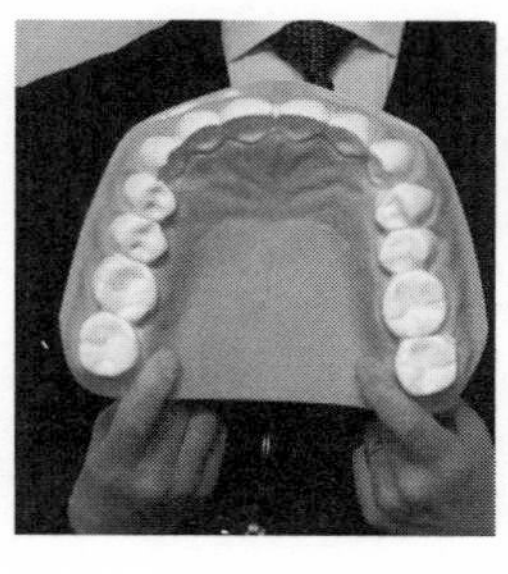

図 9.1 /r/ を言うときに舌が触れる場所；両手で示したところ (The spots on the teeth ridge that the tongue touches in the articulation of /r/—shown with both hands)

〈こんなときは (If you face a challenge ...)〉

たとえば，主たる指導者が北米系発音を使い，ALT がイギリス系の発音をする人だった場合，混乱が生じる可能性があるので注意が必要です．上記は北米系の英語における /ɚː/[1] の音の説明でしたが，イギリス系の英語においては /ɚː/ の場所で別の音が使われます．イギリス系の音はしばしば /əː/[2] と表記される音で，この音を説明しなくてはならない場合，「アゴを閉じ気味にして出すア」と言えば分かりやすいかもしれません．アゴを閉じ気味に，という指示をするときに，歯型で示したり（図 9.2），アゴの開きを示すボードで示したり（図 9.3）することができます．

There is a possibility of confusion arising in class if the main instructor for the class uses pronunciation of the North American-type and an ALT uses British-type pronunciation, for example. The above paragraph describes /ɚː/[1] as used in North American-type pronunciation, but, where /ɚː/ would be used in that type of pronunciation, a different sound is used in British-type pronunciation: what is often represented by the symbol /əː/.[2] If you need to explain to learners how it is articulated, a simple explanation is that it is an "a"-like sound that one articulates by making the opening between the jaws small. When you explain that the jaws are rather closed, you may want to do so with a jaw model (Figure 9.2) or a board with an illustration of the jaws (Figure 9.3).

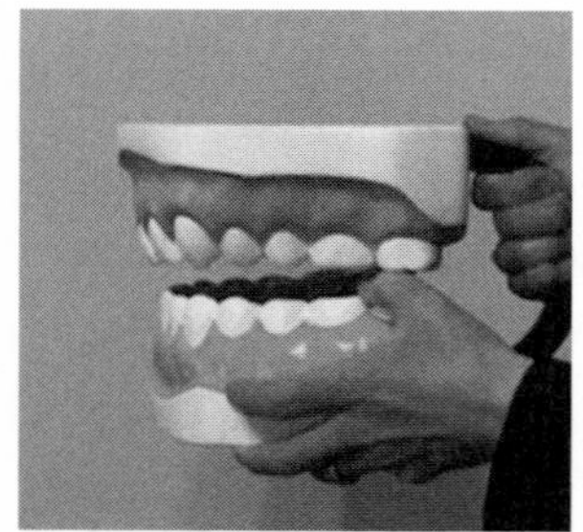

図 9.2 /əː/ の際のアゴの開き (Opening between the jaws for /əː/)

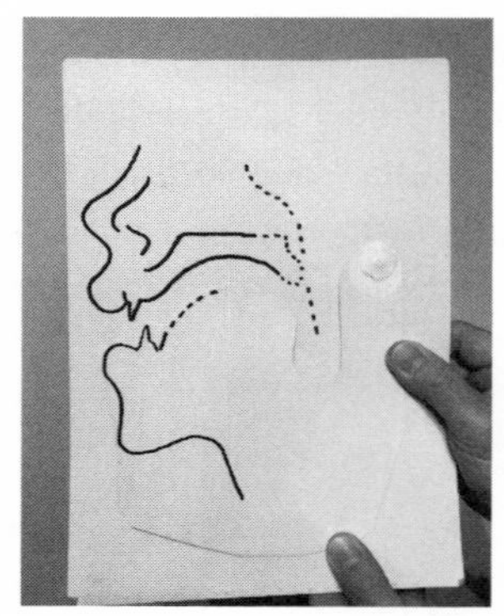

図 9.3 /əː/ の際のアゴの開き (Opening between the jaws for /əː/)

2. /ɑɚ/ の指導のポイント (How to teach /ɑɚ/)

〈まずはここから (To begin with ...)〉

/ɑɚ/ の音は，heart，park，star などに出て来ます．この音は，/ɑ/ という母音で始まり，その母音の最後のほう（始めからではなく，最後のほう）に /r/ の響きを添えた音です．この最後の /r/ の響きは発音記号としては /ɚ/ で表すことにします．まず，/ɑ/ から説明します．この音は日本語のアとほぼ同じであると説明して結構です．（このセクションの後のほうで「うがいの音」という呼び名を使ってこの音について説明しますが，初級の学習者にとってはこの説明の必要度は低いと思います．）

/ɑɚ/ appears in words like *heart*, *park*, and *star*. This sound begins as /ɑ/ and changes toward /r/ as you approach the end. This final /r/ is represented by the symbol /ɚ/. When you explain /ɑ/ to learners, you can say that it is virtually the same as the Japanese "a" vowel (I will provide further explanation of this sound later in this section by describing it as a "gargling sound," but the need for this explanation is not so great for beginning learners).

次に，/ɚ/ について説明します．この音は，/ɑɚ/ という二重母音の第二要素です．英語には，二重母音と呼ばれる音がいくつかあり，第一要素と第二要素から成っています．私は，二重母音の第二要素は，「その方向に音が動き始めれば十分」と教えることにしています．/ɑɚ/ の場合も，この音を発音する際には，最初に /ɑ/ を言い，その後で，音を /ɚ/ の方向，すなわち /r/ の方向に動かせばよいのです．第 1 章で述べた通り，/r/ は上の奥歯の内側の歯ぐきを左右同時になめる音ですから，/ɑɚ/ を言うときには，/ɑ/ を言ってから，舌で上の奥歯の内側の歯ぐきを左右同時になめようとすればよい，ということになります．ただし，第二要素の /ɚ/，すなわち /r/ と同じ音については，完全にその音が聞こえるまで音が変わらなくとも，その音の方向に音が動き始めれば十分です．[3)]

/ɚ/ is the second element of the diphthong /ɑɚ/. There are some sounds in English called diphthongs, which are each made up of a first and a second element. When I explain the symbol for the second element of a diphthong to learners I say that it only indicates the direction in which the sound should begin to change before the articulation of the diphthong is finished. This applies to /ɑɚ/: You should have learners say /ɑ/ then have them change the sound toward /ɚ/. We saw in Chapter 1 that /r/ is a sound that one produces by placing the sides of the tongue against the upper teeth ridge, right inside the back teeth on the right and on the left. This means that, when one says /ɑɚ/, one should first say /ɑ/ and then begin to change the shape of one's tongue in the direction of the aforementioned /r/ shape, not necessarily reaching it.[3)]

〈こんなときは (If you face a challenge ...)〉

するどい学習者は，heart，park，star などに出て来る母音のアタマの音である /ɑ/ が日本語のアとは違っていることに気づいて，コメントするかもしれません．実際，/ɑ/ は，日本語のアに少しオの響きが入った音です．この音の出し方は，舌を口の後ろのほうに引き気味にしながらアと言う，というものです．私はこの音に「うがいの音」という名前をつけています．われわれは，うがいをするときに，口を開けて上を向きます．すると，舌がそれ自身の重みで口の後ろのほうに寄ります（説明には図 9.4 の板書がよいでしょう）．このときに声を出すと自然に /ɑ/ の音が出ます．ただ，/ɑ/ とアが違うという知識は，コミュニケーションの観点からは不要ですので，教えるには及びません．あくまでも学習者が質問したときに指導者が説明できるようにしておく，という程度で十分です．

Astute learners may notice that /ɑ/ is different from the Japanese "a" vowel and make a comment on this. In fact, /ɑ/ is an "a" which slightly tends toward "o." To say this vowel, one says "a" but draws the tongue toward the back at the same time. I call this sound a "gargling sound." When one gargles, one opens one's mouth and looks up. Then the tongue, because of its own weight, hangs downward toward the back of the head (draw an illustration like Figure 9.4 to explain this to learners). If one said a vowel in this way, one would be saying /ɑ/. But, as the information about the difference between /ɑ/ and the Japanese "a" vowel is not significant from a communicative point of view, there is no need to teach it. Just be prepared to answer a question about it if you get one from learners.

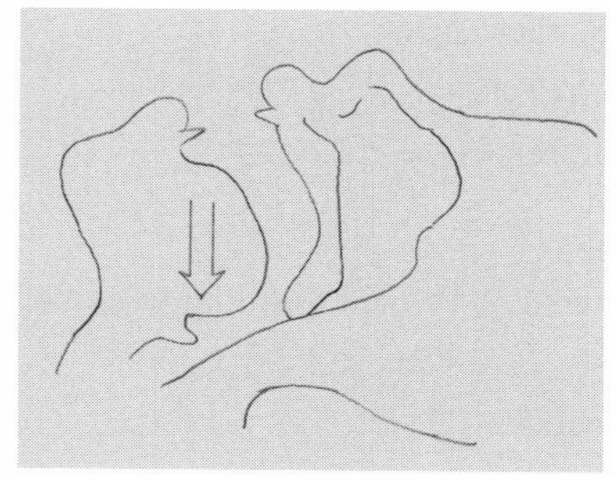

図9.4　うがいの音 (The gargling sound)

上記は北米系の英語における /ɑɚ/ の説明でしたが，イギリス系の英語においては /ɑɚ/ の場所で /ɑː/（/ɑ/ を /ɑɚ/ の長さで言う音）が使われます．

/ɑɚ/ is part of the sound system of the North American-type pronunciation. In British-type pronunciation, /ɑː/ (it is the same as /ɑ/ in quality and is pronounced as long as /ɑɚ/) is used in its place.

3.　練習のための言語材料 (Materials for practice)

下線部に注意して発音するよう指示してください．一重下線は /ɚː/，二重下線は /ɑɚ/ です．

Make learners pay attention to the underlined part(s) of each item.

単語

(1)　bird　(2)　third　(3)　shirt　(4)　turn　(5)　learn

(6)　park　(7)　car　(8)　far　(9)　heart　(10)　star

フレーズ

(1)　start the car（車のエンジンをかける）

(2)　the third turn（3番目のターン）

(3)　learn by heart（覚える）

(4)　birds in the park（公園の鳥たち）

センテンス

(1)　The church is near the park.（教会は公園の近くです.）

(2) Free cookies will be served at the market.
(マーケットで無料のクッキーがふるまわれます.)

(3) The first term is starting now. (最初の期が始まるところです.)

会話

A: We're having a party at home on Thursday. Would you like to come?
(木曜日にうちでパーティーをします. いらっしゃりたいですか?)

B: Yes, thank you. Is there a place to park?
(はい, ありがとう. 駐車場所はありますか?)

A: There's a parking lot near the service station.
(ガソリンスタンドの近くに駐車場があります.)

B: Oh, I remember. It's not far from your house, is it?
(ああ, 覚えています. お宅から遠くないですよね?)

5. アクティビティー見本 (Idea for an activity)

「私は誰でしょう?」(Who am I?)

「私は誰でしょう?」ゲームです. 学習者同士, または指導者と学習者で会話を行ってください. ひとりの人がヒントを出し, 他の人が当てます. 「私」は人間ではありません. 例として, 次のようなヒントが考えられます.

Engage learners in a conversation with each other or with you and have them play a guessing game. One person gives clues for the answer, which is something other than a person. Possible clues and answers are as follows.

1. I am very big. I look like a ball. The moon goes around me.
(私はとても大きいです. 私はボールのようです. 月は私の回りを回ります.)
Answer: I am the earth. (私は地球です.)

2. I am very distant from you. You can see me only at night. I am in the sky. I have lots of friends in the sky that look like me.
(私はあなたから遠いところにいます. あなたには夜にだけ私が見えます. 私は空にいます. 空には私のような友達がたくさんいます.)
Answer: I am a star. (私は星です.)

3. I can fly. I can sing. I eat worms. I make a nest in a tree.
（私は飛べます．私は歌えます．私は虫を食べます．私は木に巣を作ります．）
Answer: I am a bird.（私は鳥です．）
4. I am big. People come to me to walk around or sit on one of my benches.
（私は大きいです．人々は歩き回ったり私のベンチのひとつに座ったりするために私のところに来ます．）
Answer: I am a park.（私は公園です．）
5. I am made of cotton. People wear me, especially young people. My sleeves are short. I have pictures or words printed on me.
（私はコットンでできています．人々，特に若い人々は私を着ます．私の袖は短いです．私には絵やことばがプリントされています．）
Answer: I am a T-shirt.（私は T シャツです．）
6. I am a building. I have a bell. People come to me for weddings.
（私は建物です．私にはベルがあります．人々は結婚式のために私のところに来ます．）
Answer: I am a church.（私は教会です．）

ここでの焦点は /ɚː/ /ɑɚ/ です．学習者の発音に問題があったら，次のように対応してください．(1) 活動が終わってから，明示的に指導する．(2) 活動の最中であれば，リキャストにより指導する（p. 10 参照）．

The focus here is on /ɚː/ and /ɑɚ/. If learners' pronunciation is problematical, do the following: (1) provide explicit instruction after the activity; (2) provide recasts (see p. 10) during the activity.

第10章
オに聞こえる音―/oʊ/ /ɔː/ の指導

たとえば boat, bought　　How to teach /oʊ/ and /ɔː/

1. /oʊ/ の指導のポイント (How to teach /oʊ/)

〈まずはここから (To begin with ...)〉

/oʊ/ の音は，たとえば boat, coat, phone に出て来ます．この音も前章で話題にした二重母音です．最初の音は日本語のオと同じです．二番目の音を出すためには，日本語のウの方向に音を動かし始めればよい，と考えれば結構です．日本の学習者にとってこの音を出すことは全く難しくありません．/oʊ/ の第二要素である /ʊ/ をもし単独で出したとすると，それはオとウの中間の音であると考えると分かりやすいと思います．図 10.1 を板書するとこのことが説明できます．ただ，前述の通り，/oʊ/ における /ʊ/ は二重母音の第二の要素ですから，それを第一の要素ほど明確に発音する必要はありません．このことをつけ加えるのを忘れないでください．

/oʊ/, a diphthong (discussed in Chapter 9), appears in words like *boat, coat,* and *phone*. Its first element is the same as the Japanese “o” vowel. After saying /o/, learners should change the vowel in the direction of the Japanese “u” vowel. For learners in Japan, /oʊ/ is an easy sound to articulate. If you are to explain /ʊ/, the second element, you can say that, if it were produced by itself, it would be a sound halfway between “o” and “u.” Figure 10.1 will help you explain this. But be sure to add that, as /ʊ/ is only the second element of a diphthong, it is not necessary to articulate it as clearly as the first.

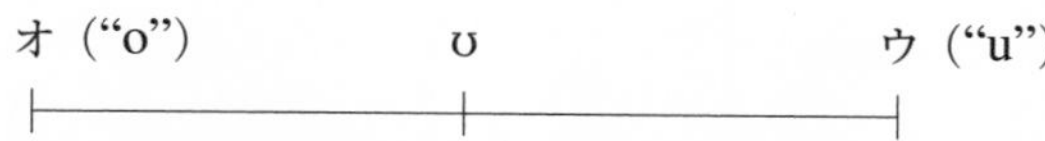

図 10.1　オからウに至る発音のものさし (Scale ranging between the Japanese "o" and "u" vowels)

〈こんなときは (If you face a challenge ...)〉

たとえば，主たる指導者が北米系発音を使い，ALT がイギリス系発音をする人だった場合，混乱が生じる可能性があるので注意が必要です．上記は北米系の英語における /oʊ/ の音の説明でしたが，イギリス系発音においては，/oʊ/ の場所で /əʊ/ というやや違った音が使われることが少なくありません．最初の /ə/ の音は，前章で取り上げたイギリス系発音の /ɜː/ にやや近い口の形で出す音なのでこの記号で表すのですが，記号は /əʊ/ であっても実際には /əʊ/ と /oʊ/ の間と言ってよいような音になることもあり，幅があります．ALT がこのような音を出したときに学習者が混乱しないように指導者がコメントすべき場面があるかもしれませんが，学習者にこの音を出させる必要はないと私は考えています．

There is a possibility that confusion may arise in class if the main instructor for the class uses pronunciation of the North American-type and an ALT uses British-type pronunciation, for example. The above paragraph describes /oʊ/ from the sound system of North American-type pronunciation, but, where /oʊ/ would be used in that type of pronunciation, a different sound may be used in British-type pronunciation: one that is often represented by the symbol /əʊ/. /ə/, its first element, is represented by this symbol as it somewhat resembles /ɜː/, discussed in Chapter 9, but /əʊ/ actually varies and may realize itself as a sound anywhere between /əʊ/ and /oʊ/. If an ALT uses /əʊ/, you may need to explain it to learners to forestall any confusion, but there is no need in my opinion to make them actually produce it.

2. /ɔː/ の指導のポイント (How to teach /ɔː/)

〈まずはここから (To begin with ...)〉

/ɔː/ の音は，たとえば talk，bought，call に出て来ます．北米系発音においては，この音はオとアの間の音で発音されたり，前章で紹介したうがいの音 /ɑ/ で発音されたりします．したがって，両者の音に挟まれた範囲のどの音で発音してもかまわない音と言うことができます（図 10.2）．ただ，全ての聞き手にとって分かりやすい発音で話すよう学習者を訓練するという観点からは，/ɔː/ を /ɑ/ とは別の音として扱うべきだと私は考えています．[1)]

/ɔː/ appears in words like *talk, bought*, and *call*. This sound realizes itself as a sound between the Japanese vowels "o" and "a"; it may be pronounced the same as /ɑ/. So you can tell learners that it will be permissible for them to say any sound within the range from "o" to "a." If learners are to be trained to use pronunciation that is easy to follow, you should in my opinion treat /ɔː/ and /ɑ/ as separate sounds.[1)]

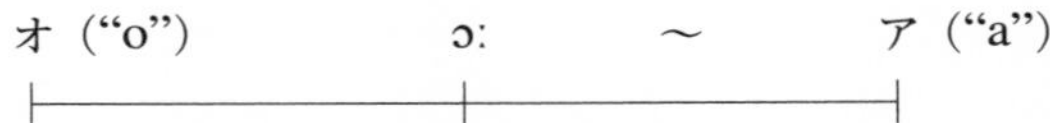

図 10.2　オからアに至る発音のものさし (Scale ranging between the Japanese "o" and "a" vowels)

教える際に気をつけるべき重要な点は，学習者がこの音をオウというような二重母音にしないように注意すべきである，ということです．/ɔː/ は始めから終わりまでひとつの音であり，途中で変化はしません．

One important point you should remember is that you should prevent learners from diphthongizing /ɔː/ and saying something like "o-u." /ɔː/ is a sound where the vowel quality remains the same from its beginning to its end.

〈こんなときは (If you face a challenge ...)〉

たとえば，主たる指導者が北米系発音を使い，ALT がイギリス系発音をする人だった場合，混乱が生じる可能性があるので注意が必要です．上記は北米系の英語における /ɔː/ の音の説明でしたが，イギリス系発音においては，/ɔː/ は日本語のオと同じ音で発音されることが少なくありません．この点で，イギリス系発音における /ɔː/ は日本の学習者には非常に楽に発音することができます．ただ，/ɔː/ をイギリス系発音に従ってオに近く言い，/oʊ/ は北米系発音に従ってオに近い音で始めるとすると，少なくとも出だしの音については両者の音が同じになってしまい，両者の区別がしにくくなります．このような発音をする初級の学習者がいた場合，少なくとも /oʊ/ を明白に二重母音として，また /ɔː/ を明白に単純なひとつの音として出すべきであることを説明してください．

There is a possibility here, too, that confusion may arise in class if the main instructor for the class uses pronunciation of the North American-type and an ALT uses British-type pronunciation, for example. This section describes /ɔː/ from the sound system of North American-type pronunciation, but, where /ɔː/ would be used in that type of pronunciation, a different sound is used in British-type pronunciation. The sound used in British-type pronunciation is the same as the Japanese "o" vowel, which is naturally easy for learners in Japan to produce. But if learners used a British-type vowel for /ɔː/, using the same sound as the Japanese "o" vowel, and used North American-type pronunciation for /oʊ/, again beginning the vowel with the Japanese "o" vowel, they would be making the two sounds rather difficult for the listener to distinguish. If you encounter such learners, tell them that they should at least make /oʊ/ unmistakably a diphthong and make /ɔː/ unmistakably a simple long vowel.

3.　練習のための言語材料 (Materials for practice)

下線部に注意して発音するよう指示してください．一重下線は /oʊ/，二重下線は /ɔː/ です．

Make learners pay attention to the underlined part(s) of each item.

単語

(1)　boat　(2)　coat　(3)　phone　(4)　soap（石鹸）
(5)　doughnut（ドーナツ）　(6)　bought　(7)　caught　(8)　walk
(9)　talk　(10)　call

フレーズ

(1)　show me your notes（あなたのメモを私に見せる）
(2)　bought some chalk sticks（チョークを何本か買った）
(3)　caught a cold（風邪をひいた）

(4)　fought for more votes（もっと票を取るために戦った）

センテンス

(1)　He drove home alone.（彼はひとりで車で帰宅した.）

(2)　We were walking along and talking.
（私たちは歩いておしゃべりしていた.）

(3)　I thought the joke was funny.（ジョークはおもしろいと思った.）

会話

A:　Look. I bought this cellphone just this morning.
（見てよ．この携帯，ついけさほど買った.）

B:　Oh, it looks nice. Have you called anybody with it?
（ああ，見た感じがいいね．誰かに電話した？）

A:　No, but I've sent a lot of text messages.
（いや．でもたくさんメッセージを送った.）

B:　My phone is three years old. I think I'll get a new one, too.
（私の電話はもう 3 年経つ．私も新しいのを買おう.）

4.　アクティビティー見本 (Idea for an activity)

「接続トラブル」(Bad connections)

「接続トラブルゲーム」です．電話の接続が悪くて相手の言葉に空白が生じます．絵をヒントにしながら，学習者同士，または指導者と学習者で会話を行ってください.

Assuming that you have a bad connection on the telephone and that a word becomes inaudible during your conversation, engage learners in a conversation with each other or with you. Use the illustrations as hints.

A の役をやる学習者に，空白のところに単語をおぎなって言わせてください．ここでは空白が埋めてあります．空白部分については，学習者は 1 ～ 2 秒だまっていれば結構です．例として，次のようなやりとりが考えられます．

The learner who plays Speaker A must supply a word in each blank. Here the blanks have been filled for you. For the silence part, the player can just remain silent for a second or two. Possible exchanges are as follows.

1. A: I bought a [*silence*] last week.（私は先週［空白］を買った.）
   B: You bought a what?（何を買ったって？）
   A: I said I bought a (coat).（コートを買った，って言ったんだよ.）
2. A: I didn't like the restaurant, so I [*silence*] out.
   （私はレストランが気に入らなかったので外へ［空白］.）
   B: You didn't like the restaurant and did what?
   （レストランが気に入らなくて何をしたの？）
   A: I (walked) out.（外へ出た.）
3. A: I [*silence*] a bad cold last week.（私は先週ひどい風邪を［空白］.）
   B: You did what last week?（先週何をしたって？）
   A: I said I (caught) a bad cold.
   （ひどい風邪をひいた，って言ったんだよ.）
4. A: I need to buy some [*silence*].（私は［空白］をいくらか買わなくては.）
   B: You need to buy some what?
   （いくらか何を買う必要があるって？）
   A: I need to buy some (soap).（いくらか石鹸を買う必要がある.）
5. A: I like [*silence*] very much.（私は［空白］がとても好きです.）
   B: You like what very much?（何がとても好き？）
   A: I said I like (doughnuts) very much.
   （ドーナツがとても好きって言ったんだ.）
6. A: I was [*silence*]-ing with him on the [*silence*].
   （私は彼と［空白］で［空白］していました.）
   B: You were doing what?（何をしてたって？）
   A: I was (talk)-ing with him on the (phone).
   （彼と電話で話してた.）

ここでの焦点は /oʊ/ と /ɔː/ です．学習者の発音に問題があったら，次のように対応してください．(1) 活動が終わってから，明示的に指導する．(2) 活動の最中であれば，リキャストにより指導する (p. 10 参照)．

The focus here is on /oʊ/ and /ɔː/. If learners' pronunciation is problematical, do the following: (1) provide explicit instruction after the activity; (2) provide recasts (see p. 10) during the activity.

第 11 章
/r/ を含む音の組み合わせの指導 (1)

たとえば bread, price, every, friend, great, cream

Clusters with /r/ (1)

1. /br/ の指導のポイント (How to teach /br/)

〈まずはここから (To begin with ...)〉

英語には, /r/ の音を含む子音の組み合わせがいくつかあります. たとえば, bread (/br-/), cream (/kr-/) などのアタマにそのような組み合わせが現れます. まずは, /br/ の組み合わせを教える方法を取り上げます. この組み合わせの指導で大事なことは, 学習者が最初の子音と次の /r/ との間に余計な母音を入れないようにすることです. たとえば, bread と言うときに, 最初の /b/ を日本語のブのような音で言ってしまうと, /b/ と /r/ の間にウという母音が入ってしまいます. このような問題を避けながら学習者に /r/ を含む組み合わせを発音させる方法を考えましょう.

There are some combinations of sounds with /r/, such as the /br/ in *bread* and the /kr/ in *cream*. An important point that you should explain to learners about /br/ is that a vowel should not be inserted between the two consonants. For example, if learners say the Japanese syllable "bu" for the initial /b/, it means that they will say an "u" vowel between /b/ and /r/. Here is how you can help learners avoid such a problem and say /br/ properly.

この組み合わせを発音する際には, 2 番目の音である /r/ をまず舌で準備しておいてから /b/ を言うように指導してください. 図 11.1 を板書するなどして, この方法を説明することができます. 図では, 話し手はまさに /b/ を言おうとして唇を閉じていますが, そのときにはすでに舌は /r/ の形になっています．こうすると，/b/ の発音が行われた瞬間にそれが別の音を間に入れることなく /r/ の音につながります．

Tell learners to get /r/ ready first with their tongue and then proceed to the articulation of /b/. It may be helpful to draw an illustration like Figure 11.1 on the board in class. In Figure 11.1 the speaker has the lips closed in preparation for /b/, and the tongue is already assuming the shape necessary for /r/. If one does this, one can begin to say /r/ as soon as one has finished saying /b/, avoiding saying another sound in between.

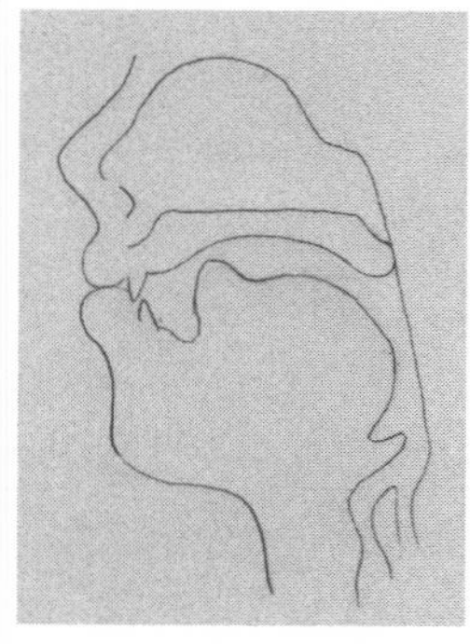

図 11.1　/br/ の発音 (Articulation of /br/)

〈こんなときは (If you face a challenge ...)〉

/br/ の組み合わせがうまく言えない学習者がいた場合，/brbrbr .../ と発音する練習を行わせるとうまく行くことがあります．口の中で舌を /r/ の形にしておいて，繰り返しバと言う練習です．

If learners cannot handle the /br/ combination, it may be helpful to make them say /brbrbr .../, keeping the tongue in the /r/ position and repeating “ba.”

/br/ などの /r/ の入った組み合わせで始まる単語を言うとき，学習者のなかにはそのあとの母音に /r/ の響きを残してしまう人がいます．たとえば，bread と言うとき，/e/ という母音をうまく言えず，/ɚː/ に近い母音を言ってしまう学習者がいます．母音をしっかり言うように指導してください．この注意は，この章で取り上げるすべての音の組み合わせに当てはまります．/r/ が入った組み合わせの直後の母音を学習者が正しく発音するようご留意ください．

When saying a word that has /br/ in it, some learners may say the vowel that follows while keeping the tongue in the /r/ position. For example, in an attempt to say *bread*, they may fail to say /e/ and say a vowel like /ɚː/ instead. Make sure that, after saying /br/, learners properly say the vowel that follows. This caveat applies to all of the clusters with /r/ that are taken up in this chapter.

2. /pr/ の指導のポイント (How to teach /pr/)

〈まずはここから (To begin with ...)〉

price などに出て来る /pr/ についても同じことが言えます．/br/ の場合同様，口のなかで舌を /r/ の形にしておいてから /p/ を発音するよう指導してください．/b/ も /p/ も唇を使って発音する音ですから，図 11.1 は /pr/ の発音の図であるとも言えます．

What was discussed in the above section also applies to /pr/, which appears in words like *price*. Tell learners to put the tongue in the /r/ position before articulating /p/. Since /b/ and /p/ are both sounds that one articulates using the lips, Figure 11.1 applies to /pr/ as well.

〈こんなときは (If you face a challenge ...)〉

/pr/ の組み合わせがうまく言えない学習者がいた場合，/prprpr ... / と発音する練習を行わせるとうまく行くことがあります．口の中で舌を /r/ の形にしておいて，繰り返しパと言う練習です．

If learners cannot handle the /pr/ combination, it may be helpful to make them say /prprpr ... /, keeping the tongue in the /r/ position and repeating “pa” with the lips.

3. /vr/ /fr/ の指導のポイント (How to teach /vr/ and /fr/)

〈こんなときは (If you face a challenge ...)〉

every などに出て来る /vr/ についても，要領は同じです．口のなかで /r/ の準備をしてから /v/ を言うように指導してください．図 11.2 を板書することによって，/r/ の準備をしておいて /v/ を発音するようすを説明することができます．

What was discussed in the above section applies to /vr/, which appears in words like *every*. Tell learners to put the tongue in the /r/ position before articulating /v/. An illustration like Figure 11.2 on the board in class may help.

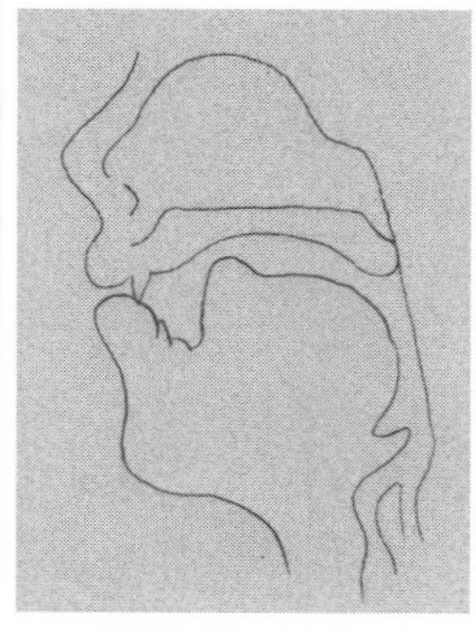

図 11.2 /vr/ の発音 (Articulation of /vr/)

friend などに出て来る /fr/ も，上の /vr/ と同じ口の動きによって発音します．/f/ は /v/ をささやき声で言ったときに出る音で，口の動きについてはふたつの音は同じですから，図 11.2 はそのまま /fr/ の図でもあると考えて頂けば結構です．舌で /r/ の準備をしておいてから /f/ を発音するよう指導してください．

/fr/, which appears in words like *friend*, is articulated in the same way as /vr/. As /f/ is a sound that is produced when one whispers /v/, Figure 11.2 is also an illustration of /fr/. Make learners put the tongue in the /r/ position before articulating /f/.

〈こんなときは (If you face a challenge ...)〉

/v/, /f/ は唇と共にほほをかなり緊張させて発音する，日本語にない音であり，学習者によっては，この状態で /r/ を言うのが楽でない，ということもあり得ます．/vrvrvr .../, /frfrfr .../ などと繰り返し言えなくとも，/vr/, /fr/ が 1 回言えれば十分ですので，無理な繰り返し練習をしないでください．

/v/ and /f/, sounds nonexistent in Japanese, both require the speaker to strain the lips and cheeks, and some learners find it particularly difficult to say /r/ while making their speech organs assume the /v/ or /f/ position. Do not make them say /vrvrvr .../ or /frfrfr .../ if such an exercise seems difficult for them. If they can say /vr/ or /fr/ once, that is a sufficient indication that they can say words with these clusters.

4. /gr/ /kr/ の指導のポイント (How to teach /gr/ and /kr/)

〈まずはここから (To begin with ...)〉

こんどは great などに出て来る /gr/ の組み合わせの説明に移ります．この場合も，口のなかで /r/ の準備をしてから /g/ と言います．図 11.3 の板書がこの説明に役立ちます．

/gr/ appears in words like *great*. In the case of this combination, too, learners should prepare /r/ first and then say /g/. An illustration like Figure 11.3 may help you explain the articulation.

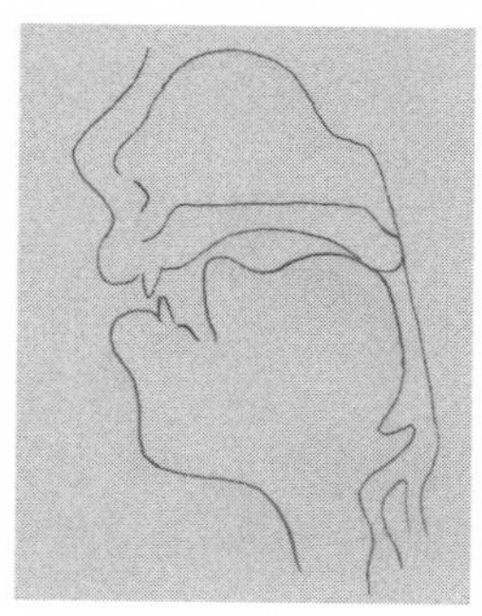

図 11.3　/gr/ の発音 (Articulation of /gr/)

cream などに出て来る /kr/ についても同じことが言えます．/gr/ の場合同様，口のなかで舌を /r/ の形にしておいてから /k/ を発音するよう指導してください．/k/ も /g/ も舌の後ろの部分で口の天井をなめる音ですから，図 11.3 は /kr/ の発音の図であるとも言えます．

This also applies to /kr/, which appears in words like *cream*. As in the case of /gr/, learners should get /r/ ready and then say /k/. As both /k/ and /g/ are sounds that one produces by placing the back of the tongue against the roof of the mouth, Figure 11.3 is an illustration of /kr/, too.

〈こんなときは (If you face a challenge ...)〉

/gr/ /kr/ は，/pr/ /br/ /fr/ /vr/ よりも発音がやや難しくなり，教えるのも難しくなります．というのは，/r/ の準備に舌を使い，/g/ /k/ の発音にもやはり舌を使うからです．初心者は，舌を慣れていない形で動かさなくてはならず，舌を緊張させないと /gr/ /kr/ が言えません．あせらないで指導してください．/br/ /pr/ の指導の際に使った方法がここでも役立ちます．すなわち，/gr/ /kr/ の組み合わせがうまく言えない学習者がいた場合，/grgrgr .../ /krkrkr .../ と発音する練習を行わせるとうまく行くことがあります．口の中で舌を /r/ の形にしておいて，繰り返し口の奥のほうで /g/ /k/ と言う練習です．

/gr/ and /kr/ are more difficult for learners to say, and more difficult for the instructor to teach, than /pr/, /br/, /fr/, and /vr/, since the tongue is used for preparing /r/ and also for saying /g/ or /k/. If learners have difficulty saying /gr/ or /kr/, be patient. Try making them say /grgrgr .../ or /krkrkr .../. In other words, make them say /g/ or /k/ repeatedly while keeping their /r/ tongue position.

5. 練習のための言語材料 (Materials for practice)

下線部に注意して発音するよう指示してください．

Make learners pay attention to the underlined part(s) of each item.

単語

(1) bread (2) price (3) every (4) friend (5) green
(6) cream (7) bridge (8) free (9) grow（育つ）
(10) crew（乗務員）

フレーズ

(1) cross the bridge（橋を渡る）
(2) break every record（すべての記録を破る）
(3) a great friend（素晴らしい友人）
(4) price of bread（パンの価格）

センテンス

(1) They painted the wall green and brown. (彼らは壁を緑と茶色に塗った.)

(2) Everybody praised the crew. (皆が乗務員を賞賛した.)

(3) The cream is free but the bread isn't.
(クリームは無料だがパンはそうでない.)

会話

A: They serve great breakfast at this hotel, don't they?
(このホテルでは素晴らしい朝食を出しますね.)

B: I agree. And the prices are reasonable.
(賛成です. それから価格もお手頃.)

A: Would you like cream in your coffee?
(コーヒーにクリームはいかがですか？)

B: Yes, thanks. I think I'll have some more fresh grapefruit juice.
(はい, ありがとう. フレッシュグレープフルーツジュースをもう少し飲もうかな.)

6. アクティビティー見本 (Idea for an activity)

「クロスワードパズル」(Crossword puzzle)

クロスワードパズルです. 学習者同士, または指導者と学習者で会話を行いながら解いてください.

Engage learners in a conversation with each other or with you and have them fill in the squares by giving answers to the clues. One possible exchange is as follows.

A: What do you think the answer to one across is?
(ヨコのカギ 1 の答えは何だと思う？)

B: It is GREAT. (GREAT だよ.)

A: Yes, that's right. Well done. (その通り. よくできました.)

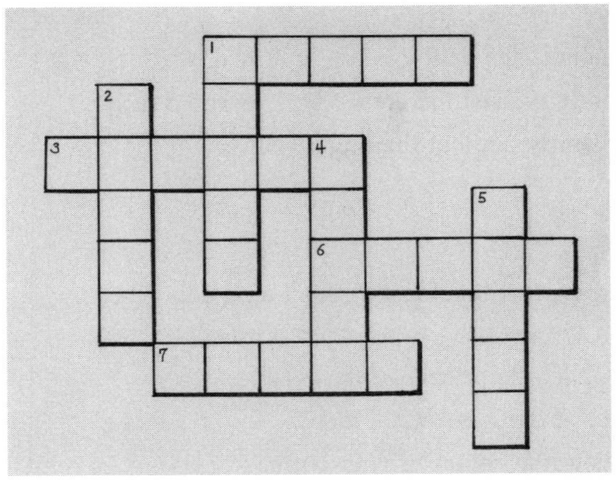

Across:

1. Very big（とても大きい）(Answer: GREAT / GRAND)
3. She is a very good ____ of mine.（彼女は私のとてもよい ___ です．）(Answer: FRIEND)
6. I jog ____ day.（私は ___ 日ジョギングをします．）(Answer: EVERY)
7. Action that breaks the law（法律を破ること）(Answer: CRIME)

Down:

1. Color of leaves（木の葉の色）(Answer: GREEN)
2. How much?（おいくらですか？）(Answer: PRICE)
4. I had a strange ____ last night.（私は昨夜変わった ___ を見た．）(Answer: DREAM)
5. The king wore a ____ on his head.（王様は頭に ___ をかぶっていた．）(Answer: CROWN)

ここでの焦点は /r/ を含む音の組み合わせです．学習者の発音に問題があったら，次のように対応してください．(1) 活動が終わってから，明示的に指導する．(2) 活動の最中であれば，リキャストにより指導する (p. 10 参照)．

The focus here is on consonant clusters with /r/. If learners' pronunciation is problematical, do the following: (1) provide explicit instruction after the activity; (2) provide recasts (see p. 10) during the activity.

第 12 章

/l/ を含む音の組み合わせの指導 (1)

たとえば blue, play, fly, lovely, glad, close　　Clusters with /l/ (1)

英語には /l/ の音を含む子音の組み合わせがいくつかあります．この章では /bl/, /pl/, /fl/, /vl/, /gl/, /kl/ の 6 種の組み合わせを取り上げます（/sl/ は第 18 章で扱います）．

There are a number of consonant clusters with /l/. This chapter covers six such clusters: /bl/, /pl/, /fl/, /vl/, /gl/, and /kl/. Another combination, /sl/, will be discussed in Chapter 18.

1．/bl/ の指導のポイント (How to teach /bl/)

〈まずはここから (To begin with ...)〉

まずは，black，blue，blog などに出て来る /bl/ の組み合わせを教える方法を取り上げます．この組み合わせで大事なことは，ちょうど第 11 章で取り上げた /r/ を含む組み合わせの発音の際に気をつけることとよく似ています．すなわち，学習者が最初の子音と次の /l/ との間に余計な母音を入れないよう指導することです．たとえば，blue と言うときに，最初の /b/ を日本語のブのような音で言ってしまうと，/b/ と /l/ の間にウという母音が入ってしまいます．このような問題を避けながら学習者に /l/ を含む組み合わせを発音させる方法を考えましょう．

The first combination that I take up is /bl/, which appears in words like *black, blue*, and *blog*. In teaching /bl/, you should make learners pay attention to the same point as in the case of clusters with /r/, discussed in Chapter 11: Learners should not put a vowel between the first consonant and the /l/ which follows it. For example, if they say the Japanese syllable "bu" at the beginning of *blue*, a vowel will occur between /b/ and /l/. The following paragraphs explain how to help learners avoid this problem.

この組み合わせを発音する際には，ちょうど第 11 章で取り上げた /r/ を含む組み合わせの発音の際と同じように，2 番目の音である /l/ をまず舌で準備しておいてから，すなわち舌先を上の歯ぐきに触れさせながら /b/ を言うように指導してください．図 12.1 はこの方法を表したものです．この図の板書が説明に役立ちます．図では，話し手はまさに /b/ を言おうとして唇を閉じていますが，そのときにはすでに舌は /l/ の形になっています．こうすると /b/ の発音が行われた瞬間にそれが別の音を間に入れることなく /l/ の音につながります．

Just as in the case of clusters with /r/, discussed in Chapter 11, learners should prepare /l/, the second sound in the combination, with the tongue (in other words, they should have the tongue tip on the upper teeth ridge) before saying /b/. Figure 12.1 explains how this is done. In this illustration, the speaker has the lips closed and is about to say /b/. At this time, the speaker's tongue is assuming the /l/ position. In this way, /l/ will be heard as soon as /b/ has been articulated.

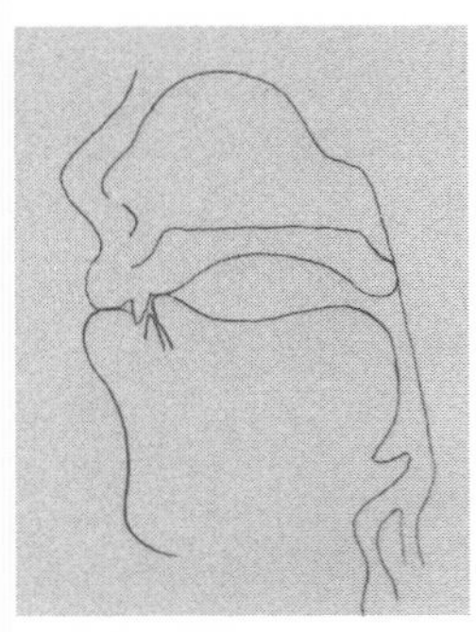

図 12.1 /bl/ の発音 (Articulation of /bl/)

〈こんなときは (If you face a challenge ...)〉

/bl/ の組み合わせがうまく言えない学習者がいた場合，/blblbl ... / と発音する練習を行わせるとうまく行くことがあります．口の中で舌を /l/ の形にしておいて，つまり，舌先を上の歯ぐきに触れさせておいて，繰り返しバと言う練習です．

If learners cannot handle the /bl/ combination, it may be helpful to make them say /blblbl ... /, keeping the tongue in the /l/ position and repeating "ba."

2. /pl/ の指導のポイント (How to teach /pl/)

〈まずはここから (To begin with ...)〉

play などに出て来る /pl/ についても同じことが言えます．/bl/ の場合同様，口のなかで舌を /l/ の形にしておいてから，つまり，舌先を上の歯ぐきに触れさせておいて，/p/ を発音するよう指導してください．/b/ も /p/ も唇を使って発音する音ですから，図 12.1 は /pl/ の発音の図であるとも言えます．

We can say the same thing about /pl/, which appears in words like *play*, as we have said about /bl/. As in the case of /bl/, learners should have their tongue in the /l/ position, that is, have their tongue tip on the upper teeth ridge, and then say /p/. As /b/ and /p/ are both articulated with one's lips, Figure 12.1 is an illustration of /pl/, too.

〈こんなときは (If you face a challenge ...)〉

/pl/ の組み合わせがうまく言えない学習者がいた場合，/plplpl ... / と発音する練習を行わせるとうまく行くことがあります．口の中で舌を /l/ の形にしておいて，繰り返しパと言う練習です．

If learners cannot handle the /pl/ combination, it may be helpful to make them say /plplpl ... /, keeping the tongue in the /l/ position and repeating "pa."

3. /fl/ /vl/ の指導のポイント (How to teach /fl/ and /vl/)

〈まずはここから (To begin with ...)〉

fly などに出て来る /fl/, lovely などに出て来る /vl/ についても，ふたつの音の間に母音を入れないように指導する必要があります．学習者は，/f/ や /v/ を言ったあとで，すぐに /l/ に移るように心がける必要があります．

In teaching /fl/, which appears in words like *fly*, and /vl/, which appears in words like *lovely*, you should also make sure that learners do not put a vowel between the two consonants in each cluster. They should move to /l/ quickly after saying /f/ or /v/.

〈こんなときは (If you face a challenge ...)〉

/f/ /v/ を言うためには /b/ /p/ の場合とは異なった形でほほや唇を緊張させる必要があり，このため，学習者のなかには /bl/ /pl/ は楽にできても /fl/, /vl/ は言いにくいという反応を示す人もいます．これは十分理解できることですので，/bl/ /pl/ の練習と /fl/ /vl/ の練習とでは，アプローチを替えることをお勧めします．あらかじめ舌を /l/ の形にして /flflfl .../, /vlvlvl .../ と言う，というあまり楽でない繰り返し練習を行うのではなく，/f/ /v/（図 12.2）が終わったらその段階ですみやかに /l/（図 12.3）に移る，という指導をするようお勧めします．

Articulation of /f/ and /v/ requires learners to strain their cheeks and lips in a way not required for the articulation of /bl/ or /pl/, and, quite understandably, they may thus find it more difficult to say /fl/ and /vl/ than to say /bl/ or /pl/. Instead of making them do a strenuous /flflfl .../ or /vlvlvl .../ repetition exercise, just try to help them learn to say /f/ or /v/ and then move to /l/ swiftly.

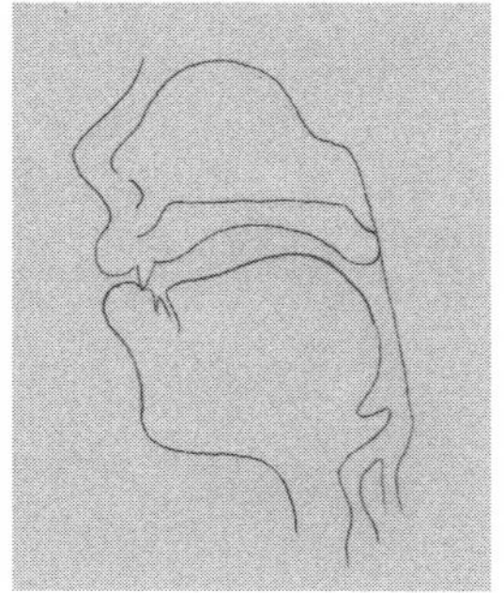

図 12.2 /f/ /v/ の発音；図 4.1，図 4.5 と同じ（Articulation of /f/ and /v/; same as Figure 4.1 and Figure 4.5）

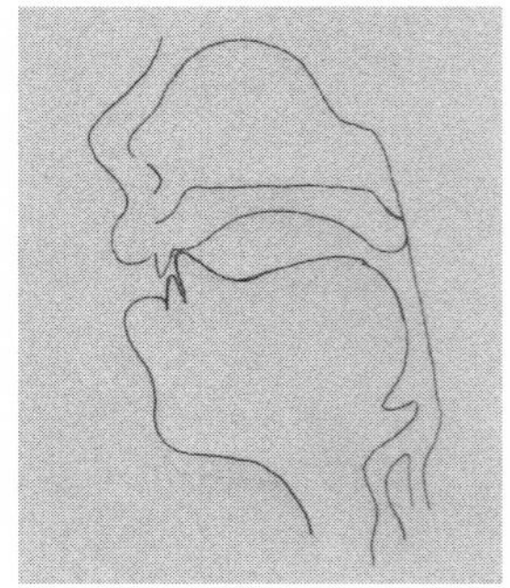

図 12.3 /l/ の発音；図 1.6 と同じ（Articulation of /l/; same as Figure 1.6）

4. /gl/ /kl/ の指導のポイント (How to teach /gl/ and /kl/)

〈まずはここから (To begin with ...)〉

clean などに現れる /kl/，glad などに現れる /gl/ の指導の際も，基本的には /pl/ /bl/ の指導の際に重視した原則が重要となります．すなわち，組み合わせになっているふたつの音を，間に母音を入れずに発音する，ということです．[1] まず，glad などに出て来る /gl/ の組み合わせを取り上げましょう．学習者が最初の /g/ を日本語のグのような音で言ってしまうと，/g/ と /l/ の間にウという母音が入ってしまいます．このような問題を避けながら学習者に /l/ を含む組み合わせを発音させる方法を考えましょう．

In teaching /kl/, as in *clean*, and /gl/, as in *glad*, you should mention to learners the same principle as in teaching /pl/ and /bl/: It is important that the two consonants in the combination should be pronounced without a vowel in between.[1] First, I take up /gl/, as in *glad*. If learners say the Japanese syllable "gu" in place of the initial /g/, an "u"-like vowel will occur between the two consonants. Here is how to avoid this problem.

これまでに指導してきた /bl/ や /pl/ 同様，/gl/ の組み合わせを発音する際には，2 番目の音である /l/ をまず口のなかで準備しておいてから，すなわち舌先を上の歯ぐきに触れさせながら /g/ を言うように指導してください．図 12.4 の板書が説明に役立つでしょう．

As in the case of /bl/ and /pl/, you should tell learners to get /l/ ready first, namely, tell them to put their tongue tip on the upper teeth ridge, and then proceed to the articulation of /g/. It may be helpful to draw an illustration like Figure 12.4 on the board in class.

この図では，話し手はまさに /g/ を言おうとして舌の後ろのほうを口の天井の後ろのほうにつけていますが，そのときにはすでに舌は /l/ の形になっています．こうすると /g/ の発音が行われた瞬間に，別の音を間に入れることなくそれが /l/ の音につながります．

In Figure 12.4 the speaker has the back of the tongue against the roof of the mouth and is about to say /g/. The tongue is already assuming the

/l/ position, namely, it is on the upper teeth ridge. If one does this, one can begin to say /l/ as soon as one has finished saying /g/, avoiding saying another sound in between.

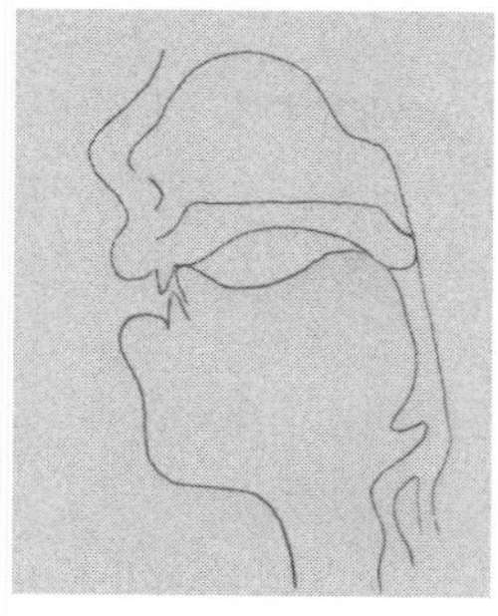

図 12.4 /gl/ の発音 (Articulation of /gl/)

clean などに出て来る /kl/ の組み合わせにおいても，/k/ と次の /l/ との間に余計な母音を入れないことが大切です．学習者が最初の /k/ を日本語のクのような音で言ってしまうと，/k/ と /l/ の間にウという母音が入ってしまいます．このような問題を避けながら学習者に /l/ を含む組み合わせを発音させる必要があります．

In teaching /kl/, as in *clean*, it is important that /k/ and /l/ should be pronounced without a vowel in between. If learners say the Japanese syllable "ku" in place of the initial /k/, an "u"-like vowel will occur between the two consonants. You should help learners say the cluster while avoiding this problem.

コツは /gl/ の場合と同じです．2 番目の音である /l/ をまず舌で準備しておいてから，すなわち舌先を上の歯ぐきに触れさせながら，/k/ を言うように指導してください．/k/ は /g/ をささやき声に替えただけの音で，舌の動きは同じですから，図 12.4 は /kl/ の発音を表した図でもあるのです．

The way to do this is the same as in the case of /gl/. Learners should have /l/ ready with their tongue, namely, they should have their tongue tip on the upper teeth ridge, before saying /k/. As /k/ is a whispered version of /g/, the tongue moving in the same way in the articulation of both sounds, Figure 12.4 is an illustration of /kl/, too.

図12.4では，話し手はまさに /k/ を言おうとして舌の後ろのほうを口の天井の後ろのほうにつけていますが，そのときにはすでに舌は /l/ の形になっています．こうすると /k/ の発音が行われた瞬間にそれが別の音を間に入れることなく /l/ の音につながります．

In this illustration, the speaker has the back of the tongue against the roof of the mouth, about to say /k/, and the tip of the tongue is already in the /l/ position. In this way, /l/ will be heard as soon as /k/ has been articulated, without a third sound in between.

〈こんなときは (If you face a challenge ...)〉

/gl/ /kl/ の組み合わせがうまく言えない学習者がいた場合，/glglgl .../ /klklkl .../ と発音する練習を行わせるとうまく行くことがあります．口の中で舌を /l/ の形にしておいて，つまり，舌先を上の歯ぐきに触れさせておいて，繰り返し舌の後ろのほうで /g/ または /k/ と言う練習です．ただ，この練習は，多くの学習者にとって，あまり楽ではありません．舌先を上の歯のすぐ後ろの歯ぐきに触れさせたまま舌の後ろのほうを口の天井の後ろのほうに触れさせることは，学習者にとっては，舌を慣れない形にすることを意味します．無理をしないでゆっくり練習させてください．

If learners cannot handle the /gl/ and /kl/ combinations, it may be helpful to make them say /glglgl .../ and /klklkl .../, keeping the tongue in the /l/ position and repeating /g/ or /k/. This is not an easy exercise to perform for many learners, however. Placing the back of the tongue against the roof of the mouth while keeping the tongue tip on the upper teeth ridge means that learners must strain their tongue in a way to which they are not accustomed. If this seems difficult for them to do, do not be overly demanding.

5. 練習のための言語材料 (Materials for practice)

下線部に注意して発音するよう指示してください．

Make learners pay attention to the underlined part(s) of each item.

単語

(1) play (2) blue (3) fly (4) climb (/klaɪm/ 登る) (5) glad
(6) please (7) black (8) flower (9) lovely
(10) glove (/glʌv/ 手袋)

フレーズ

(1) fly on a plane (飛行機で飛ぶ)
(2) black gloves (黒い手袋)
(3) have lunch (昼食をとる)
(4) play with close friends (親友と遊ぶ)

センテンス

(1) I am planning to take an early flight. (早い飛行機の便に乗る計画です.)
(2) I'll be glad to teach the class. (よろこんで授業を教えます.)
(3) The clouds are low, and the wind is blowing hard.
(雲は低く，風は強く吹いている.)

会話

A: Can you please help me? (助けて頂けませんか？)
B: Yes. What can I do for you? (はい．何をして差し上げましょうか？)
A: Can you tell me where the post office is?
(郵便局がどこだか教えて頂けませんか？)
B: I'll be glad to. Go three blocks this way. You'll come to a big building with a clothing store facing the street. The post office is on the third floor of that building.
(よろこんで．こちらに 3 ブロック行ってください．路面店の洋服屋のある大きなビルに来ます．郵便局はそのビルの 3 階です.)

6. アクティビティー見本 (An idea for an activity)

「ダメな生徒」(Bad student)

ダメな生徒の答案を見て，学習者同士，または指導者と学習者で会話を行ってください．単語は正しいがつづりに余計な 1 文字が入っているので，正しい単語を当ててください．例として，次のようなやりとりが考えられます．

Assuming that the illustration shows the answer sheet written by a bad student, engage learners in a conversation with each other or with you. Make learners guess the correct words. The words on the sheet are correct but are spelled with one unnecessary letter in each case.

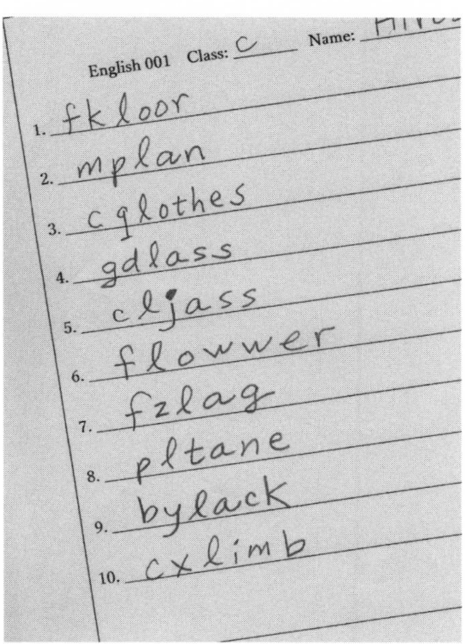

Answers:

1. floor　2. plan　3. clothes　4. glass　5. class
6. flower　7. flag　8. plane　9. black　10. climb

ここでの焦点は /l/ を含む音の組み合わせです．学習者の発音に問題があったら，次のように対応してください．(1) 活動が終わってから，明示的に指導する．(2) 活動の最中であれば，リキャストにより指導する (p. 10 参照)．

The focus here is on consonant clusters with /l/. If learners' pronunciation is problematical, do the following: (1) provide explicit instruction after the activity; (2) provide recasts (see p. 10) during the activity.

第Ⅱ部

Part Two

第13章

/r/ を含む音の組み合わせの指導 (2)

たとえば three, train, dress, Henry　　Clusters with /r/ (2)

1. /θr/ の指導のポイント (How to teach /θr/)

three, throw, through などに出て来る /θr/ は，舌の動きが大きいために多くの学習者にとって発音が難しい組み合わせです．/θ/ は，第 2 章で説明した通り，舌を上の前歯に触れさせて出す音ですので，/θ/ を言うときには舌は相当前に寄っています．/r/ は逆に舌を後ろに寄せないと言えない音ですので，/θr/ の組み合わせを言うときには，どうしても舌を前から後ろに移動させないといけません．図 13.1 を板書すればこの移動の説明に役立ちます．実線の舌の形は /θ/ の舌の形，点線の舌の形は /r/ の形を表しています．矢印が示す通り，舌先を急に移動させる必要があります．

/θr/, which appears in words like *three, throw,* and *through*, is a difficult combination of sounds for many learners to articulate because it requires a big movement of the tongue as the speaker goes through it. As I explained in Chapter 2, /θ/ is a sound that one produces by making the tongue touch the upper front teeth. This means that the tongue must be pushed toward the front as one says the sound. By contrast, /r/ is a sound that requires the tongue to be drawn toward the back. When one says /θr/, then, one must move the tongue from front to back. You can explain this movement of the tongue by drawing an illustration like Figure 13.1 on the board in class. The solid line and the dotted line represent the shapes of the tongue for /θ/ and /r/, respectively. The tongue tip must be moved quickly in the direction indicated by the arrow.

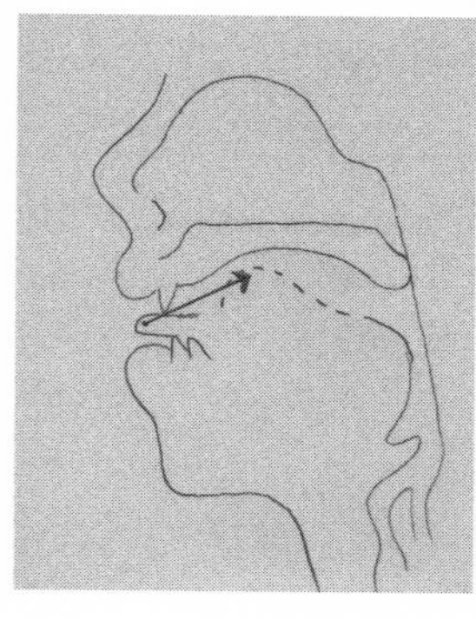

図 13.1　/θ/ から /r/ への舌先の移動 (The tongue tip moves from the /θ/ position to the /r/ position)

学習者は，時として，次のふた通りの変則的な発音をすることがあります．第一に，/r/ をきちんと発音しようとするあまり，/θ/ の際に舌を十分前に出さず，代わりに /s/ の音を出すことがあります．こんなときには舌を十分前に出して /θ/ を発音するよう指導してください．必要なら第 2 章で説明した /θ/ の発音の仕方を復習してください．第二に，学習者は，/θ/ を正しく出したあとで普通の /r/ を発音せず，日本語のラ，リ，ル，レ，ロのアタマの音を出すことがあります．この問題については，あまり神経質にならないでください．英語のネイティブスピーカーもこのような発音をすることがあります．/θ/ の状態から舌先を急に後ろに移動させる際，舌先が口の天井に触れることがあるからです．/θr/ がこのように発音されてもそれが /θr/ であることは聞き手に分かりますので，この発音にはコミュニケーション上の問題はありません．

Learners sometimes do one of two kinds of irregular articulations when trying to say /θr/. First, they may focus so much on /r/ that they may fail to push their tongue forward to a sufficient degree for saying /θ/, ending up saying /sr/ instead. You should tell them that, when they try to say /θ/, they should have their tongue pushed forward enough to be able to articulate it properly. If necessary, review the correct way of articulating /θ/, which was discussed in Chapter 2. Secondly, they may say /θ/ correctly and then, instead of articulating an ordinary /r/, produce in its place something like the Japanese /r/, namely, a sound like the one at the beginning of the syllables “ra,” “ri,” “ru,” “re,” and “ro.” If learners say /θr/ in this way, do not be overparticular, as even native English speakers sometimes do this. What happens is that, in the process of moving the tongue tip from the /θ/ position to the /r/ position, the speaker may inadvertently let it touch the roof of the mouth, resulting in a tapping sort of sound. If /θr/ is articulated in this way, the listener can still tell what the sounds are and communication failure does not occur.

2. /dr/ /tr/ の指導のポイント (How to teach /dr/ and /tr/)

初級の学習者は，drive，dress などに出て来る /dr/ の組み合わせを，単に /d/ の後に /r/ を言う形で言いがちです．この結果，drive が derive = /dəraɪv/「引き出す」のように聞こえたり，dress が duress = /dʊres/「脅迫」のように聞こえたりします．

この問題を防ぐためには，/dr/ が別々の音の連なりではなく /dr/ というひとつの独特の音と考えるべきである，と教えるとよいでしょう．/dr/ は，juice, Japan などのアタマの音である /dʒ/ を使って教えると効果的です．たとえば，dress (/dres/) は，まず Jess (/dʒes/，ジェス) という名前（男女両方あり得る）を発音させ，アタマの /dʒ/ を言うときに舌先の位置を学習者に覚えてもらいます．この /dʒ/ の音は日本語を母語とする学習者なら楽に言えます．歯型や歯列弓の絵があれば，学習者に舌先の位置を指で示してもらうのもよいでしょう．たとえば，学習者は，図 13.2 のような位置を示すかもしれません．このとき，指が本来の /dʒ/ の場合の舌先の位置を正しく指していなくともよいのです．/dʒ/ の舌先の位置を問題にするのがこの指導の目的ではありませんから，指導者は学習者が指した位置についてコメントしたり訂正したりしないでください．次に指導者がすべきことは，学習者に，舌先の位置をなるべく口の後ろにずらしてもう一度 Jess (/dʒes/) と発音してもらうことです．たとえば，図 13.3 のような位置に舌先を移すように言ってみましょう．こうすると，学習者は Jess でなく dress に近い発音をします．[1)]

Beginning learners tend to articulate /dr/ (as in *drive* and *dress*) as a sequence with /d/ followed by /r/, with the result that *drive* sounds like *derive* = /dəraɪv/ and *dress* sounds like *duress* = /dʊres/. You can prevent this by telling them that /dr/ should be thought of as a sound of its own rather than a sequence of two separate sounds. To teach /dr/, you can use /dʒ/ (as in *juice* and *Japan*) as a starting point. For example, you can teach how to say *dress* (/dres/) by making learners first say the name *Jess* (/dʒes/) and telling them to remember where the tongue tip is when they begin to say it. Any Japanese-speaking learner can produce this /dʒ/ sound easily. If a jaw model or a picture of the dental arch is available, have learners use it to show where their tongue tip is when they say /dʒ/. They may point to a spot as in Figure 13.2. Whether the spot that they point to is the correct spot for saying /dʒ/ or not does not matter. Do not correct their answer or comment on it because the purpose of having learners do this is not to discuss the correct tongue position for /dʒ/. What you should do next is to tell them to move their tongue back and say *Jess* (/dʒes/) again. You can show a specific spot by using a jaw model, as in Figure 13.3, and tell them to say *Jess* starting with that tongue position. Learners will then find themselves saying something very close to /dres/, the target word.[1)]

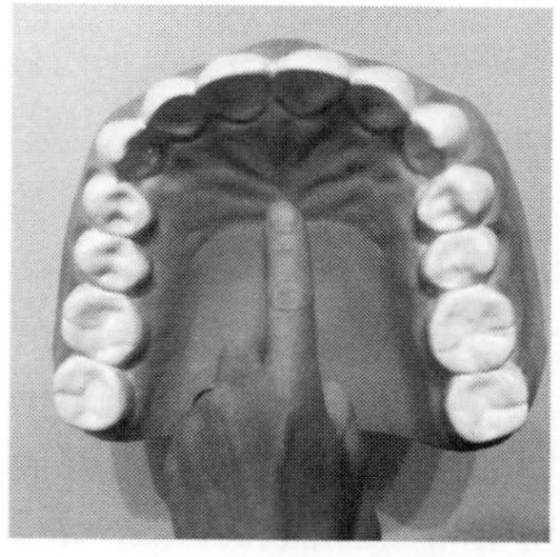

図 13.2　学習者が示す /dʒ/ の舌先の位置 (Learners' perception of the location of the tongue tip in the articulation of /dʒ/)

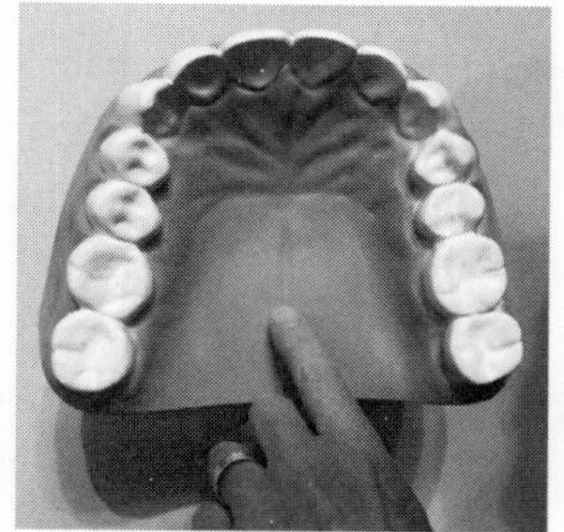

図 13.3　指を後ろにずらす (The instructor's finger moved back)

/dr/ の指導方法と同じ方法で，こんどは /tr/ を教えましょう．/tr/ は，tree，train，travel などのアタマの音ですが，単に /t/ の後に /r/ が続く組み合わせなのではなく，ひとつの独特の音です（もし /t/ と /r/ を別々に発音して train と言ったら，terrain＝/təreɪn/「地形」に聞こえる可能性があります）．この /tr/ という組み合わせは，chair，chain などのアタマの音である /tʃ/ を出発点として教えましょう．たとえば，train を教えるために，学習者に chain（/tʃeɪn/）を発音させ，アタマの /tʃ/ を言うときに舌先の位置を学習者に覚えてもらいます．歯型や歯列弓の絵があれば，学習者に舌先の位置を指で示してもらうのもよいでしょう．このとき，指が本来の /tʃ/ の場合の舌先の位置を正しく指していなくともかまいません．自分が chain のアタマの音のときの舌先の位置だと思う位置を学習者が示したら，次に，舌先の位置をなるべく口の後ろにずらしてもう一度 chain と発音してもらいます．こうすると，学習者は chain でなく train に近い発音をします．

Now, apply the method for teaching /dr/ to the instruction of /tr/. You should tell learners that /tr/, which appears in words like *tree, train,* and *travel*, is not just a sequence of /t/ followed by /r/, but is a sound of its own (if /t/ and /r/ were pronounced separately, *train* could sound like *terrain*＝/təreɪn/, for example). /tr/ can be taught by using /tʃ/, as in *chair* and *chain*, as a starting point. For example, you can teach how to say *train* by the following method: Have learners say *chain* (/tʃeɪn/) and tell them to remember where the tongue tip is when beginning to say /tʃ/. This sound is easy for Japanese-speaking learners to say, just as /dʒ/ is. It may be a good idea to have learners point to the spot where their tongue tip is by using a jaw model or an illustration of the dental arch. Whether the spot that they point to is the correct spot for saying /tʃ/ or not does not matter. After having learners point to the spot that they think is the appropriate position of the tongue tip for /tʃ/, tell them to move their tongue back and say *chain* again. They will then find themselves saying something very close to /treɪn/, the target word.

3. /nr/ の指導のポイント (How to teach /nr/)

/nr/ は Henry（/henri/ 男子の名「ヘンリー」），sunrise（/sʌnraɪz/「日の出」），in Rome（/ɪn roʊm/「ローマで」）などに出て来ます．/nr/ について説明するために，今，この Henry という名前を使いましょう．この名前をを言おうとする学習者は，次の 3 通りのどれかのことをします（正しいのは最後のものだけです)．第一に，完全にカタカナ発音をして「ヘンリー」と言う初級者は大勢います．この場合，ンのときには舌先が口の天井に触れ，リの発音の瞬間にその舌が天井から離れます．第二に，/r/ の発音をマスターした学習者は，Henry のなかの /r/ を正しく発音しますが，その直前の /n/ が言えない可能性があります．このような学習者は，/n/ を言うべき場所で日本語のホンヤ（本屋)，ハンハン（半々）などに出て来るンの音を使います．このことはすでに第 6 章セクション 2 (h) の「/n/ が /r/ の直前に来る場合」の項でくわしく取り上げました．第三に，/nr/ の組み合わせの発音をマスターした学習者は，舌先を上の歯ぐきに触れさせて正しく /n/ を発音し，それに続けて舌を口の後ろのほうに移動させて正しく /r/ を発音することができます．この第三の発音を目指して指導して頂く必要があります．図 13.4 はこの第三の発音の説明に役立ちます．実線の舌の形は /n/ の形です．点線の舌の形は /r/ の形です．矢印が示す通り，舌先を急に移動させる必要があります．

/nr/ appears in *Henry*, *sunrise*, and *in Rome*, for example. To explain how to articulate /nr/, let me take *Henry* as an example. Trying to pronounce this name, learners will do one of three things (the last one being the only correct one). First, many learners, especially beginning learners, use Japanese syllables and say “henrii.” When the name is pronounced in this way, the speaker’s tongue touches the roof of the mouth when “n” is said and it leaves the roof as soon as he or she says “ri.” Secondly, learners who have mastered the English /r/ will say the /r/ in *Henry* but may fail to say /n/ properly. Instead of the correct English /n/, these learners produce the Japanese /n/ as in “honya” (“bookshop”) and “hanhan” (“half and half”). This was discussed in Section 2 (h) of Chapter 6, which was about the articulation of /n/ in an environment in which it is followed by /r/. Third, learners who have mastered /nr/ will articulate /n/ properly by making the tongue tip touch the upper teeth ridge and then moving the tongue back to say /r/ properly. You should aim at this last stage as you teach /nr/. Figure 13.4 will help you explain what one does at this last stage. The solid line and the dotted line indicate the tongue positions for /n/ and /r/, respectively. The tongue tip should be moved quickly in the direction indicated by the arrow.

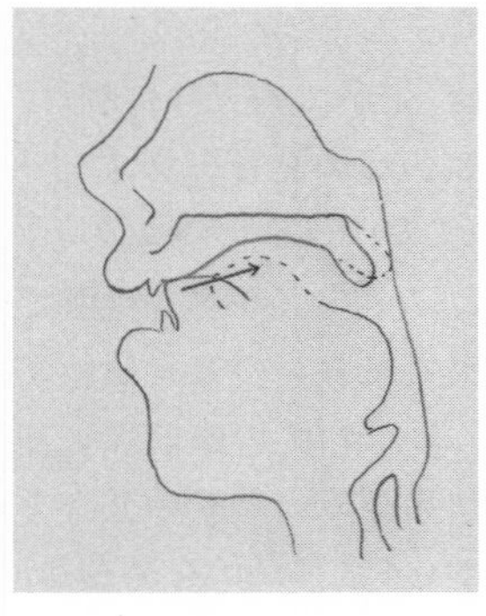

図 13.4 /nr/ の発音 (Articulation of /nr/)

4. 練習のための言語材料 (Materials for practice)

下線部に注意して発音するよう指示してください．

Make learners pay attention to the underlined part(s) of each item.

単語

(1) three (2) throw (投げる) (3) true (4) train (5) try
(6) dress (7) dream (8) dry (9) Henry (10) sunrise (日の出)

フレーズ

(1) ten roses (バラ 10 個)
(2) three-o'clock train (3 時の列車)
(3) try the dress on (ドレスを試着する)
(4) travel through a desert (砂漠を旅する)

センテンス

(1) Henry tried to throw the ball. (ヘンリーはボールを投げようとした.)
(2) She drank three cups of coffee. (彼女はコーヒーを 3 杯飲んだ.)
(3) Nine runners dropped out. (9 人のランナーが脱落した.)

会話

A: I'm going to take a trip to Lake Towada. (十和田湖に旅行します.)
B: Sounds great. I was there three years ago.
(いいですね. 私は 3 年前に行ったんですよ.)

A: Really? Did you take the train? (本当に？ 列車で行きましたか？)

B: No. I drove up there. I ate in really nice restaurants on the way.
(いいえ．車で行きました．途中とてもよいレストランで食事しました．)

5. アクティビティー見本 (Idea for an activity)

「フェイクニュース」(Fake news)

フェイクニュースを報道してばかりいるレポーターの報道をチェックしてください．報道の間違いを指摘させながら，学習者同士，または指導者と学習者で会話を行ってください．次のような答えが考えられます．

Checking the report below by a reporter who is always reporting fake news, engage learners in a conversation with each other or with you. Possible answers are as follows.

1. The report says two thieves stole money, but the fact is that three thieves stole money.
(報道は 2 名の泥棒となっているが，事実は 3 名です．)
2. The report says the bank is in London, but the fact is that the bank is in Rome.
(報道はロンドンの銀行となっているが，事実はローマの銀行です．)
3. The report says the thieves arrived by plane, but the fact is that they arrived by train.
(報道は泥棒が飛行機で着いたとなっているが，事実は列車です．)
4. The report says the thieves walked to the bank, but the fact is that they drove to the bank.
(報道は泥棒が歩いて銀行へ行ったとなっているが，事実は車で行ったのです．)
5. The report says about 200 people gathered in front of the bank, but the fact is that about 300 people gathered there.
(報道は 200 人くらいが銀行の前に集まったとなっているが，事実は 300 人くらいです．)
6. The report says the thieves didn't say anything to the police, but

the fact is that they told the police the whole truth.

（報道は泥棒たちは警察に何も言わなかったとなっているが，事実は彼らが真実を話したということです.）

The facts: 事実

Three thieves stole money from a bank in Rome. They arrived in the city at nine o'clock on Sunday night by train, drove to the bank by taxi, and broke into the bank. Staff noticed the theft on Monday morning and reported it to the police. About 300 people gathered in front of the bank and watched as the police began their investigation. The thieves were caught and questioned by the police. They told the police the whole truth.

3 名の泥棒がローマの銀行からお金を盗みました．日曜の夜 9 時に列車で到着し，タクシーで銀行に行き，押し入りました．月曜の朝にスタッフが盗難に気づき，警察に連絡しました．警察が捜査を開始していたときには，300 人くらいの人々が銀行の前に集まって捜査を見守りました．泥棒は警察に捕まり，質問されました．彼らは警察にすべての真実を話しました.

The reporting: 報道

Two thieves stole money from a bank in London. They arrived in the city at nine o'clock on Sunday night by plane, walked to the bank, and broke into the bank. Staff noticed the theft on Monday morning and reported it to the police. About 200 people gathered in front of the bank and watched as the police began their investigation. The thieves were caught and questioned by the police. But they told the police nothing.

2 名の泥棒がロンドンの銀行からお金を盗みました．日曜の夜 9 時に飛行機で到着し，銀行まで歩いてき，押し入りました．月曜の朝にスタッフが盗難に気づき，警察に連絡しました．警察が捜査を開始していたときには，200 人くらいの人々が銀行の前に集まって捜査を見守りました．泥棒は警察に捕まり，質問されました．泥棒は警察に何も話しませんでした.

ここでの焦点は /θr/ /tr/ /dr/ /nr/ です．学習者の発音に問題があったら，次のように対応してください．(1) 活動が終わってから，明示的に指導する．(2) 活動の最中であれば，リキャストにより指導する (p. 10 参照).

The focus here is on /θr/, /tr/, /dr/, and /nr/. If learners' pronunciation is problematical, do the following: (1) provide explicit instruction after the activity; (2) provide recasts (see p. 10) during the activity.

第14章

/l/ を含む音の組み合わせの指導 (2)

たとえば final, would like, little, girl　　Clusters with /l/ (2)

1. /nl/ の指導のポイント (How to teach /nl/)

final, original などの最後の部分は, /n/ と /l/ の間に弱い母音を入れて /-nəl/ と発音しても結構ですが, ここでは, 母音を入れない /-nl/ という発音の教え方を説明します. この発音を取り上げる理由には2つあります. 第一に, 母音を入れない発音のほうがスピードのある話し方に役立ち, 多用されます. 第二に, 学習者にこの発音を教えると, この章で取り上げる /dl/ /tl/ と第18章で取り上げる /sl/ が教えやすくなります. 舌の動きがよく似ているからです. /nl/ は, 舌先を上の歯ぐきにつけたままナと言う指導をするとうまく教えられます. 教え方は以下の通りです.

Words like *final* and *original* may be pronounced /-nəl/, with a vowel between /n/ and /l/, but in this chapter I explain how to teach the other pronunciation, one without a vowel in between: /-nl/. I have two reasons for doing this. First, the pronunciation without a vowel helps one to speak fast and is thus used frequently. Second, if you have taught learners to say /nl/, you can easily teach /dl/ and /tl/, which I also take up in this chapter, and /sl/, which I discuss in Chapter 18. All these clusters require similar movements of the tongue. A good way to teach learners to say /nl/ is to have them put the tongue tip on the upper teeth ridge and have them say "na" while keeping the tongue tip there. Here is how to teach this.

まず, 学習者に, 舌先を上の前歯のすぐ後ろの歯ぐきにつけるように指示し, /l/ の形を作らせます (図14.1). そして, その舌先を歯ぐきから離さないようにして，ナと言うよう指示します．そうすると，ナの発音の準備段階で舌のヘりは歯ぐきにつきます（図 14.2）が，ナと言う瞬間に，舌先が歯ぐきについたまま，舌の脇が下がり（図 14.3），結果として，/nl/ を言うときの舌の動きと同じような動きを舌がすることになります．私は図 14.1–14.3 の 3 枚の絵を板書しながら口の動きを教えることにしています．図 14.3 は図 14.1 に矢印を加えればできます．

First, have learners make their tongue assume the /l/ position, that is, have them put their tongue tip on the upper teeth ridge, right behind the upper front teeth (Figure 14.1). Then tell them to say "na," without taking the tongue tip off the teeth ridge. If they begin to do this, they will, in preparation for saying "na," first find themselves putting the edge of the tongue all along the upper teeth ridge (Figure 14.2), resulting in a horseshoe-shaped area of contact between the tongue and the teeth ridge. When they proceed to the vowel in the syllable "na," the sides of the tongue will be lowered (Figure 14.3). That is how the tongue moves when one says /nl/. I draw illustrations like Figures 14.1–14.3 on the board when teaching the movement of the tongue in this process. You can get Figure 14.3 just by adding arrows to Figure 14.1.

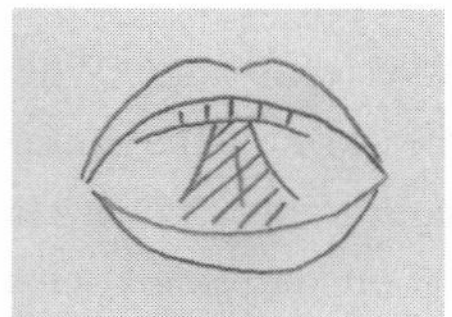

図 14.1　/l/ の発音
(Articulation of /l/)

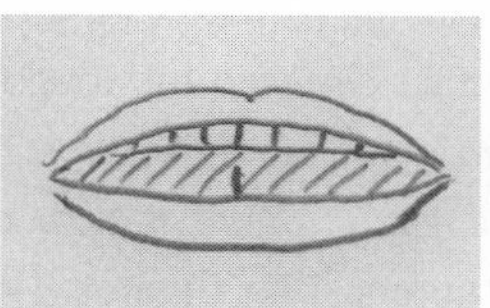

図 14.2　/n/ の発音
(Articulation of /n/)

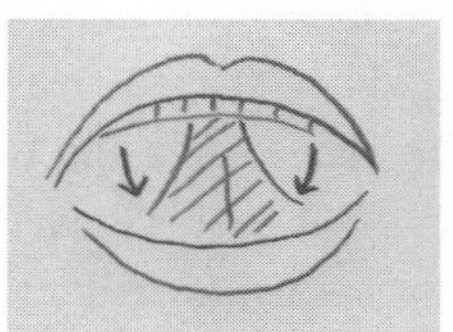

図 14.3　/l/ の発音
(Articulation of /l/)

2. /tl/ /dl/ の指導のポイント (How to teach /tl/ and /dl/)

little の最後の部分や，might like の 2 語の境目などに出て来る /tl/ の組み合わせを取り上げます．/tl/ も，/nl/ 同様，/l/ の直前に母音を入れないで発音するのが典型的です．この発音のほうがスピードのある話し方に役立ち，多用されます．ここでは母音を入れない /tl/ の発音の教え方を説明します．

/tl/ appears in words like *little* and at the word boundary in phrases such as *might like.* Just like /nl/, the cluster /tl/ is typically said without a vowel right before /l/. This pronunciation helps one speak fast and is thus used frequently. Here is how to teach it.

まず，上述の /nl/ の場合のように，学習者に，舌先を上の前歯のすぐ後ろの歯ぐきにつけるように指示し，/l/ の形を作らせます（図 14.4）．そして，その舌先を歯ぐきから離さないようにして，タと言うよう指示します．そうすると，タの発音の準備段階で舌のへりは歯ぐきにつきます（図 14.5）が，タと言う瞬間に，舌先が歯ぐきについたまま，舌の脇が下がり（図 14.6），結果として，/tl/ を言うときの舌の動きと同じような動きを舌がすることになります．図 14.4–14.6 を板書すればこの舌の動きを説明することができます．図 14.6 は図 14.4 に矢印を加えればできます．

First, have learners make their tongue assume the /l/ position, that is, have them put their tongue tip on the upper teeth ridge, right behind the upper front teeth (Figure 14.4). Then tell them to say “ta,” without taking the tongue tip off the teeth ridge. If they begin to do this, they will, in preparation for saying “ta,” first find themselves putting the edge of the tongue all along the upper teeth ridge (Figure 14.5), resulting in a horseshoe-shaped area of contact between the tongue and the teeth ridge. When they proceed to the vowel part of the syllable “ta,” the sides of the tongue will be lowered (Figure 14.6). That is how the tongue moves when one says /tl/. I draw illustrations like Figures 14.4–14.6 on the board when teaching the movement of the tongue in this process. You can get Figure 14.6 just by adding arrows to Figure 14.4.

図 14.4　/l/ の発音
(Articulation of /l/)

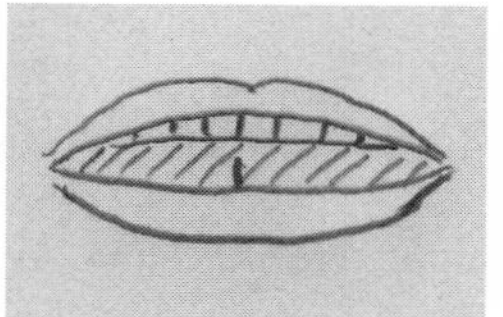
図 14.5　/t/ の発音
(Articulation of /t/)

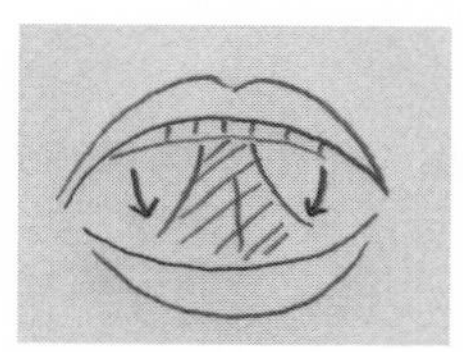
図 14.6　/l/ の発音
(Articulation of /l/)

saddle の最後の部分や would like の 2 語の境目などに出て来る /dl/ の組み合わせを取り上げます．上述の /tl/ の説明と以下の /dl/ の説明はほとんど同じです．なぜならば /t/ は /d/ をささやいて言ったものであり，舌の動きという点で言えば同じ音だからです．/tl/ の場合同様，/dl/ の組み合わせを言う際には，/d/ と /l/ の間に母音を入れないのが典型的な発音です．この発音のほうがスピードのある話し方に役立ち，多用されます．

> /dl/, which appears in words like *saddle* and at the word boundary in such phrases as *would like,* is articulated in the same way as /tl/, as the movement of the tongue is exactly the same in /dl/ as in /tl/. The only difference is that /t/ is a whispered version of /d/. As in the case of /tl/, /dl/ is typically pronounced without a vowel between the two consonants. This pronunciation helps one to speak fast and is therefore used frequently.

すなわち，母音を入れない /dl/ の発音の教え方は，上述の /tl/ の場合と同じです．ただひとつの違いは，/t/ がささやき声の音であるのに対して /d/ は普通に声を出す音である，という点だけです．/tl/ のときと同じ舌の動きを教えてください．すなわち，舌先を上の歯ぐきにつけたままダと言うよう指導してください．

> Thus the way to say /dl/ is the same as the way to say /tl/ except that, while /t/ is a sound that one produces by whispering, /d/ is a voiced sound. To teach /dl/, teach the movement of the tongue for /tl/, but tell learners to say "da" instead of "ta" while keeping the tongue tip on the upper teeth ridge.

3. /iː/ /uː/ /ɚː/ に続く /l/ の指導のポイント (How to teach /l/ preceded by /iː/, /uː/, or /ɚː/)

第 1 章で母音の前に出て来る /l/ について説明しました．ここでは，feel にあるような，母音に続く /l/ のいくつかのケースについて説明します．ここで紹介する /l/ を言うためには，図 14.7 にある通り，口の中のほうで，点線で示したあたりのスペースをある程度確保しなくてはなりません．[1] この図は極端に誇張されており，実際には舌はこれほど湾曲するわけではないのですが，この誇張が学習者への説明に役立ちますので，私はこのような図を描くことにしています．図のポイントは，舌と歯ぐきとの接面が小さくなっているべきであり，そのためには舌先がやや上に向かってとがっているべきであり，またそのためには，舌が平らになることを防ぐためにアゴが少し開いているべきである，ということです．多くの学習者は舌をこの形にすることがなかなかできません．むしろ，/l/ から日本語のルを連想し，発音の際に口を閉じ気味にして唇を丸める傾向にあります．この問題が起きると /l/ が /r/ に近く聞こえることがあります．指導者は学習者に唇を丸めないよう指導する必要があります．

In Chapter 1 we looked at /l/ as it occurs before a vowel. Here in Chapter 14, I discuss how to deal with some cases of /l/ occurring after a vowel, as in *feel*. One needs to secure some empty space in the mouth, as indicated by the dotted line in Figure 14.7, for saying /l/.[1)] Figure 14.7 is an extremely exaggerated illustration, and in reality the tongue will not be curved so sharply. But I draw this sort of illustration because the exaggeration seems to help convey the message well. The important message is that the area of contact between the tongue and the upper teeth ridge should be small, which means the tongue tip should be slightly pointed upward, which in turn means that the jaws should be open to a certain extent to prevent the tongue from becoming flat. Learners often do not have their tongue in this shape and instead have their mouth rather closed while rounding their lips when they try to articulate /l/ because they associate /l/ with the Japanese syllable “ru.” You should prevent learners from doing this.

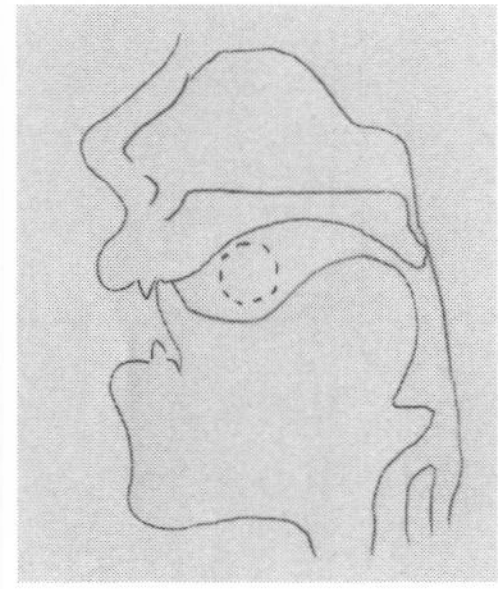

図 14.7 口を開き気味にして /l/ を発音 (Having the mouth rather open for /l/)

学習者は，/l/ が /iː/ /uː/ /ɚː/ のあとに来た場合，たとえば *feel*，*cool*，*girl* の場合，特に発音が難しいと感じるようです．これらの母音はアゴを閉じ気味にして発音する音です．多くの学習者は母音を言い終わって /l/ に移ったときに，そのままアゴを閉じ気味のままにし，その結果 /l/ が /r/ に聞こえることがあります（たとえば，学習者の言う feel が fear に聞こえることがあります）．そこで，私は，学習者に，/l/ に移るときにアゴをむしろ開くよう指示することにしています．前述の通り，図 14.7 は大げさな絵ですが，学習者は，このような図を見たほうが，母音から /l/ への移行の仕方を速く覚えられるようです．

Learners seem to find it particularly difficult to say /l/ when it is preceded by one of three vowels, /iː/, /uː/, and /ɚː/, as in *feel, cool,* and *girl*. These vowels require learners to have their jaws rather closed. Many learners keep their jaws that way even when they proceed to the articulation of /l/. This will make their /l/ sound like /r/ (for example, *feel*, as pronounced by some learners, may sound like *fear*). I thus tell learners to *open* their jaws when they proceed to /l/. As I said, Figure 14.7 presents an exaggerated picture, but a picture like this seems to enable them to quickly learn to handle the transition from the vowel to /l/.

学習者にアゴを開き気味にして問題の /l/ を発音させるためには，/l/ の直前に /ə/ を入れさせてもうまく行きます．すなわち，たとえば，feel は /fiːəl/，cool は /kuːəl/，girl は /gɚːəl/ と発音させればうまく発音させることができます．

To help learners have their jaws rather open for saying the /l/ in question, you can also tell them to put /ə/ before /l/, as in /fiːəl/ (*feel*), /kuːəl/ (*cool*), and /gɚːəl/ (*girl*).

girl，world の場合は，/ɚːə/ の部分が /rə/ に聞こえるはずです．つまり，girl は /gɚːrəl/，world は /wɚːrəld/ と聞こえます．なぜなら，/ɚːə/ を発音するときの舌の動きを示すと図 14.8 のようになるからです．/ɚː/（すなわち /r/）のために口の後ろのほうに寄っていた舌先が急に前に移動して /l/ を発音します．その移動の途中に，舌が /ə/ のときのような形になる，というわけです．図 14.8 を板書すればこの舌の動きを説明することができます．実

線の舌の形は /ɚ:/ の舌の形，点線の舌の形は /l/ の形を表しています．矢印が示す通り，舌先を急に移動させる必要があります．

In the case of *girl* and *world*, /rə/ is often heard in the /ɚ:ə/ part of the word, as in *girl* (/gɚ:rəl/) and *world* (/wɚ:rəld/). What happens is that, when the speaker says /ɚ:ə/, the tongue moves in the way illustrated by Figure 14.8. The tongue is drawn toward the back for the articulation of /ɚ:/(which is the same as /r/) and then pushed toward the front for /l/. When the tongue tip moves from back to front, it is likely to assume the /ə/ position at one stage. You can explain this to learners by drawing an illustration like Figure 14.8 on the board in class. The solid line indicates /ɚ:/, and the dotted line /l/. The tongue tip moves forward quickly in the direction of the arrow.

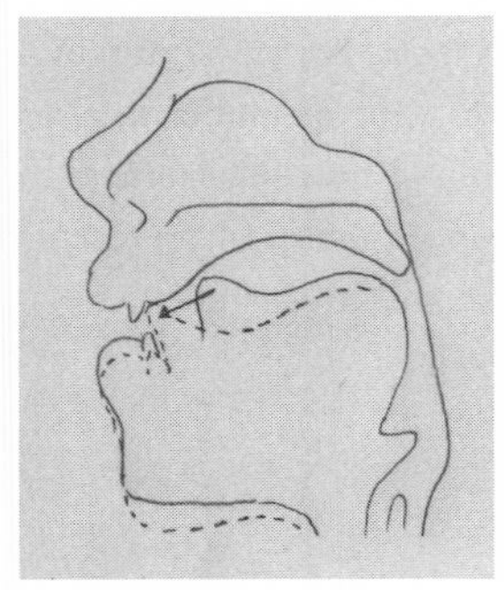

図 14.8　/ɚ:rəl/ の発音 (Articulation of /ɚ:rəl/)

北米系の発音で /ɚ:/ を含む girl (gɚ:l/)，world (/wɚ:ld/) のような単語は，イギリス系の発音の場合は，girl (gə:l/)，world (/wə:ld/) となりますので，上記の /r/ が単語の途中に出現する話は当てはまりません．

This does not apply to British-type pronunciation, where *girl* is pronounced /gə:l/ rather than /gɚ:l/ and *world* is pronounced /wə:ld/ rather than /wɚ:ld/.

4. 練習のための言語材料 (Materials for practice)

下線部に注意して発音するよう指示してください．

Make learners pay attention to the underlined part(s) of each item.

単語

(1) final (2) national (3) saddle（サドル） (4) little
(5) kettle（やかん） (6) feel（感じる） (7) meal（食事） (8) cool
(9) girl (10) world

フレーズ

(1) old lady（年配の女性）
(2) a little kettle（小さなやかん）
(3) traditional meal（伝統的な食事）
(4) a girl with a pearl necklace（真珠のネックレスをつけた若い女性）

センテンス

(1) You might like to have your meal now.
（お食事を今なさってもいいかもしれません.）
(2) He could live anywhere in the world.
（彼は世界のどこでも住める.）
(3) I feel personal information should be better protected.
（個人情報がもっと守られるべきだと私は感じている.）

会話

A: I'd like to take lessons at this swimming pool. Actually, I can't swim at all.
（このプールでレッスンを受けたいのですが. 実は全く泳げないんです.）
B: Well, I wish you all the luck in the world. Fill out this form.
（がんばってくださいね. この書式に記入してください.）
A: OK. I'd like to bring a guest from time to time. May I?
（分かりました. 時々ゲストを連れて来たいのですが, いいですか？）
B: Sure, but there's a fee. Here's a little book about the pool. It gives you all the information you need.
（いいですよ. でも料金がかかります. ここにプールについての小冊子があります. 必要な情報が全部入っています.）

5. アクティビティー見本 (Idea for an activity)

「絵画展」(Art exhibition)

絵画展を見に行った4人が互いに好きな絵の話をしています．John, Gladys, Phyllis, Bill の4人の会話をもとに，誰がどの絵を好きなのか当てるゲームです．話題になっている絵は，「決勝戦」「卓上のケトル」「舞台上の少女」「鞍にまたがる男」の4枚です．学習者同士，または指導者と学習者で会話を行ってください．

Assuming that four people, John, Gladys, Phyllis, and Bill, have visited an art exhibition and are now talking about the kinds of paintings they each like, have learners try to guess who likes which picture on the basis of the conversation given below. The paintings that the characters are talking about are: "Final Match," "Kettle on the Table," "Girl on the Stage," and "Man in the Saddle." Engage them in a conversation with each other or with you.

Possible exchanges are as follows.

A: Which painting does John like? (ジョンはどの絵が好きですか？)
B: I think he likes "Man in the Saddle."
(彼は「鞍にまたがる男」が好きなんだと思います．)

A: Which painting does Gladys like?
(グラディスはどの絵が好きですか？)
B: I think she likes "Final Match."
(彼女は「決勝戦」が好きなんだと思います．)

A: Which painting does Phyllis like? (フィリスはどの絵が好きですか？)
B: I think she likes "Kettle on the Table."
(彼女は「卓上のケトル」が好きなんだと思います．)

A: Which painting does Bill like? (ビルはどの絵が好きですか？)
B: I think he likes "Girl on the Stage."
(彼は「舞台上の少女」が好きなんだと思います．)

4 人の会話 (Conversation between the four characters)

John: I love paintings where you can see the beauty of nature. When scenes out of doors are captured in good paintings, I feel as if I were out of doors myself.

(自然の美しさが見られる絵が好きだね．屋外の風景がいい絵に描かれると，自分も屋外にいるように感ずる.)

Gladys: I like themes about sports. It's wonderful to see athletes in good paintings.

(スポーツのテーマが好きだわ．いい絵でアスリートを見るのは素晴らしい.)

Phyllis: I like paintings about everyday things—things in the house, things in the garden, that sort of thing.

(日常の物事の絵が好きだわ．家の中のもの，庭にあるもの，なんか.)

Bill: I liked the painting of someone that looks like my daughter. She's not as old as the woman in the painting is, but their faces kind of look like each other.

(娘に似た人の絵がよかったよね．娘は絵の女性ほどの年齢じゃないけど，顔が似てる.)

ここでの焦点は /nl/ /dl/ /tl/ /ɚːl/ です．学習者の発音に問題があったら，次のように対応してください．(1) 活動が終わってから，明示的に指導する．(2) 活動の最中であれば，リキャストにより指導する (p. 10 参照).

The focus here is on /nl/, /dl/, /tl/, and /ɚːl/. If learners' pronunciation is problematical, do the following: (1) provide explicit instruction after the activity; (2) provide recasts (see p. 10) during the activity.

第 15 章

ズに聞こえる音 — /z/ /dz/ の指導

たとえば cars, cards　　How to teach /z/ and /dz/

1. /z/ /dz/ の指導のポイント (How to teach /z/ and /dz/)

cars の最後の音は /z/ です．これに対し cards の最後の音は /dz/ です．size の最後の音は /z/ ですが sides の最後の音は /dz/ です．/z/ と /dz/ は異なる音ですが，そもそも音が異なることを知っている学習者は多くありません．これらの音の違いを教えるには，これらの音を声を出さずに言ったらどうなるかを説明するのが近道です．

Cars ends in /z/, while *cards* ends in /dz/. *Size* ends in /z/, while *sides* ends in /dz/. Not many learners know that different sounds are used in these pairs of words. The best way to teach the difference between /z/ and /dz/ is to explain what these sounds would be like if they were whispered.

cars (/kɑɚz/) を学習者の前でささやき声で言ってみてください．最後の音は /s/ になります．一方，cards (/kɑɚdz/) をささやき声で言うと，最後の音は /ts/ になります．/s/ と /ts/ は日本語の音体系にある音ですから，日本の学習者は /s/ と /ts/ を簡単に区別することができます．普通の声で言おうとささやき声で言おうと舌の動きは同じですから，cars と cards を言う際の舌の動きを学習者に確認させるために，まずこれらの単語をささやき声で言わせ，/s/ と /ts/ との差を感じさせることをお勧めします．

Whisper *cars* (/kɑɚz/) for learners and show that the last sound comes out as /s/. Do the same with *cards* (/kɑɚdz/) and show that the last sound turns out to be /ts/. Learners in Japan can easily distinguish between /s/ and /ts/ because they are both in the Japanese sound system. As the movement of the tongue is the same whether one says something with or without voice, I recommend that you make learners whisper these words and get the feel of the difference between /s/ and /ts/ so that they can understand how the tongue moves when one says *cars* and *cards*.

さて，(a) /z/（またはそれをささやいたときの /s/）と (b) /dz/（またはそれをささやいたときの /ts/）との舌の動きの違いをどう教えればよいでしょうか．この差は，/s, s, s ..../ /ts, ts, ts .../ と繰り返して言えば分かりやすくなります．繰り返しながら舌先がどのような動きをするかを考えさせると，/s, s, s ..../ のときは舌先が上の歯のすぐ後ろの歯ぐきに近づくことを理解させることができます．ただし，舌先は歯ぐきに触れません．これに対して，/ts, ts, ts .../ のときは，/ts/ の数だけ舌先が上の歯のすぐ後ろの歯ぐきに繰り返し触れることが分かります．舌先が歯ぐきに近づくだけなのか触れるのかが違いなのです．学習者にこのことをしっかり理解させてください．

Now, how should one teach the difference between /z/ and /dz/ in terms of the movement of the tongue? You can make the difference easy to understand if you have learners say /s, s, s .../ and /ts, ts, ts .../. By having them think about how the tongue moves in these simple repetition exercises, you can help them realize that, when they say /s, s, s .../, the tongue tip comes close to the upper teeth ridge, right behind the front teeth, but does not touch the ridge, while, when they say /ts, ts, ts .../, the tongue tip does touch the teeth ridge, as many times as they say /ts/. The difference is thus whether the tongue tip touches the ridge or not. Make sure that learners understand this.

学習者が舌の動きを理解したところで，次に，声を伴った発音をすることを教えます．/s, s, s ..../ はささやき声で行う発音ですが，これに普通の声をつけると /z, z, z .../ になります．舌先は上の歯ぐきに近づくだけで触れることはありません．また，/ts, ts, ts .../ もささやき声で行う発音ですが，これに普通の声をつけると /dz, dz, dz .../ になります．舌先は /dz/ のたびに上の歯ぐきに触れます．学習者にささやかせたり声を出させたりして練習させてください．

When learners have understood the movement of the tongue, you should then teach how to produce sounds with voice. /s, s, s .../ becomes /z, z, z .../ when voice is added. The tongue tip comes close to the upper teeth ridge but does not touch it. /ts, ts, ts, .../ becomes /dz, dz, dz .../, with voice. The tongue tip touches the upper teeth ridge every time /dz/ is said. Have learners do these whispered and voiced exercises.

/z/ または /s/ の場合と，/dz/ または /ts/ の場合とで，舌が口の天井のどの部分に触れるのか，図で説明するのもよい方法です．/z/ または /s/ の場合，舌は口の天井に馬蹄形に触れますが，真ん中は開いていて（図 15.1），そこから息が外に出て行きます．出て行った息は前歯に当たってノイズを作ります．これが /z/ または /s/ の音です．/dz/ または /ts/ の場合，舌は，まず，真ん中が開いていない形で口の天井に触れます（図 15.3）．息は出て行きません．次に，/dz/ または /ts/ の発音と同時に真ん中が開いて，息が外に出て行く道ができます．このとき，舌の形は /z/ または /s/ の場合の形（図 15.1）と同じになります．図 15.1，図 15.3 の情報を板書で伝えるには，それぞれ図 15.2，図 15.4 のようなもので十分でしょう．

Another good way of teaching /z/, /s/, /dz/, and /ts/ is to use illustrations and show what part of the roof of the mouth the tongue touches in each case. In the case of /z/ and /s/, the tongue touches the roof of the mouth, the area of contact looking almost like a horseshoe, except that there is an opening at the very center (Figure 15.1), where air goes out. Air hits the front teeth and makes noise—the /z/ or /s/ sound. In the case of /dz/ and /ts/, the tongue first touches the roof of the mouth without an opening (Figure 15.3). Air therefore does not go out. Then, at the time of the articulation of /dz/ and /ts/, the opening at the center occurs and air goes out. When the opening has been created, the shape of the tongue is the same as that in the case of /z/ and /s/ (Figure 15.1). If you want to convey the information given in Figure 15.1 and Figure 15.3, you can draw simpler illustrations like Figure 15.2 and Figure 15.4, respectively.

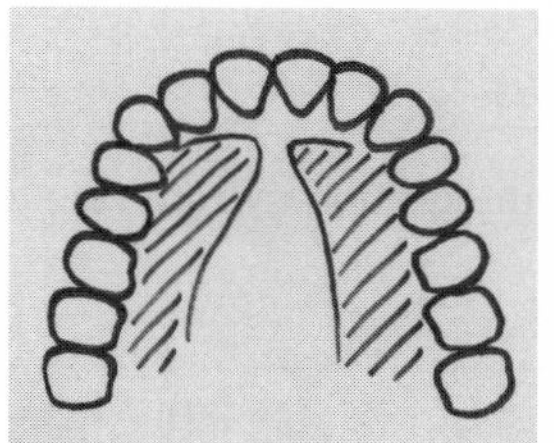

図15.1　/s/ /z/ の発音（Articulation of /s/ or /z/）

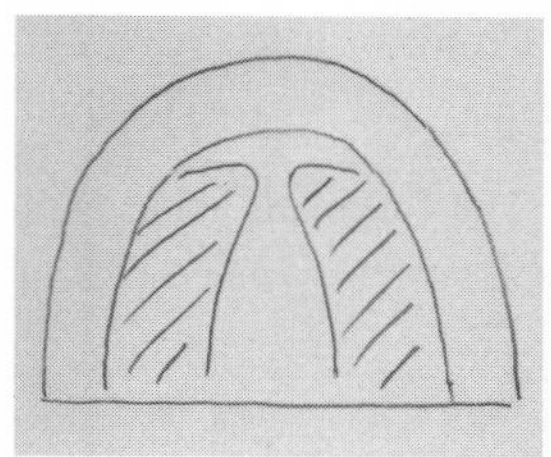

図15.2　図15.1の簡易版（Simplified version of Figure 15.1）

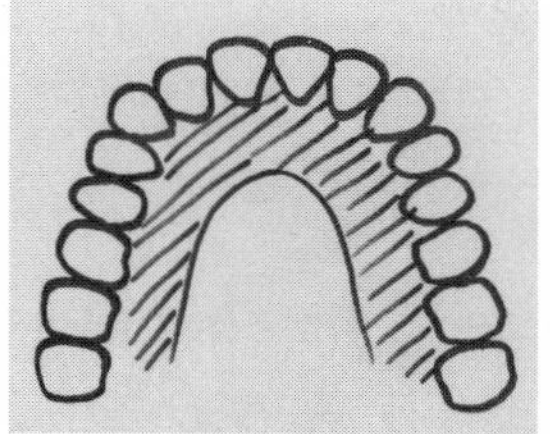

図15.3　/ts/ /dz/ の発音の準備段階（Preparatory stage of the articulation of /ts/ or /dz/）

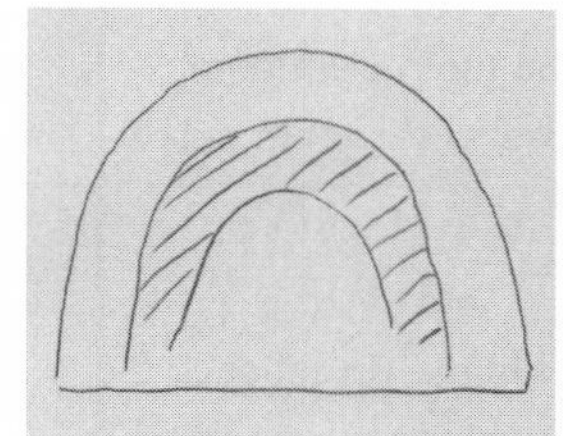

図15.4　図15.3の簡易版（Simplified version of Figure 15.3）

2.　ささやき声と普通の声（Voiceless and voiced sounds）

本章の理解には，ささやき声と普通の声との関係の理解がカギになります．このことが理解できない学習者に対しては，第2章セクション2で説明した声の有無に関する説明をしてください．学習者に自分ののどに指を当てて声の有無を確認させてください．

The key to the comprehension of the content of this chapter is the comprehension of the relation between whisper and voice. If learners have trouble understanding it, go back to Section 2 of Chapter 2 and provide them with the explanation given there. Make learners put their fingers on their throat and check the presence and absence of voice.

少し理屈っぽくなりますが，上記のことを整理すると次のようになります．/z/ と /dz/ について，raise（/reɪz/ 高さを上げる），race（/reɪs/ レース），

raids（/reɪdz/「攻撃」の複数），rates（/reɪts/「割合」の複数）という 4 個の単語を例にとって説明します．下の表をご覧ください．

The following table explains the relation in question by referring to four words: *raise, race, raids,* and *rates*.

	声を出す Voiced	声を出さない Whispered (voiceless)
舌先を歯ぐきに 近づける The tongue tip comes close to the teeth ridge	/z/ たとえば raise の 最後	/s/ たとえば race の 最後
舌先を歯ぐきに 触れさせる The tongue tip touches the teeth ridge at one stage	/dz/ たとえばの raids の 最後	/ts/ たとえば rates の 最後

表を横に見て頂ければ分かりますが，/z/ を出すためには /s/ に声をつけて出せばよいし，/dz/ を出すためには /ts/ に声をつけて出せばよいわけです．また，表を縦に見て頂ければ分かりますが，/z/ と /dz/ の違いも，/s/ と /ts/ の違いも，ともに舌を歯ぐきに近づけるだけなのか，あるいは触れさせるか，という違いです．

Horizontal comparison will show that one can produce /z/ by adding voice to /s/ and that one can produce /dz/ again by adding voice to /ts/. Vertical comparison will show that the difference between /z/ and /dz/ is the same as the difference between /s/ and /ts/: The tongue tip does not touch the teeth ridge in the case of /z/ and /s/, while it does in the case of /dz/ and /ts/.

3. 練習のための言語材料 (Materials for practice)

下線部に注意して発音するよう指示してください．一重下線は /z/，二重下線は /dz/ です．

Make learners pay attention to the underlined part(s) of each item.

単語

(1)　cars　(2)　knees（ひざ）　(3)　guys　(4)　rise（昇る）
(5)　rose（バラ）　(6)　cards　(7)　needs（ニーズ）　(8)　guides（案内人）
(9)　rides（乗ること，乗り物）　(10)　roads

フレーズ

(1)　cars on the roads（道路の車）
(2)　size of the seeds（種の大きさ）
(3)　ties for young guys（若い男性用のネクタイ）
(4)　prizes for the best guides（最高の案内人たちへの賞）

センテンス

(1)　They gave out roses as prizes.（彼らは賞としてバラを与えた.）
(2)　He feeds the birds every day.（彼は毎日鳥に餌をやっている.）
(3)　The prices of goods and services are rising fast.
（商品とサービスの価格が急上昇している.）

会話

A:　There used to be a small amusement park here, but it was closed down two years ago.
（ここに小さな遊園地がありましたが，2 年前に閉園になりました.）

B:　Really?　What was it like?
（本当ですか？　どんな遊園地でしたか？）

A:　The place was filled with roses.　There were rides for kids.　And they had parades, too.
（バラで一杯でした．子供のための乗り物があって，パレードもありました.）

B:　Too bad it was closed down.
（閉園になって残念ですね.）

4. アクティビティー見本 (Idea for an activity)

「コーヒーのしみ」(Coffee stains)

下に挙げる日記の文章にコーヒーのしみがあります．しみで隠れた単語を当てるゲームをしてください．毎回，サイコロを振り，出た目の数の番号の空欄を，リスト（cars, roads, rose, knees, needs, cards の 6 語）のなかの単語を使って答えさせてください．先に正しい単語を言えた学習者がその回の勝者です．

Assuming that someone's diary entry has coffee stains on it, have learners guess what word is covered by each stain. For each round, players roll a die and try to guess the word for the stain for the number they got, choosing a word from a 6-word list: *cars, roads, rose, knees, needs,* and *cards*. The first player who has said the correct word for the stain is the winner for that round.

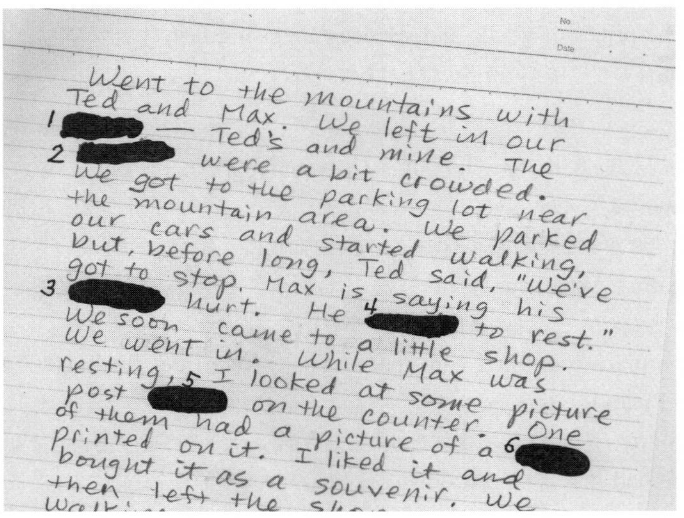
No
Date
Went to the mountains with
Ted and Max. We left in our
1 — Ted's and mine. The
2 were a bit crowded.
We got to the parking lot near
the mountain area. We parked
our cars and started walking,
but, before long, Ted said, "We've
got to stop. Max is saying his
3 hurt. He 4 to rest."
We soon came to a little shop.
We went in. While Max was
resting, I looked at some picture
post 5 on the counter. One
of them had a picture of a 6
printed on it. I liked it and
bought it as a souvenir. We
then left the shop.

Text with the answers:

Went to the mountains with Ted and Max. We left in our (1. cars) —Ted's and mine. The (2. roads) were a bit crowded. We got to the parking lot near the mountain area. We parked our cars and started walking, but, before long, Ted said, “We’ve got to stop. Max is saying his (3. knees) hurt. He (4. needs) to rest.” We soon came to a little shop. We went in. While Max was resting I looked at some picture post (5. cards) on the counter. One of them had a picture of a (6. rose) printed on it. I liked it and bought it as a souvenir ...

先週，テッドとマックスと一緒に山に行った．我々の車—テッドのとぼくの—で出発した．道は少し混んでいた．山岳地帯の近くの駐車場に着いた．駐車して歩き始めたが，程なくテッドが「止まらなきゃ．マックスが膝が痛いって言ってる．彼は休みが必要だ．」と言った．すぐに小さな売店に来た．中に入った．マックスが休んでいる間，カウンターの絵葉書を見た．そのうち 1 枚にはバラの絵がプリントされていた．気に入ったのでおみやげにそれを買った．

ここでの焦点は /z/ /dz/ です．学習者の発音に問題があったら，次のように対応してください．(1) 活動が終わってから，明示的に指導する．(2) 活動の最中であれば，リキャストにより指導する (p. 10 参照)．

The focus here is on /z/ and /dz/. If learners’ pronunciation is problematical, do the following: (1) provide explicit instruction after the activity; (2) provide recasts (see p. 10) during the activity.

第 16 章

グに聞こえる音―/g/ /ŋg/ /ŋ/ の指導

たとえば magazine，finger，singer　　How to teach /g/, /ŋg/, and /ŋ/

1. /g/ の指導のポイント (How to teach /g/)

/g/ は go，get，magazine（アクセントは mag- にも -zine にも置き得る），again などの語の "g" の部分に出て来ます．学習者は，/g/ の音を簡単に出すことができます．日本語にある音だからです．たとえば，この音は，日本語のガッコウ（学校）のアタマの音と同じ音です．この発音をするとき，話し手は舌の後ろを高くし，その高くなった部分を口の天井に触れさせます．図 16.1 を板書することによりこのことを説明することができます．

/g/ is a sound used in *go*, *get*, *magazine*, and *again*. Learners will have no trouble articulating /g/, as it is in the Japanese sound system. For example, it is the sound that appears at the beginning of the Japanese word "gakko" ("school"). When this sound is articulated, the speaker raises the back of the tongue and makes that part of the tongue touch the roof of the mouth. You can explain this by drawing an illustration like Figure 16.1.

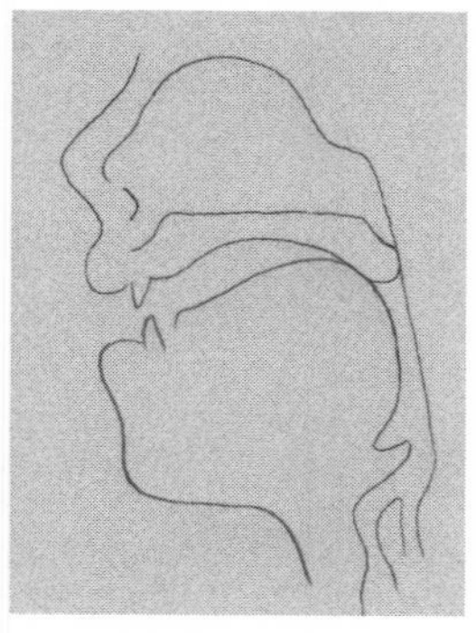

図 16.1　/g/ の発音 (Articulation of /g/)

学習者は，英語を話すとき，(a) 単語のアタマの “g”（たとえば go のアタマの音）と (b)「ッグ」で終わる外来語になっている単語のグの部分（たとえば egg＝「エッグ」の “gg”）は正しく /ɡ/ で発音できます．しかし，それ以外の “g” については，学習者が正しい /ɡ/ を使わず，鼻濁音と呼ばれている /ŋ/ (-ing に出て来る) を使うことがあります（たとえば magazine や hug の “g”；/ŋ/ については次のセクションをご参照ください）．/ɡ/ を使うべきところで /ŋ/ を使ってしまう学習者に対しては，正しい /ɡ/ を使うように注意を与えてください．ほとんどの学習者はこの注意を聞いたとき直ちに /ŋ/ を /ɡ/ に直すことができます．

Learners can correctly use (a) /ɡ/ at the beginning of a word, such as the initial sound in *go*, and (b) /ɡ/ at the end of a word which has found its way into Japanese and become a loanword ending in “-ggu,” such as “eggu” (“egg”). On the other hand, they may not be able to say /ɡ/ for the letter “g” and may use /ŋ/ (used in the *-ing* ending) instead. They may say *magazine* and *hug* using /ŋ/, for example. See the following section for further discussion of /ŋ/. If you find learners using /ŋ/ where /ɡ/ should be used, tell them to use the correct /ɡ/. Most of them will be able to change /ŋ/ to /ɡ/ once they have been told to do so.

2. /ŋ/ の指導のポイント (How to teach /ŋ/)

/ŋ/ は，たとえば singer の真ん中の音であり，going の最後の音です．日本語で言う「鼻濁音」と同じです．日本語では，「私が」と言うときの助詞のガも鼻濁音で言うのが伝統的な発音です．しかし，日本語話者の間には鼻濁音を使わない人が大勢いて，このような人は英語を話すときに /ŋ/ を使うのを苦手とする可能性があります．げんに，たとえば，singer (/sɪŋɚ/) の /ŋ/ が出せずに /ŋɡ/ を使う学習者は多いです．

/ŋ/ is a sound which appears in the middle of *singer* and at the end of *going*, for example. It is the same sound as what is called “bidakuon” in Japanese, the velar nasal sound. The particle “-ga” in Japanese is traditionally supposed to be pronounced /ŋa/, for example. However, there are a fair number of speakers of Japanese who do not use /ŋ/, and these people may very well find it difficult to use /ŋ/ when speaking English. In fact, many learners of English in Japan cannot say *singer* (/sɪŋɚ/) properly and use /ŋg/ instead of the correct /ŋ/.

ひとつの練習方法は，次のようなフレーズを使ってリピート練習することです．モデルを提供する指導者は「ガ」に鼻濁音を使わなくてはなりません．

ニャガニャガニャガ …

ニュガニュガニュガ …

ニョガニョガニョガ …

この練習法は，発音方法において /ŋ/ が /n/ の仲間（どちらも鼻から息を出す音）の音であることを利用したものです．学習者がガのアタマの音として /g/ を使うと，上記のフレーズのなかに発音方法において異なる子音が混じることになり，フレーズを言うのが楽ではありません．/ŋ/ を使ったほうがずっと言いやすいのです．このことを利用し，学習者が発音しやすい方法でフレーズを言うようになることを狙った練習です．

One way to have learners practice saying /ŋ/ is to make them do a repetition exercise using the following nonsense phrases. Learners can repeat after the instructor and say the phrases, where the point is that they should say /ŋa/ for "ga."

"nyaga, nyaga, nyaga ..."

"nyuga nyuga, nyuga ..."

"nyoga, nyoga, nyoga ..."

This practice takes advantage of the fact that /ŋ/ and /n/ are the same in terms of the manner of articulation (both are nasals). These phrases are more difficult to say with /g/ than with /ŋ/ because /g/ and /n/ are different in terms of the manner of articulation. Thus, the phrases are intended to help learners to say /ŋ/ in phonetic environments favorable for saying it.

3. /ŋg/ と /ŋ/ との使い分け (Where to use /ŋg/; where to use /ŋ/)

/ŋg/ と /ŋ/ との使い分けを間違えてもコミュニケーション上困るということは考えにくいので，学習者が使い分けがなかなかできなくともあまり深刻に考える必要はありません．ただ，学習者が将来上級者になって行くことを考えれば，学習者が初級の時点で，使い分けについて基本情報を与えることには価値があると思います．

> If learners are faced with a choice between /ŋg/ and /ŋ/ and choose the wrong item, do not be overly demanding of them, because the mistake is not likely to lead to a failure in communication. But, considering that learners will eventually reach an advanced level of English in the future, it will be a good idea to provide them with basic information about this matter while they are still beginning learners.

私は次の 3 点に分けて使い分けの問題を扱うことにしています．

第一に，つづりが -ng で終わる単語の最後では /ŋ/ が使われ，このような語の頻度は高いので，このつづりと発音との関係は重視するよう教えます．along，among，evening，hang，king，long，morning，ring，sing，song，spring，strong，swing，wing，young などの例を挙げることができます．

> First, I attach importance to words ending in *-ng*, the final consonant of which is pronounced /ŋ/, as these words are relatively high-frequency words. See the above list of words for examples.

第二に，これらの語から派生した単語の場合，元の語の /ŋ/ が，派生した語の真ん中に入ることになりますが，学習者が元の語の /ŋ/ が言えても単語の真ん中の /ŋ/ が言える保証はありませんので注意が必要です．

> Secondly, forms derived from those words have /ŋ/ in the middle, as in the following items. You need to be careful as some learners can say /ŋ/ when it is at the end of a word but not when it is in the middle of a word.

sing（/sɪŋ/）+ er = singer（/-ŋɚ/，「歌手」）
sing（/sɪŋ/）+ ing = singing（/-ŋɪŋ/，「歌うこと，歌唱」）
long（/lɔŋ/）+ ing = longing（/-ŋɪŋ/，「あこがれ」）

上に挙げた語の場合のように，ふたつの部分（元の語と接尾辞）に分けられる語で元の語が /-ŋ/ で終わるのであれば，接尾辞の直前は /-ŋ/ のままです．しかし，そのような構造でない anger（/æŋgɚ/，怒り），finger（/fɪŋgɚ/，指），hunger（/hʌŋgɚ/，空腹）などには，/ŋg/ が使われます．

As in the above examples, if a word is made up of two parts—a stem, ending in /-ŋ/, and a suffix—then /-ŋ/ is unchanged. If a word does not have such a structure, then the *ng* in the spelling is pronounced /ŋg/, e.g. *anger* (/æŋgɚ/), *finger* (/fɪŋgɚ/), and *hunger* (/hʌŋgɚ/).

第三に，形容詞や副詞の比較級，最上級を教える必要があります．longer，longest，stronger，strongest といった /-ŋ/ で終わる形容詞や副詞の比較級と最上級は，いずれも -er，-est という接尾辞を含んでいますので，上記の原則で行くと /-ŋɚ/，/-ŋɪst/ となりそうですが，これらの比較級，最上級は /-ŋgɚ/, /-ŋgɪst/ となります．

Thirdly, you need to teach the comparative and superlative forms of adjectives and adverbs ending in /-ŋ/, such as *longer*, *longest*, *stronger*, and *strongest*, which are pronounced with /ŋg/ despite the second principle above.

4. 練習のための言語材料 (Materials for practice)

下線部に注意して発音するよう指示してください．一重線が /g/，二重線が /ŋ/ です．

Make learners pay attention to the underlined part(s) of each item.

単語

(1) tag（札） (2) finger (3) longest (4) magazine (5) stronger
(6) spring (7) wedding (8) coming (9) singer
(10) belongings（所持品）

フレーズ

(1) wedding in spring（春の結婚式）
(2) the strongest argument you can think of（考えられる最強の議論）
(3) longer-term savings（より長期の貯金）
(4) recipe for pudding in a magazine（雑誌に載ったプディングのレシピ）

センテンス

(1) Stronger workers had to work for longer hours.
(より強い労働者はより長時間働かなくてはならなかった.)

(2) He pointed the finger at the singer. (彼は歌手を名指しで非難した.)

(3) She put a tag on each of her belongings.
(彼女は自分の所持品のすべてに札をつけた.)

会話

A: I was impressed by the singer at the wedding.
(結婚式で歌手に感動しました.)

B: So was I. I sometimes see her in a magazine.
(私もです. 時々彼女を雑誌で見ますね.)

A: I wish she had sung a longer piece.
(もっと長い曲を歌ってくれたらよかったのに.)

B: That would have been nice. Oh, I remember she's giving a concert very soon.
(そうだったらよかったのにね. あ, 思い出した. 彼女はまもなくコンサートをやりますよ.)

5. アクティビティー見本 (Idea for an activity)

クロスワードパズル (Crossword puzzle)

クロスワードパズルです. 学習者同士, または指導者と学習者で会話を行いながら解いてください.

Engage learners in a conversation with each other or with you and have them fill in the squares by giving answers to the clues. One possible exchange is as follows.

A: What do you think the answer to one across is?
(ヨコのカギ 1 の答えは何だと思う？)

B: It is BOXING. (BOXING だよ.)

A: Yes, that's right. Well done. (その通り. よくできました.)

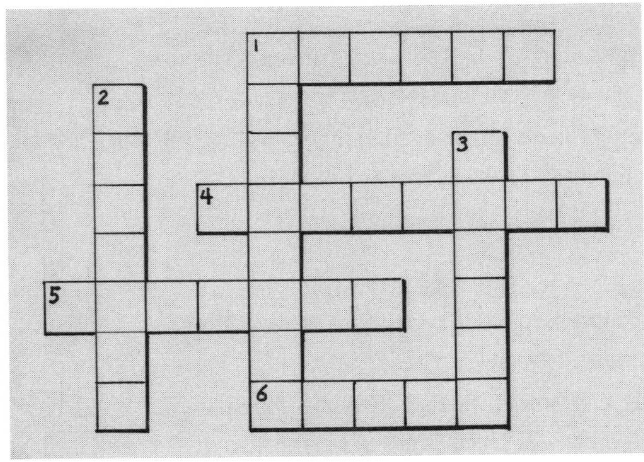

Across:

1. Sport with two people punching each other（ふたりが打ち合うスポーツ）
Answer: BOXING

4. Making sweaters, gloves, etc.（セーター，手袋などを作る）
Answer: KNITTING

5. Music made with the voice（声で作る音楽） Answer: SINGING

6. Hi! How's it ____ ?（やあ！調子は ____ ?） Answer: GOING

Down:

1. I am ____ up this topic as a reminder.
（私はリマインダーとしてこの話題を ____.） Answer: BRINGING

2. The phone is ____.（電話が ____.） Answer: RINGING

3. Ouch! The dog is ____ me.（痛っ！犬が私を ____.） Answer: BITING

ここでの焦点は /ŋ/ です．学習者の発音に問題があったら，次のように対応してください．(1) 活動が終わってから，明示的に指導する．(2) 活動の最中であれば，リキャストにより指導する（p. 10 参照）．

The focus here is on /ŋ/. If learners' pronunciation is problematical, do the following: (1) provide explicit instruction after the activity; (2) provide recasts (see p. 10) during the activity.

第 17 章

音のくずれの指導（1）

Sound reduction（1）

この章と次の第 18 章では，音のくずれを紹介します．この第 17 章では，どちらかと言えば初級の学習者も学んだ方がよいと思われる項目，第 18 章ではそれよりもやや高度な事例を取り上げます．

In this and the next chapter—Chapters 17 and 18—cases of sound reduction are discussed. Here in Chapter 17 I take up cases of reduction which beginning learners should learn about in my opinion; more advanced cases of sound reduction will be explained in Chapter 18.

音のくずれをどう扱うかは，指導者として判断しにくい場合がありますが，いくつかヒントを述べるとすれば，(a) 学習者にとってリスニングに役立つと思われる知識は，自分で発音できなくともよいというコメントつきで紹介する，(b) 学習者が英語の発音を学ぶモチベーションにつながる知識があれば紹介する，(c) 速くしゃべりたい，なめらかにしゃべりたい，という学習者の希望があれば，そのために役立つくずれの知識を紹介する，といったことが考えられます．くずれを重視しすぎると発音の勉強が難しくなりすぎる恐れがありますので，教師は，どこまで教えるべきか，目前の学習者をよく見ながら判断する必要があります．

"How should the instructor treat sound reduction?" is not an easy question to answer. Here are a few principles that may be worth considering: (a) If there are cases of sound reduction that may help learners perform better in listening comprehension, you can teach them with a comment that they themselves do not have to learn to put those cases of sound reduction into practice. (b) If knowledge about certain cases of sound reduction is likely to raise learners' motivation, you should perhaps provide them with such knowledge. (c) If learners have a strong desire to learn to speak faster or speak more smoothly, you can teach cases of sound reduction that are likely to help them achieve their goal. But if you overemphasize sound reduction, you could make the study of pronunciation difficult for learners. Observe learners' performance carefully as you decide what to teach.

1. /dj/ /tj/ /zj/ /sj/ のくずれ (Reduction of /dj/, /tj/, /zj/, and /sj/)

初級の学習者も恐らくしばしば耳にする音のくずれに次のようなものがあります．例文とともにお示しします．

(a) /dj/ が /dʒ/ となる．たとえば，Would you help me?（「手伝ってくれませんか？」）の would you /wʊd juː/ が /wʊdʒuː/ となる．/dʒ/ は，チャ，チュ，チョのアタマの音を声を伴う形で言ったときの音．

(b) /tj/ が /tʃ/ となる．たとえば，How about you?（「あなたはどうなのですか？」）の about you /əbaʊt juː/ が /əbaʊtʃuː/ となる．/tʃ/ はチャ，チュ，チョのアタマの音．

(c) /zj/ が /ʒ/ となる．たとえば，Is your work finished?（「あなたの仕事は終わりましたか？」）の is your /ɪz jʊɚ/ が /ɪʒʊɚ/ となる．/ʒ/ は，シャ，シュ，ショのアタマの音を声を伴う形で言ったときの音．

(d) /sj/ が /ʃ/ となる．たとえば，I'll miss you.（「あなたがいなくなって寂しくなります.」）の miss you /mɪs juː/ が /mɪʃuː/ となる．/ʃ/ は，シャ，シュ，ショのアタマの音．

Here are cases of sound reduction that even beginning learners are likely to be familiar with.

(a) /dj/ changes into /dʒ/, as in *Would you help me?*, where /wʊd juː/ (*would you*) changes into /wʊdʒuː/. /dʒ/ is the voiced version of the initial consonant in the Japanese syllables "cha," "chu," and "cho."

(b) /tj/ changes into /tʃ/, as in *How about you?*, where /əbaʊt juː/ (*about you*) changes into /əbaʊtʃuː/. /tʃ/ is the same as the initial consonant in the Japanese syllables "cha," "chu," and "cho."

(c) /zj/ changes into /ʒ/, as in *Is your work finished?*, where /ɪz jʊɚ/ (*is your*) changes into /ɪʒʊɚ/. /ʒ/ is the voiced version of the initial consonant in the Japanese syllables "sha," "shu," and "sho."

(d) /sj/ changes into /ʃ/, as in *I'll miss you*, where /mɪs juː/ (*miss you*) changes into /mɪʃuː/. /ʃ/ is the same as the initial consonant in the Japanese syllables "sha," "shu," and "sho."

2. 発音に至らない /b/ /d/ /g/ /p/ /t/ /k/

(Incomplete articulation of /b/, /d/, /g/, /p/, /t/, and /k/)

英語のいくつかの音は，特定環境のもとで，発音が始まるものの発音が完結せず，聞こえないことがあります．次の項目の下線部が例です．

(a) cabdriver (/kæbdraɪvɚ/, タクシー運転手)
(b) bedtime (/bedtaɪm/, 就寝時刻)
(c) eggbeater (/egbiːtɚ/, タマゴ泡立て器)
(d) clipboard (/klɪpbɔɚd/, クリップボード)
(e) shotgun (/ʃɑtgʌn/, 散弾銃)
(f) blackboard (/blækbɔɚd/, 黒板)

上の例のそれぞれの音は，本来，息の流れを一度止めて，息を勢いよく口の外に出して発音します．しかし，場合によっては，息の流れを止めたところで，発音が終わりになってしまいます．たとえば，上の (a) の場合，話し手は /b/ を言うべく唇を閉じますが，/b/ を言うことなく，次の音である /d/ に移って行ってしまいます．これは初級の学習者にもさほど難しくないことであると思われますので，指導を試みてください．

Certain consonants in certain phonetic environments become inaudible because the articulation is incomplete. In all of the above examples, the consonant on which each one focuses would ordinarily be a sound that one articulates by stopping the flow of air and then letting air out in a plosive manner. Articulation of such a consonant is sometimes halted. For example, in (a) above, the speaker closes the lips in preparation for /b/ but, without saying /b/, moves on to /d/. The articulation of the incomplete sound followed by another sound should not be too difficult even for beginning learners. Try teaching it.

3. **“gonna” と “wanna”** (*gonna* and *wanna*)

会話でよく出て来るフレーズである be going to（〜するつもりである．これから〜する.）の going to がしばしば /gənə/ とくずされます（くずれた発音にはバラつきがありますが，ここでは典型的な発音をご紹介します)．これをことさらつづりで表す場合は，gonna とつづられます．また，want to（〜したい）はしばしば /wɑnə/ とくずされます．これをことさらつづりで表す場合は，wanna とつづられます．どちらも非常に使用頻度の高いフレーズであり，また，くずれた発音が使われる頻度も高いので，初級の学習者もこのくずれについて知っておいたほうがよいと思います．また，この発音を使って英語を話すことが学習者にとって楽であれば，学習者はこの発音を使って積極的に会話すべきだと思います．

The second and third words in the phrase *be going to* (meaning *will*) are often reduced to various degrees, the result of ultimate reduction being /gənə/. If this reduction needs to be made explicit in spelling, it is spelled *gonna*. Similarly, *want to* is often reduced to /wɑnə/, which may be written *wanna*, if necessary. As *going to* and *want to* are frequently used phrases, and the reduced forms are heard frequently, learners should know about the reduced pronunciations. If the use of these forms makes it easy for learners to speak English, they should certainly be encouraged to use them in their interactions with others.

4. **ラ行子音に似た /t/ の発音** (Reduction of /t/ to a tap)

北米系の発音では，/t/ が，ある条件[1] のもとで，ほぼ規則的にラ，リ，ル，レ，ロのアタマの音に似た /t/ になります．たとえば，city の -ty の部分はリのように聞こえます．この発音は，できなくともコミュニケーション上何の問題もありませんが，できるようになりたい学習者には指導してください．

この発音を行いたい学習者が，代わりに /l/ を出してしまうことがあります．たとえば，次のような誤りが考えられます．

city を /sɪli/(silly に聞こえる) と発音

better を /belɚ/ と発音

cutter を /kʌlɚ/(color に聞こえる) と発音

この誤りについて指導する場合，舌が触れる場所を学習者に認識させると有効かもしれません．今話題にしている /t/(図 17.1) と，誤って発音される /l/(図 17.3) を学習者に比較させてください．板書する場合は図 17.2，図 17.4 のようなもので十分でしょう．

In North American-type pronunciation, /t/ changes almost sytematically into a sound similar to the Japanese /r/ under a certain condition.[1] For example, the last part of *city* sounds like the Japanese syllable "ri." There is no problem if learners cannot use this sort of /t/, but teach it if they want to learn to use it.

In an attempt to use this sort of /t/, some learners say /l/ instead, so that *city* sounds like /sɪli/ (*silly*), *better* sounds like /belɚ/, and *cutter* sounds like /kʌlɚ/ (*color*). If this problem arises, help learners realize what part of the roof of the mouth the tongue touches when one says the reduced /t/ (Figure 17.1) and when one says /l/ (Figure 17.3). If you want to convey the information given in Figures 17.1 and 17.3, you can draw illustrations like Figures 17.2 and 17.4, respectively.

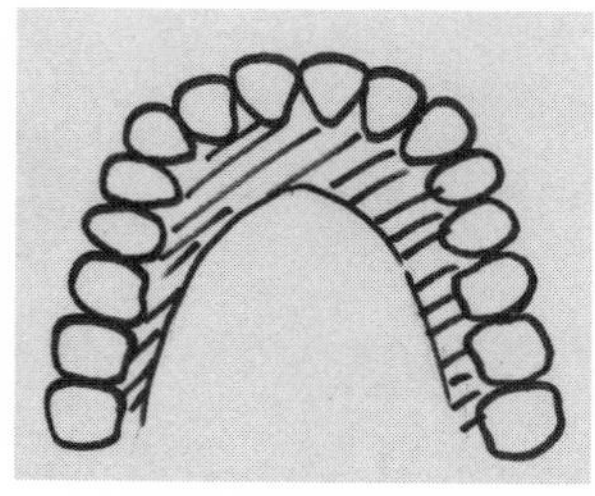

図 17.1　/t/

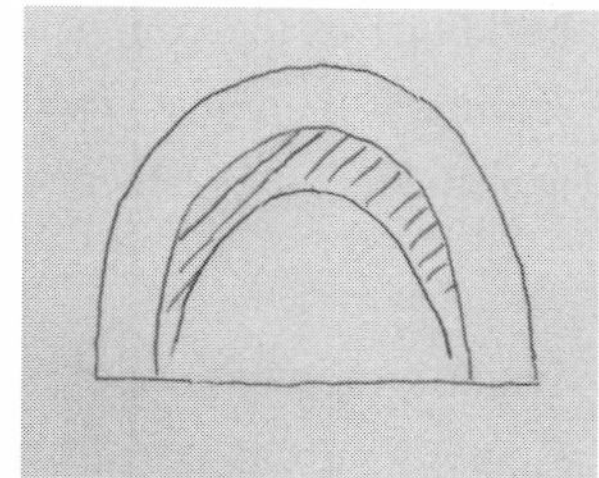

図 17.2　図 17.1 の簡易版 (Simplified version of Figure 17.1)

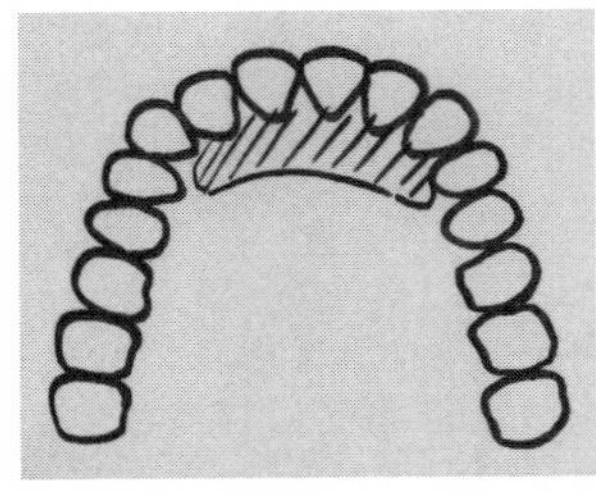

図 17.3 /l/

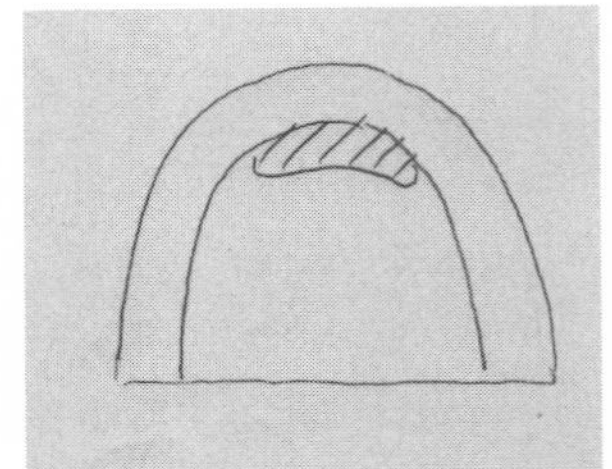

図 17.4 図 17.3 の簡易版 (Simplified version of Figure 17.3)

5. 練習のための言語材料 (Materials for practice)

下線部に注意して発音するよう指示してください.

Make learners pay attention to the underlined part(s) of each item.

単語

(1) captain (2) objection (反対意見) (3) football (4) handbook
(5) blackboard (6) rugby (7) better (8) party
(9) ceiling (天井) (10) seating (座席配置)

フレーズ

(1) count your blessings (あなたの幸運を数える)
(2) backbone of the company (会社のバックボーン)
(3) seating at the party (パーティーでの座席配置)
(4) need better dog trainers (もっとよい犬の訓練士が必要)

センテンス

(1) Would you please help me? (手伝ってくださいませんか ?)
(2) How's your daughter? (お嬢さんはお元気ですか ?)
(3) I'm gonna treat you to lunch. (昼食をご馳走します.)

会話

A: I wanna talk to you about something. Is your work finished?
(話がある. 仕事終わった ?)

B:　Sure.　What is it?　I hope it's not about next week's meeting.
（うん．何？来週の会議のことじゃないだろうね．）

A:　You guessed it.　Some people have objections about the content of the handbook we're putting together.
（当たり．作っているハンドブックの内容に何人かが反対意見を持ってる．）

B:　Oh, no.　What're you gonna do about it?（困ったね．どうするつもり？）

6.　アクティビティー見本 (Idea for an activity)

「どちらが高い？」(Which is more expensive?)

2 つのサイコロを振るか，1 つのサイコロを 2 回振るかして，番号を 2 つ得てください．その番号の項目を下のリストから取り出し，どちらが高い（費用がかかる）かを話し合ってください．可能なら理由も話題にしてください．学習者同士，または指導者と学習者で会話を行ってください．例として，次のような発言が考えられます．

Players roll two dice, or role one die twice, and obtain two numbers. They then take two of the items from the list below for the numbers obtained and discuss which costs more.　If the players' English permits it, they may want to give reasons as well.　Engage learners in a conversation with each other or with you.　Possibilities are as follows.

Going to a theater is more expensive than sending a letter to Europe.
（劇場に行くのは手紙をヨーロッパに送るよりお金がかかる．）
Going to a party may be as costly as eating at a restaurant, because you may need to take a taxi to go to the party.
（パーティーに行くのはレストランで食事をするのと同じくらいお金がかかるかもしれない．パーティーに行くのにタクシーに乗る必要があるかもしれないから．）

1.　Sending a letter to Europe.（ヨーロッパに手紙を送ること）
2.　Going to a party.（パーティーに行くこと）
3.　Eating at a restaurant.（レストランで食事をすること）
4.　Printing out a photograph.（写真をプリントアウトすること）

5. Going to a theater.（劇場に行くこと）
6. Buying a sweater.（セーターを買うこと）

ここでの焦点はラ行子音に似ている英語の /t/ です．上の項目 1-6 に下線があります．ただ，この音を使わなくてもかまいませんので，使わない学習者がいても批判しないでください．学習者がこの音を使いたいと思っており，かつ学習者の発音に問題があったら，次のように対応してください．(1) 活動が終わってから，明示的に指導する．(2) 活動の最中であれば，リキャストにより指導する（p. 10 参照）．Going to a party [to a theater] の going to は gonna にはなりません．ここでの going to は「〜するつもり」という意味ではありません．go は「行く」の意味です．

The focus here is on the tapped /t/. It appears in the underlined part(s) of each of the items 1–6 above. But don't criticize learners for not using it, as this sound reduction is optional. If learners want to learn to use it and their /t/ is not tapped, do the following: (1) provide explicit instruction after the activity; (2) provide recasts (see p. 10) during the activity. Note that *going to* in *going to a party* and *going to a theater* is not reduced to *gonna*.

第 18 章
音のくずれの指導 (2)

Sound reduction (2)

第 17 章冒頭で述べた通り，第 17 章では基本的なくずれの知識をカバーしましたが，第 18 章ではそれ以外のくずれの事例を取り上げます．ここで話題にするくずれは初級の学習者にはさほど必要はないかもしれませんが，英語学習歴が浅くとも発音には非常に興味を持っている，という学習者もいますので，発音の指導者としては，この第 18 章で取り上げる項目は知っておくべきだと思います．

As I mentioned at the beginning of Chapter 17, I covered basic kinds of sound reduction in that chapter. Here in Chapter 18 I take up other cases of reduction. Beginning learners may not need to learn about what is discussed in this chapter, but you as the instructor should know about it because there may be learners who are keenly interested in pronunciation, even among those who do not have a long experience of learning English.

1. /l/ のくずれ (Reduction of /l/)

第 1 章で，/l/ を教える際には，舌先で上の前歯のすぐ後ろ，または前歯のはえぎわをなめるよう指導することが有効であると述べました．しかし，時として，/l/ はこのようには発音されません．第 14 章で取り上げた，舌先と歯ぐきの接面の小さい /l/（第 14 章注 1 で「暗い L」という用語を紹介しました）については，/l/ を言おうとする話し手は，単に舌先を上の歯ぐきに近づけるだけにする，ということがあり得ます．図 18.1 を板書すればこのことを説明することができます．

I said in Chapter 1 that, when you teach /l/, you should tell learners to put the tongue tip on the upper teeth ridge, right behind the upper front teeth or right where the upper teeth ridge borders on the upper front teeth. /l/ is sometimes not pronounced in that way, however. As regards the /l/ characterized by a small area of contact between the tongue tip and the upper teeth ridge, taken up in Chapter 14 (the term "dark /l/" is introduced in Note 1 to Chapter 14), the speaker, trying to say /l/, may only make the tongue tip come close to the upper teeth ridge. You can draw an illustration like Figure 18.1 to explain this.

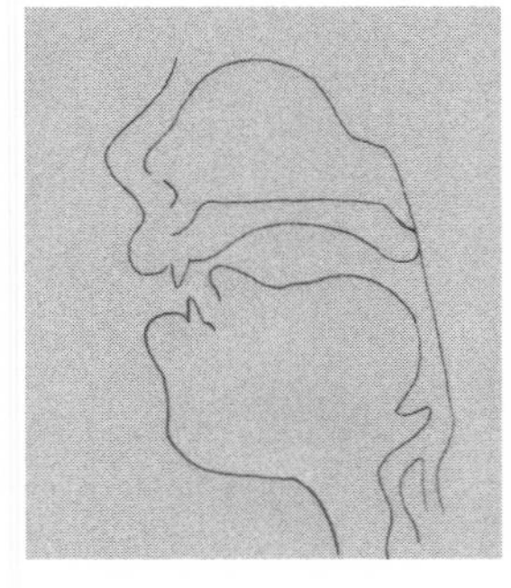

図 18.1 /l/ の不完全な発音 (Incomplete articulation of /l/)

たとえば，all right をいま説明した通りの方法で発音し，ことばを通じさせることは十分可能です．こうすると all の /l/ は /o/ または /ʊ/ に近く聞こえます．この例を含め，このような /l/ のくずれが起きる例を以下に列挙します．

(a) /w/, /r/ の前.

/lw/: たとえば shall we（〜しませんか）

/lr/: たとえば all right（よし）

(b) /s/, /z/, /ʃ/ の前

/ls/: たとえば else（他の）

/lz/: たとえば sells（sell「売る」＋ s）

/lʃ/: たとえば bell-shaped（鐘形の）

これらの例の特徴は，/l/ とその直後の音を同時に発音することが不可能または困難であるということです（たとえば /l/ と /r/ は同時に言えません．/l/ と /s/ も同じです．/l/ と /w/ を同時に言うのはつらいです）．このくずし

た発音方法は，学習者が日本語のルを使って /l/ を発音するよりはずっと自然で通じやすい発音になりますので，私はこの /l/ のくずれについては，実行しても全くかまわないと学習者に言うことにしています．

For example, if one pronounced *all right* in that way (/l/ would then sound like /o/ or /ʊ/), the listener would still understand. Including this example, let me give a list of cases in which /l/ reduction of this sort is likely to happen.

(a)　followed by /w/ and /r/, as in *shall we* and *all right*

(b)　followed by /s/, /z/, and /ʃ/, as in *else, sells*, and *bell-shaped*

What these examples all have in common is that it is impossible or very difficult to say /l/ and the following sound at the same time (one cannot say /l/ and /r/ at the same time; nor can one say /l/ and /s/ simultaneously; pronouncing /l/ and /w/ at the same time is not easy, to say the least). Reduced pronunciation of this kind is far more natural and easier to comprehend than the pronunciation using the Japanese syllable "ru" as a substitute for /l/, often done by Japanese-speaking learners. I thus tell learners that it is perfectly permissible to speak with this sort of /l/ reduction.

上記のケースに加え，他にもくずれの可能性があります．[1)] たとえば，help が /heop/ または /heʊp/ に近く発音されることがあります．こうしたくずれは，上記のケースほど必要度は高くありません．/l/ とその直後の音を同時に発音することがさほど困難ではないからです．このようなくずれについては，教えるとすればリスニングのための情報としてのみ教えるべきですが，ただ，どうしても /l/ を日本語のラ，リ，ル，レ，ロで発音してしまう学習者や，/l/ を自然にくずしてスピードのある話し方をしたい学習者には，例外的にこの /l/ のくずれを教える選択肢を考えるのもよいかもしれません．

There are other cases of the reduction of /l/, such as *help*, reduced to something like /heop/ or /heʊp/.[1)] The necessity of these cases of reduction is not as high as that of (a) and (b) above, because simultaneous articulation of /l/ and the following consonant is not as difficult. Information about this latter sort of sound reduction should rather be given to learners only as a tip for listening comprehension, but, if there is a learner who keeps using the Japanese /r/ for the English /l/, or a learner who wants to master /l/ reduction and learn to speak fast, you may want to make an exception and teach the /l/ reduction discussed here.

2. 消える /h/ (Inaudible /h/)

代名詞 he, his, him, her のアタマの /h/ の音は，速い話し方やくだけた話し方の場合，センテンスの途中では，弱くなり，究極的には消えることがあります．たとえば，He likes coffee. の he や Her room is upstairs. の her の /h/ は消えませんが，一方，Does he like coffee? の he や She is in her room now. の her の /h/ は消えるかもしれません．初級の学習者に練習させる必要はありませんが，リスニングに役立つ知識として教えたほうがよい場合もあります．

The initial /h/ in the pronouns *he, his, him,* and *her* occurring mid-sentence may be weakened and ultimately dropped. For example, /h/ does not disappear in *He likes coffee* or *Her room is upstairs*, but it may in *Does he like coffee?* and *She is in her room now*. You do not need to make learners actually do this /h/ reduction, but it may be a good idea to teach it, as this knowledge may help them with listening comprehension.

3. /nt/ のくずれ (Reduction of /nt/)

/nt/ という音の組み合わせにおいて，しばしば /t/ が抜け落ちます．たとえば，Internet は本来 /ɪntɚnet/ ですが，しばしば /ɪnɚnet/ と発音されます．この発音を聞いて「イナネットって何だろう」と思う学習者もいることでしょう．いくつか例を挙げましょう．

/t/ in /nt/ is often dropped. For example, *Internet* (/ɪntɚnet/) often changes into (/ɪnɚnet/). Here are some examples.

international /ɪntɚnæʃənl/ > /ɪnɚnæʃənl/
Internet /ɪntɚnet/ > /ɪnɚnet/
twenty /twenti/ > /tweni/
center /sentɚ/ > /senɚ/
winter /wɪntɚ/ > /wɪnɚ/

4. 歯を使う音 (Dentalization)

/d/, /t/, /n/, /l/ の 4 個の音は，いずれも，舌先を上の歯ぐきに触れさせて発音する音です．しかし，これらの音が /ð/ /θ/ の直前に来ると，話し手は，舌先を少し，またはしっかりと，歯に触れさせながら発音することが少なくありません．たとえば，in the (/ɪn ðə/) というフレーズにおいて，/n/ は，舌を上の前歯に触れさせて発音されることが多いのです．図 18.2 の板書がこのことの説明に役立ちます．

Ordinarily, /d/, /t/, /n/, and /l/ are all articulated with the tongue tip touching the upper teeth ridge. It will benefit learners to know that these sounds may be articulated with the tongue tip touching the upper teeth, either slightly or firmly, if they are followed by /θ/ or /ð/. For example, /n/ in *in the* (/ɪn ðə/) is often articulated in that fashion. You can explain this by drawing an illustration like Figure 18.2 on the board in class.

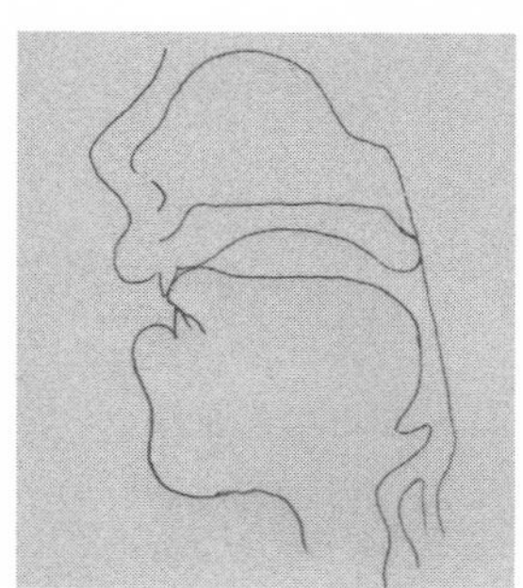

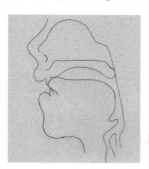

図 18.2　歯を使った /n/ (Dentalized /n/)

こうすると，/n/ の段階ですでに舌先は /ð/ の位置まで前に出るので，/n/ から /ð/ への移行がなめらかになります．たとえば，次のようなフレーズを使ってこのことを教えることができます．

By allowing this sound change to occur, learners can go from /n/ to /ð/ smoothly, as the tongue is already touching the upper teeth in preparation for /ð/ when /n/ is being said. You can teach this sound reduction by using the following items, for example.

/θ/ の前

(a) /lθ/ の /l/ Bill thought（ビルは考えた）
health（健康）

(b) /dθ/ の /d/ Ted thought（テッドは考えた）
add three（3 を加える）

(c) /tθ/ の /t/ that theory（あの理論）
what theater（どの劇場）

(d) /nθ/ の /n/ in theory（理論上）
one third（三分の一）

/ð/ の前

(e) /lð/ の /l/ bell the cat（ネコに鈴をつける）
Will that do?（それでいいですか？）

(f) /dð/ の /d/ read this（これを読む）
said the word（その単語を言った）

(g) /tð/ の /t/ ate that apple（あのリンゴを食べた）
set the clock（時計を合わせる）

(h) /nð/ の /n/ in the house（家の中で）
in that case（その場合は）

さらなる変化もあり得ます．例：/dð/ は歯を使った，または普通の /d/ に（たとえば read this において），/nð/ は歯を使った，または普通の /n/ に（たとえば in the house において）．

Further changes may take place: /dð/ to a dentalized or plain /d/ (as in *read this*) and /nð/ to a dentalized or plain /n/ (as in *in the house*), for example.

5. のどを使う /t/ (Glottal /t/)

/t/ の音をのどを使って発音することがあります．たとえば，次の 2 つのセンテンスにおいて，いずれの /t/ も，通常の /t/ を使って，すなわち舌先を上の歯ぐきにふれさせて発音してもかまいませんが，北米系の発音においては，ほぼ規則的に，以下に説明する，のどを使った発音になります．[2)]

/t/ may be articulated in the throat—at the glottis. For example, in each of the following two sentences, /t/ is almost systematically articulated in the throat in North American-type pronunciation, as I explain below, although it may of course be articulated as a regular /t/ sound.[2)]

(a)　That was good.

(b)　Is it raining?

のどを使った音は，実は日本語にも存在しています．私は次のような漫画を描いて説明することにしています．ストーブのほうにはいはいして行く赤ちゃんを見た母親が，「あっあっあっ ...（危ない！）」と言ったとします．この日本語のことばの，小さい「っ」で表されるものは，物理的には，のどの奥の息の通り道をふさぐ行為です．自分で「あっあっあっ ...」と言ってみればすぐに分かります．小さい「っ」が出て来る回数だけ，のどの奥が締まるのが分かるはずです．北米系の発音では，この方法で /t/ を言うことがあるのです．

/t/ articulated in the throat exists in Japanese, too. I often explain this by drawing a cartoon like the following. A baby is crawling toward a heater, and the mother, alarmed, is saying “Uh, uh, uh” (transcribed「あっ，あっ，あっ」). The sound represented by the little「っ」is a glottal sound articulated by closing the glottis—the space between the vocal cords—and thus stopping the flow of air.

上の例にある通り，北米系の発音では，/t/ は /w/ の前に来るとき（上の例では that was に出て来る /t/）と /r/ の前に来るとき（上の例では it raining に出て来る /t/) にのどで発音されることがほとんどです．のどで作る /t/ を，漫画の例に沿って小さな「っ」で表すとすれば，上のセンテンスの that と it は，/ðæ っ/, /ɪ っ/ と表すことができるかもしれません．

As in the above examples, /t/ is almost always reduced in this way in North American-type pronunciation when it is followed by /w/, as in *That was good* (example (a) above), and when it is followed by /r/, as in *Is it raining?* (example (b) above). If /t/ articulated in the throat is to be represented by「っ」, as in the above cartoon, then *that* and *it* in the above sentences may be represented as /ðæ っ/ and /ɪ っ/.

6. **/tən/ /dən/ のくずれ** (Reduction of /tən/ and /dən/)

英語の動詞の過去分詞 eaten, written, ridden などの最後に /tən/ と /dən/ がよく出てきます．それ以外にも，kitten, Britain, button, Sweden など，/tən/ と /dən/ で終わる単語があります．このような /tən/, /dən/ がくずれるとき，二通りのくずれ方があります．第一に，舌を上の歯ぐきにつけたまま鼻から息を抜く方法があります．息を抜く前に，口から鼻への息の通り道をふさぎ（図 18.3)，次にその通り道を急に開けて息を鼻に逃がします（図 18.4)．図 18.3 と図 18.4 を板書して説明してください．

There are many words that end in /tən/ or /dən/, such as *eaten, written, ridden, kitten, Britain, button,* and *Sweden*. /tən/ or /dən/ may be reduced in one of two ways. First, one can put the tongue tip on the upper teeth ridge and let air out through the nose. Before letting air out, one should close the passage from the mouth to the nose (Figure 18.3) and then suddenly open the passage (Figure 18.4). You may want to draw illustrations like these figures on the board in class to explain this process.

第二のやり方は，前項のセクション 5 で取り上げた，のどを使う /t/ の音を使う方法です．舌を上の歯ぐきにつけたまま，前項で小さい「っ」を使って説明したやり方でのどの奥を締めて息の流れを止め，次に締めておいたのどを急にゆるめて息を通します．舌が上の歯ぐきについていますので，息は口からは逃げず，鼻から逃げて行きます．

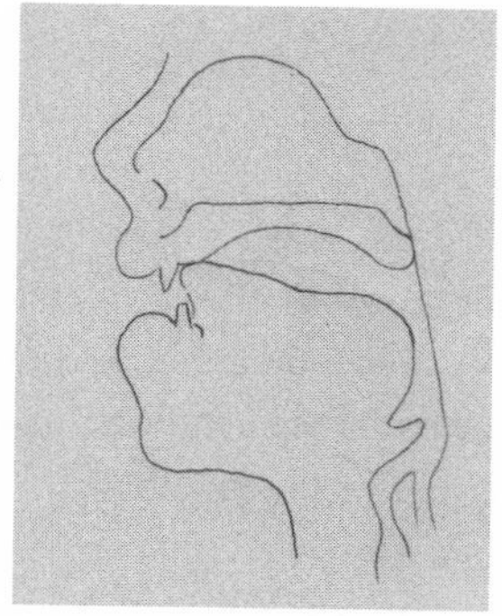

図 18.3　口から鼻への息の通り道をふさぐ (Closing of the passage from the mouth to the nose)

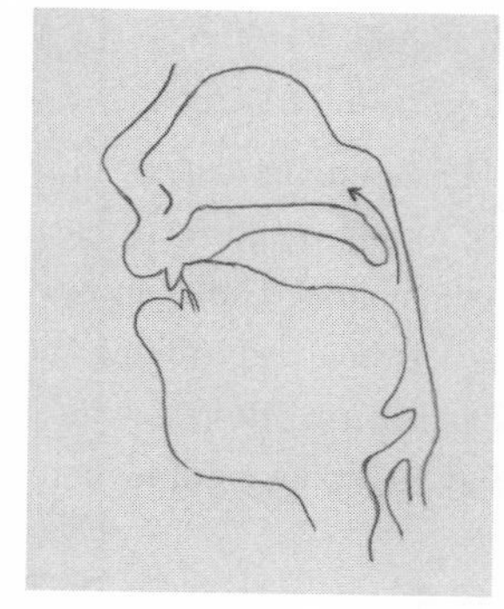

図 18.4　口から鼻への息の通り道を開けて息を鼻へ (Letting air into the nose through the passage)

The second way is to use the glottal sound discussed in Section 5 above. One puts the tongue tip on the upper teeth ridge, closes the passage of air at the throat, and then opens the passage suddenly. As the tongue tip is on the teeth ridge, air does not escape through the mouth but goes out through the nose.

/tən/ と /dən/ を，くずさずに普通に /n/ の前に母音を入れて発音しても全くかまいません．ただ，速く話すとき，話し手はしばしば上に述べた方法で /tən/ や /dən/ をくずすものです．

It is perfectly acceptable to say /tən/ and /dən/, with a vowel between the two consonants, but English speakers often reduce /tən/ and /dən/ in one of those two ways when they speak fast.

7．/sl/ の言い方 (How to say /sl/)

/l/ の発音を正しく行おうとするとき，sleep や slow に出て来る /sl/ の組み合わせは言いにくいものです．/s/ から /l/ に移る際に余計な母音が入りがちです．そこで，/s/ から /l/ に移るときに，間に /t/ を入れ，ちょうど第 14 章セクション 2 で取り上げた /tl/ の場合と同じ舌の動きをすれば，余計な母音を入れずにすみます．このことを，舌が口の天井にどのように触れるか，という切り口で説明します．

Pronouncing /sl/, as in *sleep* and *slow*, is often difficult for learners who try to say /l/ correctly, as they are liable to put a vowel between the two consonants. They can prevent this unwanted vowel insertion by putting /t/ in between and moving their tongue in the way mentioned in Section 2 of Chapter 14. Below is an outline of this process, explained in terms of the way the tongue comes into contact with the roof of the mouth.

図 18.5 に示す通り，/s/ を言うときは，舌のヘリが上の歯ぐきに触れ，舌先だけは少し離れています．この舌先のすきまから息が勢いよく外に押し出され，その息が前歯に当たってノイズを作ります．これが /s/ です．/sl/ を発音するためには，次に，舌のヘリだけでなく舌先も上の歯ぐきにつけて，舌先と歯ぐきとのすきまをふさぎます（図 18.6）．最後に，舌先を歯ぐきにつけたまま，舌の両脇をおろします（図 18.7）．この最後の動作は，まさに第 14 章セクション 2 で説明した /tl/ の発音の際の舌の動きそのものです．

When one says /s/, the edge of the tongue comes into contact with the upper teeth ridge, with the opening at the center, as shown in Figure 18.5. Air is pushed out of the mouth through this opening and hits the front teeth, creating noise—the /s/ sound. To say /sl/, one then makes the tongue tip touch the upper teeth ridge, closing the passage of air (Figure 18.6). Finally, one lowers the sides of the tongue while keeping the tongue tip on the upper teeth ridge (Figure 18.7). This movement of the tongue is the same as that explained in Section 2 of Chapter 14.

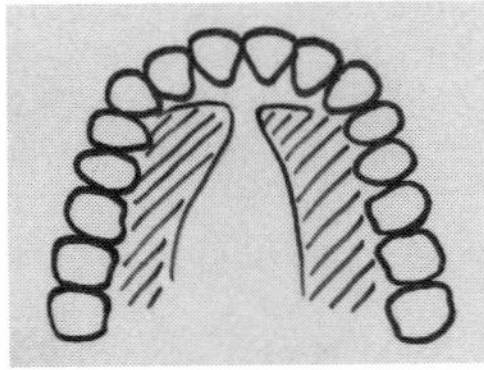

図 18.5 /s/ の発音 (Articulation of /s/)

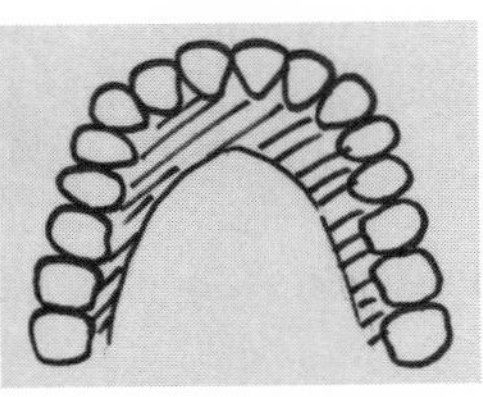

図 18.6 /t/ の発音の第一段階 (First stage in the articulation of /t/)

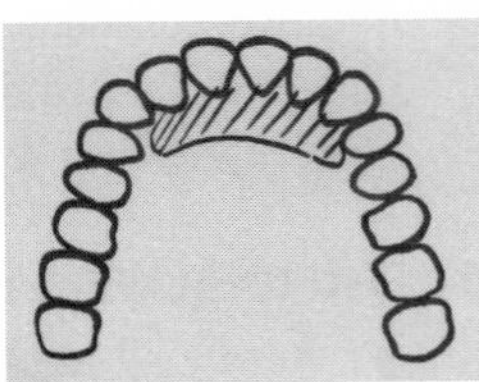

図 18.7 /l/ の発音 (Articulation of /l/)

もし，/s/ と /l/ の間に /t/ を入れることをしないで /sl/ を言おうとすると，/s/ と /l/ の間で一度舌を上の歯ぐきから離さざるを得ず（図 18.8），[3] こうして舌を離したときに母音を言ってしまうのです．[4]

If one were to say /sl/ without /t/ in between, one would then need to remove the tongue tip from the upper teeth ridge at one stage (Figure 18.8),[3] inserting a vowel between /s/ and /l/.[4]

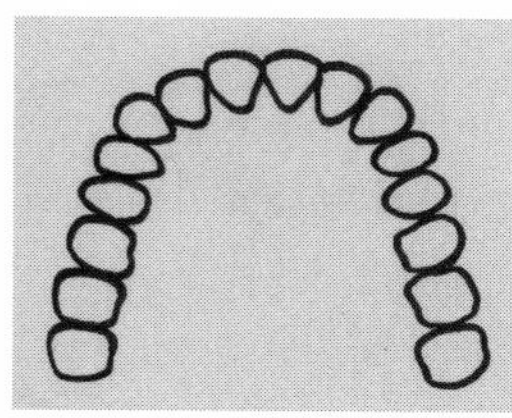

図 18.8　母音の発音 (Articulation of a vowel)

8.　練習のための言語材料 (Materials for practice)

下線部に注意して発音するよう指示してください．音のくずれの練習の機会を提供するための項目が並んでいますが，音をくずすかどうかは学習者に委ねてください．ただ，単語の（10）とフレーズ（1）のように，同じ単語内で後に母音が来る /sl/ については，間に母音を入れないで発音させるようご注意ください．

Make learners pay attention to the underlined part(s) of each item. Although the items here are given for providing learners with opportunities for practicing sound reduction, learners should be allowed to decide whether to reduce sounds or not in each item. But be sure to have learners say /sl/ without a vowel in between if the cluster is followed by a vowel in the same word, as in (10) in the vocabulary items section and (1) in the phrases section.

単語

(1) milk (2) false（正しくない） (3) wolf（オオカミ） (4) twenty
(5) health (6) tenth (7) eighth (8) eaten (9) sudden（突然の）
(10) sleep

フレーズ

(1) slightly too slow（少し遅すぎ）
(2) sudden change in her health（彼女の健康の突然の変化）
(3) twenty pairs of cotton gloves（20 組の木綿の手袋）
(4) the eighth discovery in his career（彼のキャリアのなかでの 8 番目の発見）

センテンス

(1) In theory it rains a lot in winter in this area.
（理屈の上ではこの地域で冬にたくさん雨が降ることになっている.）
(2) I'd written that letter before the tenth of December.
（私は 12 月 10 日より前にあの手紙を書いてしまっていた.）
(3) That was false information floating around on the Internet.
（それはインターネットに出回っている正しくない情報でした.）

会話

A: That was a really good speech. Good job. I couldn't do that myself.
（とてもいいスピーチだった. よくやった. 私だったらできないね.）

B: Well, I said a few things I shouldn't have said.
（言うべきでなかったことを少し言ったけど.）

A: No, you didn't. Hey, have you eaten lunch? If not, I want to take you to a place where they serve really healthy food. I found it on the Internet.
（いや, 言ってないよ. そうだ. 昼ごはん食べた？まだだったら, とてもヘルシーな食べ物を出すところにお連れしたい. ネットで見つけた.）

B: All right. Can I see you downstairs around twelve twenty?
（いいよ. 下の階で 12 時 20 分に会うのでいい？）

9. アクティビティー見本 (Idea for an activity)

「感謝のことば」(A word of thanks)

学習者が次の人々に感謝のことばを述べるとの想定で，ふさわしい花束を選ばせ，そこにある言葉を使って "Without your help, I wouldn't ____ now." という形の感謝の言葉を言わせてください．

Assuming that learners are expressing their thanks to the following people, have them choose the right bouquet and say, "Without your help, I wouldn't ____ now," by choosing words from the bouquet.

1. Advisor to the school drama club (学校の演劇部の顧問)
2. Music teacher at school (学校の音楽の先生)
3. Rescuer at the beach (海岸の救助員)
4. Coach for the local baseball team (地元野球チームのコーチ)
5. Loan officer at a bank (銀行の融資係)
6. Mountain guide (山岳ガイド)

Answers:

Advisor to the school drama club: Bouquet 4: Without your help, I wouldn't be an actor now.（あなたの助けがなかったら，私は今俳優にはなっていないでしょう.）

Music teacher at school: Bouquet 1: Without your help, I wouldn't be a singer now.（あなたの助けがなかったら，私は今歌手にはなっていないでしょう.）

Rescuer at the beach: Bouquet 6: Without your help, I wouldn't be alive now.（あなたの助けがなかったら，私は今生きてはいないでしょう.）

Coach for the local baseball team: Bouquet 3: Without your help, I wouldn't be a professional baseball player now.（あなたの助けがなかったら，私は今プロ野球選手にはなっていないでしょう.）

Loan officer at a bank: Bouquet 5: Without your help, I wouldn't have my own company now.（あなたの助けがなかったら，私は今自分の会社を持ってはいないでしょう.）

Mountain guide: Bouquet 2: Without your help, I wouldn't be at the top of this mountain now.（あなたの助けがなかったら，私は今この山の頂上にはいないでしょう.）

ここでの焦点は /dən/ です．母音を入れずに /dn/ と発音する機会を提供するための活動ですが，母音を入れる発音でもかまいませんのであまり厳しく要求しないでください．学習者の発音に問題があったら，次のように対応してください．(1) 活動が終わってから，明示的に指導する．(2) 活動の最中であれば，リキャストにより指導する（p. 10 参照）．

The focus here is on /dən/. This activity is meant to provide learners with an opportunity to practice saying /dn/ without a vowel in between, but, since the pronunciation with a vowel also exists, do not be too demanding. If learners' pronunciation is problematical, do the following: (1) provide explicit instruction after the activity; (2) provide recasts (see p. 10) during the activity.

第 19 章
アクセント，リズム，イントネーションの指導

Stress, rhythm, and intonation

発音には，個々の音のレベルとは別の側面があります．それは，よく「プロソディー」と呼ばれ，アクセント，リズム，イントネーションが含まれます．三者は密接に関連しています．プロソディーは，個々の音が伝えないようなメッセージを伝えるという点で重要ですので，指導者はプロソディーについても教えるべきだと思います．本章では，指導の実際にかかわるいくつかの事柄を取り上げます．

There is an aspect of pronunciation which is separate from the level of individual sounds. It is often called “prosody” and covers stress, rhythm, and intonation, which are closely linked to each other. In this chapter, I take up some practical issues related to prosody which in my opinion should be taught to learners, as it conveys messages in ways in which individual sounds do not and is therefore important in its own right.

1. 単語の提示について (Presenting vocabulary items)

アクセント，リズム，イントネーションの指導は，学習者が長いセンテンスを扱うようになるときまで待って始めるのではなく，学習者が初級の段階にいるときから始めるべきであると思います．指導の出発点は，指導者が単語を口頭で提示すること，というすべての語学指導者にとって基本中の基本の事柄にあると私は考えています．単語の提示を丁寧に行うことにより，学習者に声域というものに意識を向けさせることができます．声域に対する意識は，アクセント，リズム，イントネーションの性質に対する理解の基本で

す（この点については，セクション7で再び触れます）.

> You should begin teaching learners about stress, rhythm, and intonation early, when they are at the beginning level, rather than wait until they are able to handle long sentences. The first step to your instruction in this area should be oral presentation of vocabulary items—something that all language instructors do as one of the very basic procedures in class. By carefully presenting words to be learned, you can help learners come to an awareness of their voice range, namely an awareness of that element of pronunciation which is basic to the understanding of the nature of stress, rhythm, and intonation (I will return to this topic in Section 7 below).

単語を口頭で提示するとき，標準的な下がり調子のイントネーションを使い，単語の最後で声域の一番下まで降りるようにしてください.

> When you present a vocabulary item orally, you should use a standard falling intonation pattern and, at the end of the word, lower your voice so that you reach the bottom of your speaking voice range.

たとえば，car と言うときには，図 19.1 のような声の使い方をしてください．単語を言い終わるときには，声が声域の一番下まで降りているようにしてください．May（5月）と言うときも同様です（図 19.2）．/me-/ と言いながら声の高さを落として行って，最後の /ɪ/ に向かうときには声域の最低レベルまで声が降りているようにしてください．日本語の「メイ」（銘）のようにならないようにしてください（日本語のメイの場合，イを言うときの声の高さは普通声域の一番下ではありません）.

> When saying *car*, for example, use the pitch of your voice as indicated by Figure 19.1. Make sure that the pitch reaches the bottom of your voice range as you finish saying the word. Similarly, when saying *May*, for example, lower the pitch of your voice and reach the bottom of your voice range as the vowel changes toward /ɪ/, the second element of the diphthong (Figure 19.2). Do not say the word in the same way as you say the two-syllable Japanese word "mei," which means "name" (voice usually does not reach the bottom of one's voice range when one says "i," the second syllable).

単語の提示の仕方はどちらかと言えば指導者に対する注意であり，学習者に同じ声の使い方を指導する必要はないと思いますが，学習者に声の使い方を明示的に示すような場面になった場合（たとえば教員研修などの場合）は，ここに掲載した図 19.1，図 19.2 のような板書をすることをお勧めします．

The presentation of vocabulary items that I am discussing here is a topic meant for the instructor rather than for learners, and learners do not need to be rigorously trained in the use of pitch of voice when saying a word. If you find yourself in a situation where you need to explicitly show learners how to say a word in isolation (in teacher training, for example), you may want to draw illustrations like Figure 19.1 and Figure 19.2.

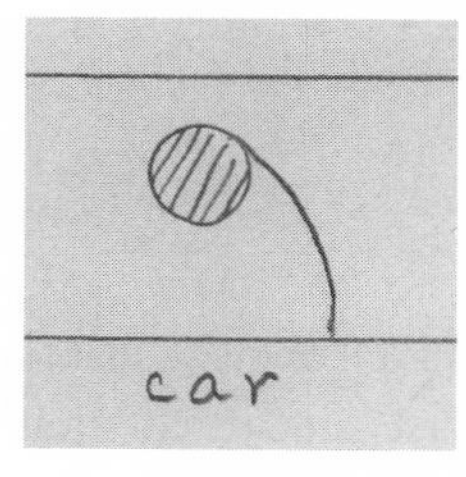

図 19.1

図 19.2

car や May は 1 拍 [1] の単語ですが，window，enjoy のような 2 拍以上の単語を提示する場合は，もちろん，アクセントの位置をしっかり教えなくてはなりません．アクセントを教える際には，単語を下がり調子で言い，アクセントのある拍のアタマが高くなるように言ってください（図 19.3，図 19.4）．

Car and *May* are monosyllables, namely one-beat words.[1] When teaching words with multiple syllables such as *window* and *enjoy*, you need to teach where the stressed syllable is in these words. When saying these words, say them with falling intonation and make sure that the initial part of the stressed syllable is said with a higher pitch than the other syllable(s) (Figure 19.3 and Figure 19.4).

図 19.3

図 19.4

アクセントを教える際に，英語の語や文には強く言うところと比較的弱く言うところがあるという説明がしばしば行われます．この説明をするとすれば，強さが絶対的な強さを表すかのような誤解を学習者がしないよう注意してください．アクセントとは相対的なものであり，「ある拍にアクセントがある」とは「それが他の部分より相対的に目立つように言われる」ということに過ぎません．[2)]

When teaching about stress, many instructors tell learners that, in words or sentences in English, there are parts that are articulated strongly and ones that are said weakly. If you choose to explain stress in this way, be careful not to mislead learners into thinking that levels of strength are absolute. Stress is relative: When a syllable is stressed, that merely means that this syllable is said in such a way that it stands out in relation to the other syllable(s).[2)]

2. 第二アクセントを大切に (Importance of secondary stress)

学習者の英語を自然なものにするためには，指導者は，特に，第二アクセントを大切にすべきです．見逃されることが多いのですが，長い単語には主たるアクセント（ここでは第一アクセントと呼びます）に加えて第二アクセントがあり，辞書に標示されています．たとえば，Japanese，international は，それぞれ図 19.5，図 19.6 のようなアクセントのパターンを持つ単語です（ここでは大きな四角は第一アクセントを，中くらいの四角は第二アクセントをそれぞれ表します）．いずれの単語の場合も，アタマの部分に第二アクセントがあります．

If you want to make learners' English sound natural, I recommend that you attach importance to secondary stress. Long words have a syllable with secondary stress as well as one with primary stress, and secondary stress is noted in dictionaries (albeit frequently overlooked by their users). For example, *Japanese* and *international* have patterns as given in Figure 19.5 and Figure 19.6, respectively (here, a big square and a middle-sized square stand for primary and secondary stress, respectively). Both words have secondary stress on the first syllable.

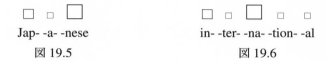

図 19.5　　図 19.6

第二アクセントを教える際には，セクション1で紹介したような板書が役立ちます．たとえば，Japanese は図19.7のような板書を，また international は図19.8のような板書を使い，図の通りの声の使い方をして教えてください．

When teaching stress patterns, you may want to draw on the board in class illustrations like the ones introduced in Section 1 above. For example, you can draw illustrations like Figure 19.7 and Figure 19.8 to teach the stress patterns on *Japanese* and *international*, respectively.

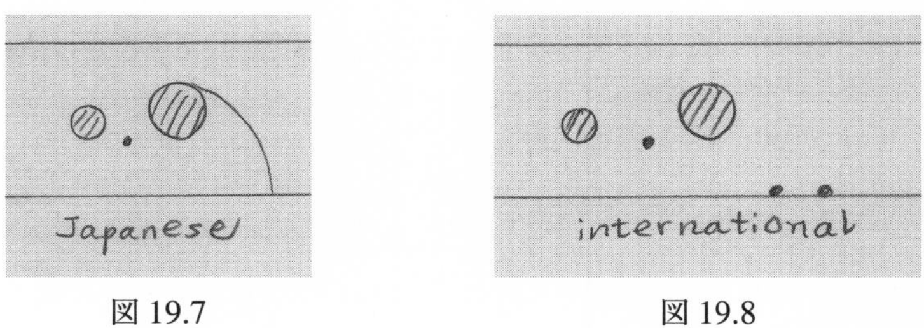

図 19.7　　図 19.8

学習者に図19.9，図19.10に示すような言い方をさせないでください．これらは悪い例であり，第二アクセントがしかるべき場所に置かれていません．

Do not let learners pronounce *Japanese* and *international* with stress patterns as in Figure 19.9 and Figure 19.10. These figures illustrate examples of poor treatment of stress: Secondary stress, which should be present, is absent.

図 19.9 悪い例 (Poor treatment of stress)

図 19.10 悪い例 (Poor treatment of stress)

第二アクセントに関する問題は日本ではほとんど英語の試験に出ないので，第二アクセントの存在に学習者の注意を向けない指導者が多いのですが，第二アクセントは次のふたつの理由により大切です．

Few instructors direct learners' attention to secondary stress because, in Japan, examinations in English at school do not customarily cover it. However, it is important for two reasons.

(a) 第二アクセントの存在はリズムやイントネーションにしっかり現れるので，自然な発音を学びたい学習者にとってどうしても学ぶべき要素です．私は，学習者に第二アクセントのある部分の発音を教えるときには，「第二アクセントは，その重みにおいて，アクセントなしの部分に近いのではなく，むしろ第一アクセントのほうに近い．第二アクセントのある部分を発音するときには，その重みを忘れないように発音すること．」と述べることにしています．たとえば，上記の international の場合，図 19.8 に示した通り，in- の部分にほぼ -na- の部分に迫るくらいの重みのアクセントを置くように指導します．乱暴な単純化かもしれませんが，この語を言うときに第一アクセントと第二アクセントとに差がつけられなければ，第二アクセントを第一アクセントと同じ強さで言ってよい，と指導します．

(a) As secondary stress is reflected in rhythm and intonation, it is something learners should learn about if they are to acquire natural pronunciation. I tell learners to pay attention to secondary stress as the weight of syllables with secondary stress is closer to that of syllables with primary stress than it is to that of unstressed syllables. For example, in the case of the word *international* cited above, I tell learners to put almost the same degree of stress on *in-* as on *-na-*. If learners seem to be finding it difficult to distinguish between primary and secondary stress, I tell them, at the risk of oversimplification, to treat secondary stress in exactly the same way as primary stress when saying this word.

(b) 第二アクセントは時としてある条件下で第一アクセントに昇格するので，その潜在的な重要度は第一アクセントに劣ることがありません．ある条件下とは，(b-1) 第二アクセントが，同じ単語内の第一アクセントより先に出て来て，かつ，(b-2) その単語の直後に第一アクセントを持つ別の単語が続く場合です．たとえば，Japanese car というフレーズがこの条件に当てはまります．このフレーズにおいては，時として，アクセントのパターンが変わり，図19.11のようなパターンが図19.12のようなパターンに変ります．

(b) As secondary stress sometimes promotes itself to primary stress under a certain condition, secondary stress is potentially no less important than primary stress. The condition is that (b-1) a syllable receiving secondary stress is followed by a syllable receiving primary stress in the same word and (b-2) that word is followed by a word that has a syllable receiving primary stress. The phrase *Japanese car* is a case in point. The stress pattern on this phrase sometimes changes from the pattern shown in Figure 19.11 to the pattern shown in Figure 19.12.

Jap- -a- -nese car
Jap- -a- -nese car

図19.11　　図19.12

このことを説明するために，図19.11に代わって図19.13を，図19.12に代わって図19.14のような板書をしても結構です．

To explain the above stress shift, you may want to write an illustration such as Figure 19.13 instead of Fig 19.11 and one such as Figure 19.14

instead of Fig 19.12 on the board.

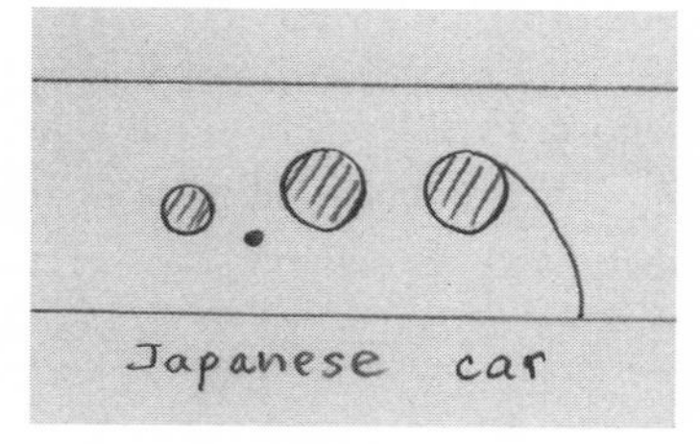

図 19.13

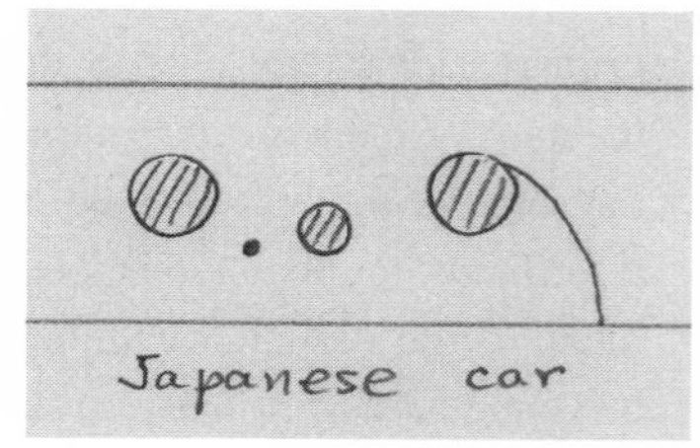

図 19.14

第二アクセントが第一アクセントに時として昇格するこの現象は，英語においてはアクセントの隣接を避けアクセント同士を離すことが好まれる，と説明することができます．

以上 2 つの理由により，第二アクセントは重要であり，指導者はそれについて教えるべきである，と言えます．

The tendency for secondary stress to be sometimes promoted to primary stress may be explained in terms of a tendency for the speaker to avoid the juxtaposition of two stressed syllables and instead favor placement of such syllables at a certain distance from each other.

For those two reasons, there is a case for saying that secondary stress is important and that you should thus teach learners about it.

3. /ə/ の扱い方 (How to treat /ə/)

アクセントのない部分に，辞書で /ə/ と表記される母音がしばしば出て来ます．この音は，音の質を特定しにくい特殊な音ですので，明示的指導にはなじまない，と私は思っています．むしろ，指導者が必要な情報を持ち，学習者の前でその情報に基づいた発音をすることにより，学習者に /ə/ を自然に身につけさせるほうが得策だと思います．

指導者が持つべき情報として，ここでは次の 2 項目を挙げたいと思います．

A vowel represented by the symbol /ə/ often appears in weakly stressed syllables. The quality of this sound is difficult to specify and is not highly susceptible to explicit instruction. Rather, the best policy will be for the instructor to acquire enough knowledge about this sound and, through exposure to his or her pronunciation based on this knowledge, have learners learn about it by osmosis.

Here are two bits of information that you should have about /ə/.

(a) 音の質について：弱く，明瞭でない母音なので，音を特定しにくい.[3] 基本的には，ほほや唇や舌から力を抜き，アゴをあまり開けずに言う「ア」のような音．弱さは程度問題で，話すスピードやくだけている度合いに影響される．

(a) The quality of /ə/: It is a weak, unclear sound and is difficult to specify.[3] Basically, it is an /a/-like sound that one produces by relaxing one's cheeks, lips, and tongue, without opening one's jaws very much. The weakness is a matter of degree and depends upon the speed at which one speaks and the degree of informality with which one speaks.

(b) どこで使われるか：2拍以上の単語のなかのアクセントのない部分において，また，強形と弱形を持つ単語[4]が弱形で言われるとき，/ə/ が使われる．いくつかの単語は，「強形」と「弱形」という2種類の発音を持っており，たとえば，that という単語の強形は /ðæt/ であり弱形は /ðət/ である．強形はアクセントのある場所で使われ，弱形はアクセントのない場所で使われる．

(b) Places where /ə/ is used: /ə/ may be used in unstressed syllables in a word of two or more syllables and in the weak form of a word which has strong and weak forms.[4] Some words are pronounced in their strong and weak forms. For example, the strong form of *that* is /ðæt/, used when the word is stressed, and the weak form of the word is /ðət/, used when the word is not stressed.

/ə/ は弱い拍に使われますが，指導者は学習者が聞き取りにくいような弱い言い方や小さな声を使わないようにしてください．/ə/ を教えるために文中で言うとき，声量は高く保ち，アクセントがないことはイントネーションで表現してください．たとえば，*About a hundred people have arrived.*

(100 人くらいの人々が到着した.) というセンテンスには /ə/ が最低 4 回出てきます. about のアタマ, 冠詞の a, 助動詞の have, それから arrived のアタマです. (hundred の -dred でも使われる可能性が高いです.) これらの場所の /ə/ を, 弱く小さな声で言うのではなく, 大きな声で, 低い高さの声を使って言ってください.

Although /ə/ is used in unstressed syllables, you should not pronounce it too weakly or softly in class for learners to be able to hear with ease. My advice is that, when you teach /ə/ by pronouncing it in context, you should keep the volume of your voice high and express the absence of stress using your intonation. For example, in *About a hundred people have arrived*, /ə/ is used at least four times: in the first syllable of *about*, the indefinite article *a*, the auxiliary *have*, and the first syllable of *arrived* (it is also highly likely to be used in *-dred* in *hundred*). Be sure to say /ə/ in these places loudly, using a low pitch of voice, not softly or weakly.

4. リズム (Rhythm)

リズムの指導は, さまざまのレベルの英語指導の場面で, マザーグースなどを使った形で行われています. 韻文のリズムは規則的で学習者にとって真似しやすいので, 韻文はリズムの指導に向いています.

Rhythm is taught in various situations in class in Japan, with Mother Goose rhymes, for example. Verse is suitable for teaching rhythm, as its rhythm is regular and easy for learners to copy.

一方, 散文を使ったリズム指導には, 韻文の場合とは異なるアプローチが必要だと思います. 散文は特定のリズムを念頭に書かれたものではなく, 散文のリズムは, センテンスのなかの音や単語の並びが自然に決めてくれる, いわば産出物です. また, 文章をどのようなリズムで読むことができるのかについては, 許容範囲が非常に広いです. したがって, 散文を使ったリズム指導を行う場合は, 質の高い音声教材を得てそれに準拠するか, 指導者自身が教材をよく研究してリズムを決めるかする必要があります.[5)]

Prose as material for teaching rhythm requires an altogether different approach. Prose is not written with specific rhythmic patterns in mind: The rhythm of prose is in fact a product of the arrangement of words and sounds in the text, and there is a wide range of acceptability for the appropriate rhythm with which the text can be read. If you want to use prose for teaching rhythm, choose good recorded materials for learners to copy, or study the text yourself and decide what sort of rhythm you want learners to use when reading it.[5)]

教材が韻文であれ散文であれ，リズム指導においては，次の 2 点が大切だと思います．

(a) ターゲットとなるリズムで学習者が英語を言えない場合は，発音上の問題が原因となっている可能性が高いので，リズムだけを修正するのでなく，単語の発音の矯正を試みる．

(b) 早口言葉のように急いで言う練習は避ける．無理な早口は発音の乱れの原因になる．[6)]

Whether you use verse or prose as material for teaching rhythm, remember the following two points.

(a) If learners cannot achieve the target rhythm, the cause of the problem may be the pronunciation of specific sounds. In that case, correct their pronunciation as well as their rhythm.

(b) Do not treat a sentence as a tongue twister and make learners say it fast. Such an exercise could cause problems with accuracy in learners' pronunciation.[6)]

5. 下がり調子と上がり調子 (Falling and rising intonation)

英語のイントネーションについては，ほとんどの教育現場で，下降調（下がり調子）と上昇調（上がり調子）の差についての指導が中心になっています．すなわち，下降調は平叙文と命令文と感嘆文と疑問詞で始まる疑問文に使われ，上昇調は yes-no 疑問文に使われること，選択疑問文においては最後の選択肢に下降調，それ以外の選択肢に上昇調が使われること，などが教えられています．初級の学習者にとってこうしたデフォルトのイントネーションについて学ぶことは意義のあることですが，[7)] 指導者はイントネーションと文構造の関係についてもう少し深い理解をしておく必要があります．げんに，リスニング指導をしていると，教材に上記の原則に合わないイントネーションが出て来ることがあり，このことについて学習者から質問が出た場合，指導者は解説をする必要があります．

Typically, in an English class in Japan, instruction in intonation focuses on falling intonation and rising intonation. It is often taught (a) that falling intonation is used for declarative sentences, imperative sentences, exclamatory sentences, and interrogative sentences beginning with an interrogative word, (b) that rising intonation is used for yes-no questions, and (c) that, in an alternative question, falling intonation is used for the last alternative and rising intonation for the other alternative(s). While teaching learners about these default patterns has its significance,[7)] you as the instructor should have a deeper understanding of the relation between intonation patterns and grammatical structures. In fact, while teaching listening comprehension, you may come across patterns of intonation that do not fit the above principles and get a question about them from learners. You should be prepared to provide an explanation.

指導者が承知しておくべきことは，イントネーションと文構造との間には固定的な関係はなく，イントネーションは話し手の気持ちの現れである，ということです．たとえば，話し手は平叙文を上昇調で言うことがあります．また，たとえば，Sit down. は命令文ですが，話し手は命令調を和らげるためにこれを上昇調で言うこともあります．スポーツの試合結果をめぐる次の会話において，答をにごす B のことばを受けて，A は下降調で 2 回目の質問をするかもしれません．

The fact is that there is no fixed relation between intonation and grammatical structure and that intonation rather reflects the speaker's feeling. For example, a speaker may say a declarative sentence with rising intonation. *Sit down* is an imperative sentence, but a speaker may say it with rising intonation to soften the imperative tone. In the following dialogue about the result of some game of sport, Participant A may use falling intonation in his or her second utterance, which is a response to the utterance by Participant B, who does not want to give a clear answer.

A:　Did you win?（勝ったの？）
B:　Well ...（それが ...）
A:　Did you win?（勝ったの？）

この2回目のAの疑問文は，下降調で言われた場合，疑問の気持ちよりも，「もう一度質問しますよ.」「勝ったのかって聞いてるんですよ.」という宣言の気持ちが込められたものだと言えるでしょう．このように，下降調と上昇調とは，文構造につきものなのではなく，むしろ，話し手の気持ちにつきものであると考えるべきです．学習者から質問が出たら，イントネーションのこの特徴を説明してください．

Rather than being a pure question, Participant A's second question may reflect his or her desire to make to Participant B a statement such as "I am repeating the question," or "I want you to tell me the result of the game," hence the falling intonation. As these examples suggest, falling and rising intonation come not with a grammatical structure but with the speaker's feeling. Explain this feature of intonation when you get a question from learners.

6. 山の位置 (Location of the peak)

イントネーションについて，下降調と上昇調の選択よりももっと答えがはっきりしているのが，イントネーションの山の位置です.[8] 下がり調子の平叙文を話題にして説明する方法が学習者にとって最も分かりやすいと思います．

One aspect of intonation which is more clear-cut than the choice between falling and rising intonation is the location of what I would like to call the "peak" in an intonation pattern.[8] An explanation using a declarative sentence said with falling intonation will be easiest for learners to understand.

ここで言う山とは，（下降調の場合なら）声の高さが最も高い部分，または他のどの部分よりも低くならない部分のことです．山は普通，そのことば通り，最高の高さの部分ですが，山より高くないものの山と同じ高さの部分が他にあるかも知れません．原則が２つあります．

By "peak" I mean the part of the intonation pattern which is the highest or which is no lower than any other part (I am assuming that the pattern is one of falling intonation; the "peak," as the name suggests, is usually the highest part of the pattern, but there may be parts which are as high as the peak, if not higher). There are two principles that govern the location of the peak.

第一に，センテンスが特別長くない限り，[9] また，センテンスに特別強調すべき場所がない限り，イントネーションの山は，普通センテンスの最後の第一アクセントのある拍に来ます．[10] たとえば，I bought a hat at a department store.（私はデパートで帽子を買った）という文は，図 19.15 のようなパターンになります．

First, as long as the sentence is not very long[9] and does not have a part that is supposed to receive special emphasis, the peak is usually on the last syllable with primary stress.[10] For example, *I bought a hat at a department store* assumes a pattern as shown in Figure 19.15.

I bought a hat at a department store.

図 19.15

第一アクセントが bought, hat, -part- にあり，第二アクセントが store にあります．最後の第一アクセントは -part- にありますから，ここがイントネーションの山になります．センテンスの他の部分は -part- より高くはなりません．このことを示すために板書をするとすれば，図 19.16 のようなものが役立ちます．

Primary stress is on *bought, hat*, and *-part-*, and secondary stress is on *store*. Since the last syllable with primary stress is *-part-*, that is where the peak is. No other part of the sentence is higher than *-part-*. If you wish to indicate this on the board in class, draw something like Figure 19.16.

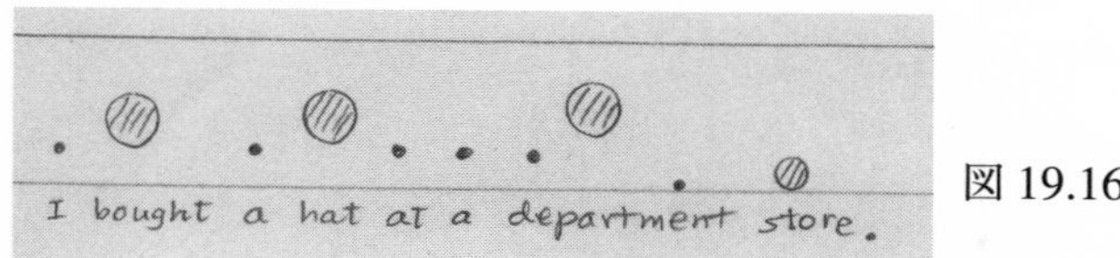

図 19.16

もうひとつ例を挙げるとすれば，He said she'd arrive at five o'clock.（彼女は5時に到着する，と彼は言った.）を板書するとすれば，図 19.17 のような書き方ができます．最後の第一アクセントは -clock にありますから，そこが山になります．

Here is another example. You can draw an illustration for *He said she'd arrive at five o'clock,* as in Figure 19.17. The last syllable with primary stress is *-clock*, and that is where the peak is.

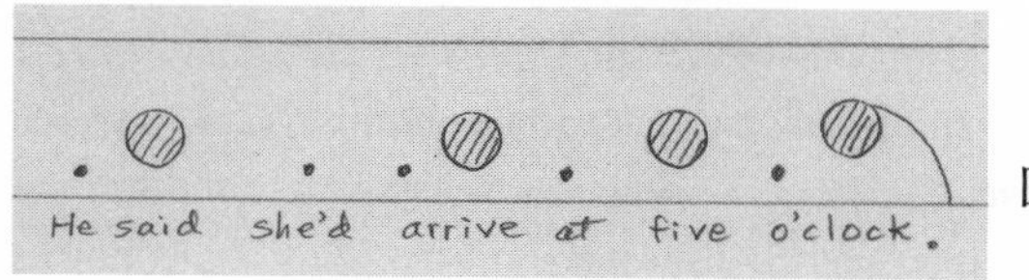

図 19.17

第二に，もしセンテンスに特に強調したい部分があった場合は，山はその部分のなかの最後の第一アクセントの位置に来ます．たとえば，このセンテンスが，Who said she'd arrive at five o'clock?（彼女が5時に着く，って誰が言ったの？）に対する答えだったら，センテンスで大事な部分は he で，この語に第一アクセントが来ますから，ここにイントネーションの山が来ます（図 19.18）．

The second principle is that, if the sentence has a part that is supposed to receive special emphasis, the peak is on the last syllable with primary stress within that part. For example, if the above sentence is a response to *Who said she'd arrive at five o'clock?*, the word *he* should receive special emphasis, i.e., receive primary stress, and that is where the peak is.

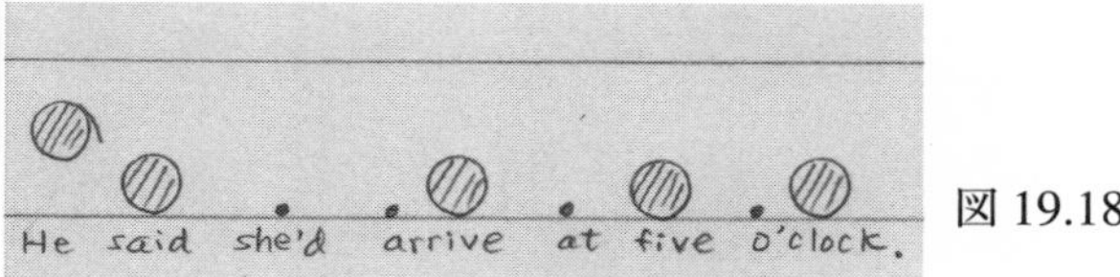

図 19.18

山の位置について指導することをお勧めしたい点のひとつは，2 つの事柄の対比の提示のために，センテンスが特に強調されるべき個所を 2 個備えていることがあり得る，ということです．このような場合，山は 2 個現れます．たとえば，次の例では，話し手は「それが好きなのはケイトではなくアンです.」と言っており，ふたりの名前が対照的に述べられますので，山はアンとケイトとの両方に現れます (図 19.19)．

One thing I recommend you to teach in connection with the location of the peak is that a sentence may have not one but two parts that receive special emphasis, because the speaker wants to present a contrast between two items. In such a case, two peaks appear in a sentence. In the following example, the speaker is saying that the person who likes something is not Kate but Anne. The two names are contrasted against each other, and a peak appears on each of the two names (Figure 19.19).

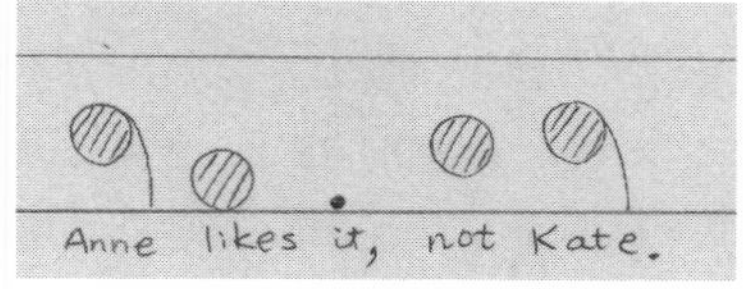

図 19.19

これまで山の位置について下がり調子を前提として説明しましたが，上がり調子のイントネーションの場合はどうなるか，も指導する必要があります．上がり調子の場合，山は，次のふた通りのどちらかの形を取って現れます．第一に，山は，しばしば，高い声が連続する部分の始まりとなります (この第一の形の説明においてのみ，山という用語は臨時に「ジャンプ」に置き換えたほうがよいかもしれません)．たとえば，次の Is that the house you're trying to buy? (あなたが買おうとしている家は，あれですか？) で，山は that にありますが，話し手は普通ここで声を高くして，そのままセンテンスの終わりまで高いレベルを維持します（図19.20）．学習者によく見られる問題は，上向きのジャンプがはっきりせず，音程の上昇がなだらかな坂になってズルズルと後のほうまで続くことです．これでは聞き手にとって山がどこにあるのか分かりにくくなります（文脈がその情報を伝える場合は別ですが）．ジャンプがはっきり分かるように学習者に話させる必要があります．

I have been discussing the location of the peak on the assumption that the intonation pattern is a falling one. But you also need to teach how to treat a peak in a rising pattern. With rising intonation, the peak appears in one of two ways. First, the speaker may raise the pitch at the point where the peak is and maintain the high pitch until the sentence is finished (in this first case only, a peak should perhaps be renamed "jump" temporarily). For example, with the sentence *Is that the house you're trying to buy?*, the pitch goes up on *that* (which is where the peak is) and is kept high for the rest of the sentence (Figure 19.20). A common problem with the way learners handle such a rising pattern is that they fail to make the upward jump clear, prolonging the gradual upward change in pitch further into the middle of the sentence. This makes it difficult for the hearer to identify the peak-carrying word (unless the context conveys that information). You need to tell learners to make the upward jump clearly recognizable.

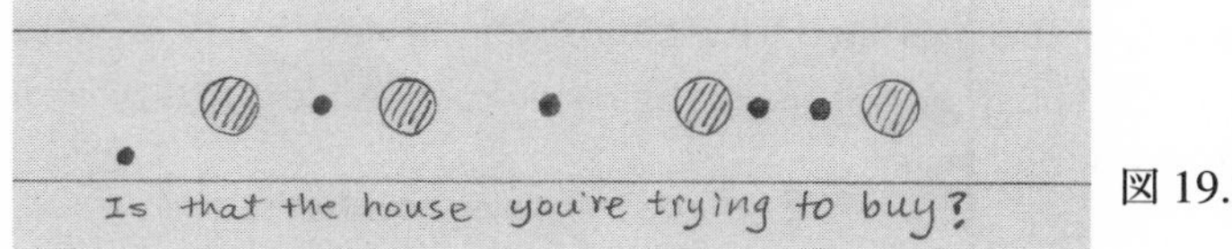

図19.20

第二に，山は，下がり調子の場合のように，センテンスのなかで声の高さが最も高い場所になるかもしれません．もっとも，この場合，文末に出て来る高い場所だけは，山より高い場合もあり得ます（図19.21）．

Secondly, just as in a falling pattern, the peak may be the part of the sentence which is said at the highest pitch, the other syllables being no higher than the peak. But, as it is a rising pattern, the last part of the sentence will have an upward jump (which is the distinctive characteristic of a rising pattern), which may reach a level higher than the peak (Figure 19.21).

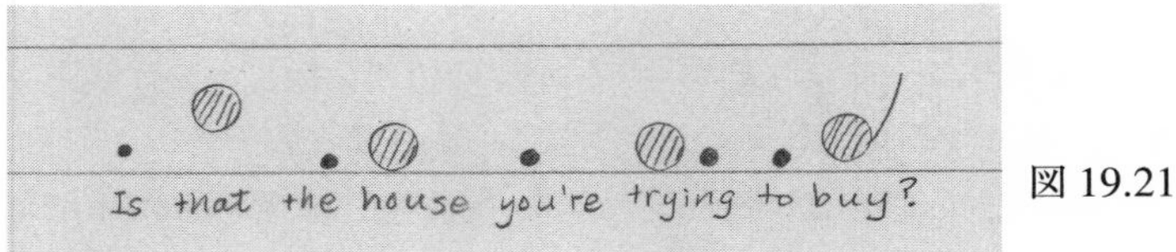

図 19.21

山の位置を教えることは，イントネーションの持つコミュニケーション上の価値を学習者に理解させるとてもよい機会です．

Teaching learners about the location of the peak provides an excellent opportunity for bringing home to them the communicative value of intonation.

7. 低い声を大切に (Importance of low pitches of voice)

これまで述べて来たイントネーションの扱いについて指導を行う場合，指導者が直面する苦労に，「学習者に低い声を出させる」ということがあります．これは 2 つの種類の苦労であると言うことができます．

As you give learners training in the use of intonation that we have discussed, you may find that they have difficulty using low levels of voice pitch when attempting to use natural intonation. Specifically, they may have two sorts of problems.

第一に，この章の冒頭で述べた，声域の下まで声を急に降ろすイントネーションが，多くの学習者にとって難しい事柄です．学習者は，たとえば，May (5 月) を日本語の「銘」のように発音したり，car で終わるセンテンスの最後で声を降ろしきれなかったりします．

First, learners may have difficulty dropping their pitch of voice from a high level to the bottom of their voice range. For example, they may say something like the Japanese word "mei" ("name") when attempting to say *May* or fail to lower their voice to the bottom of the voice range when finishing a sentence whose last word is *car*.

声域の下まで声を降ろすことが苦手な学習者は，リズムの扱いがうまく行かなくなる可能性があります．たとえば，They have a car. というセンテンスにおいて，普通，山は car の部分に来ます．この場合，声の高さという切り口で見れば，car を言うときに声が声域の上のほうから最低レベルまで降ります．また，リズムという切り口で見れば，car を言うのに時間がかかり，They have a の部分は速く発音されます（板書で図解するとすれば，このセンテンスの言い方は図 19.22 のようになりますが，car の部分の扱いを特によく学習者に理解させるためには，図 19.23 のような表しかたもよいでしょう）．しかし，声域の最低のレベルが使えない学習者は，センテンスの最後を短く切り（たとえば第 18 章の「のどを使う /t/」の項で述べたような，のどの息の通り道を閉じることをセンテンスの終わりで行い），センテンスを不自然なリズムで言ってしまいます．

ただ，この第一の問題は，解決できなくともさほど深刻なコミュニケーション上の支障にはつながらないので，このことに関してはあまり完璧主義にならないようにしてください．

Learners who have trouble lowering the pitch of their voice to the bottom of their voice range may have trouble saying a sentence with natural rhythm. When saying the sentence *They have a car*, for example, one needs to say *car* with a falling tone, using a high pitch to begin to say *car* and dropping the pitch all the way to the bottom of the voice range. From the point of view of rhythm, *car*, namely the stressed part, is said relatively long, and the rest of the sentence, consisting of the words *they have a,* is said relatively short (you can explain this to learners by drawing something like Figure 19.22, or, if you wish to emphasize the rhythm, Figure 19.23). However, learners who cannot use the lowest part of their voice range clip the last part of the sentence short (with a glottal stop, discussed in Chapter 18 in connection with the glottal /t/, for example) and end up saying the sentence with an unnatural rhythm.

The problem of this first kind does not lead to serious communicative trouble, however. Thus, my advice is that you should not be overly meticulous about the use of the lowest part of one's voice range.

図 19.22

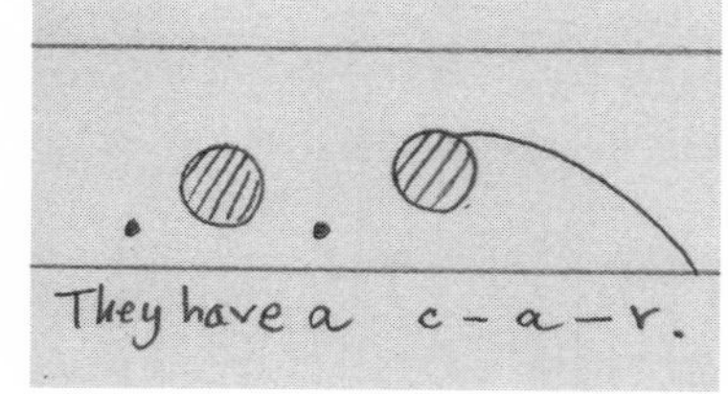

図 19.23

学習者が直面しやすい第二の問題は，山でないところを低く言うのが難しい，という問題です．たとえば，セクション 6 で例に挙げたばかりの，he に山が来る He said she'd arrive at five o'clock. の場合（図 19.18），said から o'clock までは，he より低い声で言わないといけません．低い声でセンテンスの長い部分を言うのは，多くの学習者にとって楽ではありません．低い声を続けることができず，five あたりで声が高くなってしまう学習者もいると思います．

Secondly, learners have difficulty highlighting a specific part of a sentence by saying the rest of the sentence at a low pitch. For example, when one says *He said she'd arrive at five o'clock*, where the peak comes on *he* (Figure 19.18), one has to say all the words from *said* to *o'clock* at a low pitch. For many learners, it is difficult to say a long portion of a sentence at a low pitch. They may fail to maintain a low pitch, raising the pitch of voice when saying *five*, for example.

学習者が第一，第二の問題をかかえやすい原因として，日本語における声の使い方が考えられます．日本語では，高いレベルで声を維持する言い方が必要とされるセンテンスが多く登場します．たとえば，「こんにちは」を言うとき，「んにちは」の部分は高い声で言います．「わたしのなまえは」を言うとき，「わ」と「な」以外は高い声で言うのが普通です．「な」も高い場合すらあります．このような声の使い方に慣れている学習者が英語を話すときに低い声がうまく使えないのは当然かもしれません．

A possible cause of the above two problems is the way in which pitch of voice is used in Japanese. Sentences that require the speaker to maintain a high pitch occur quite often in Japanese. For example, when one says "konnichiwa" ("hello"), one says the last four syllables, namely "n," "ni," "chi," and "wa," at a high pitch. "Watashi no namae wa" ("My name is") should be said with all the syllables except "wa" and "na" at a high pitch. Sometimes even "na" is high, making the intonation pattern high all the way from "ta" to the end of the phrase. It may be little wonder that Japanese-speaking learners have difficulty using low pitches of voice when speaking English.

この問題の解決方法としては，学習者に自分の声の高さをコントロールする能力を身につけてもらうことが考えられます．特に低い声を自在に出せるようになってもらう必要があります．私は，まず，学習者に，「アー」と言いながら声の高さを下げて行って，自分の声の最低の高さまで降りてもらう指導法を使います．

One good way to solve this problem is to have learners acquire an ability to control the height of the pitch of voice, especially an ability to use low pitches freely. When I teach intonation I have learners say a long tone with the "a" vowel, lowering the pitch gradually until it reaches the bottom of their voice range.

学習者にこれができるようになったら，次に，降りるスピードを上げて，学習者がすばやく最低の高さまで降りられるようにします．そして最後に，いきなり始めから最低の高さの声を「アー」と出してもらいます．こうした練習を通して，声の高さをコントロールできるようになったら，学習者は，今問題にしているような，低い部分が長く続くセンテンスも楽に言えるようになるはずです．

When learners have learned to do this, I then have them lower the pitch quickly. Finally, I have them say a tone, beginning at a low pitch and staying low until the end of the tone. When learners have learned to control the pitch of their voice, they should be able to say with ease sentences where a low pitch should be maintained.

山の位置はコミュニケーション上非常に大事な情報を伝えるものなので，

学習者が山を正しい場所に置きながら英語を話せるよう指導してください.

As the location of the peak in an intonation pattern conveys information which is communicatively important, do make sure that learners can speak with peaks in intonation in correct places.

8. 練習のための言語材料 (Materials for practice)

次の練習をさせてください.

Make learners do the following exercises.

1. 次の語を図 19.24 のようなパターンで言いなさい.

Say the words below following the pattern shown in Figure 19.24:

(a) Japanese (b) represent (代表する) (c) understand

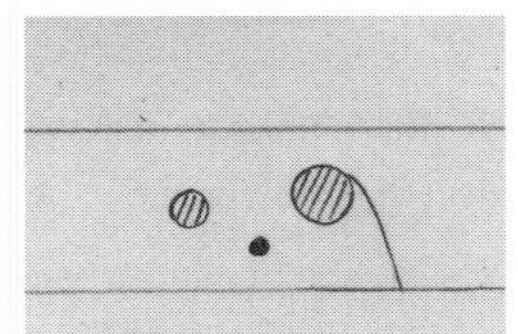

図 19.24

2. 次の語を図 19.25 のようなパターンで言いなさい.

Say the words below following the pattern shown in Figure 19.25:

(a) examination (b) communication (c) imagination

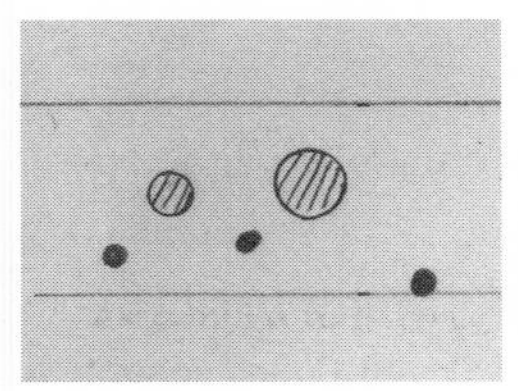

図 19.25

3.　次のセンテンス（Sheila received a letter from Ken.＝シーラはケンから手紙をもらった.）を，What happened yesterday? に対する答えだとして，図19.26に示すように正しい位置に山を置いて言いなさい.

Assuming that the following sentence is a response to *What happened yesterday?*, say it with the intonational peak put in the right place, as shown in Figure 19.26.

図 19.26

4.　次のことば(No. I bought the book. ＝いいえ．私は本を買ったのです.）を，Did you borrow the book from the library?（あなたはその本を図書館から借りたのですか？）に対する答えだとして，図19.27に示すように正しい位置に山を置いて言いなさい.

Assuming that the following utterance is a response to *Did you borrow the book from the library?*, say it with the intonational peak put in the right place, as shown in Figure 19.27.

図 19.27

5.　次のことば（No. Steve went to the post office with her. ＝いいえ．スティーブが彼女と一緒に郵便局に行きました.）を，Did Bill go to the post office with her?（ビルが彼女と一緒に郵便局に行きましたか？）に対する答えだとして，図19.28に示すように正しい位置に山を置いて言いなさい.

Assuming that the following utterance is a response to *Did Bill go to the post office with her?*, say it with the intonational peak put in the right place, as shown in Figure 19.28.

図 19.28

9. アクティビティー見本 (Idea for an activity)

「怠惰なルームメート」 (Lazy roommate)

学習者に次の会話を演じさせてください．下線部に特に注意を払わせ，そこを自然なイントネーションで言うように注意してください．ここでは，山の位置を二重下線にしてあります．学習者には下線のない教材を渡してください．(1) と (4) では，not がかなり高くなり，次の語と同じくらいの高さになる可能性もありますが，次の語より高くはなりません．

Have learners perform the following dialogue, paying particular attention to the underlined sentences so that they say them with natural intonation. Here the location of the peak is indicated by a double underline. Provide learners with a written version of the dialogue without underlines. In (1) and (4), *not* may be fairly high, possibly as high as the following word, but not higher.

A: I'm going out. Can you tidy up the room while I'm gone?
(外出する．留守中に部屋を片付けておいて．)

B: Wait a minute. (1) You should do it, not me. I did it yesterday.
(ちょっと待ってよ．ぼくじゃなくて，君がやるべきだろう．ぼくはきのうやったよ．)

A: Well, OK. (2) I'll do it. By the way, can you take this parcel to the post office for me when you have time?
(分かった．ぼくがやるよ．ところで，時間があるとき，この小包を郵便局に持って行ってくれないか？)

B: (3) Why don't you do it? (4) You're the one that's going out, not me.

（君がやったらどうなんだい？ 外出するのはぼくじゃなくて君だよ.）

A: Well, I'm not passing the post office. Also, can you put these clothes into the wash for me?

（それが，郵便局の前は通らないんだ．それから，この衣類を洗濯に入れといてくれないか？）

B: (5) You put them into the wash. (6) Those are your clothes.

（君が入れろよ．君の衣類だよ.）

A: OK. Now, can you do this homework for me?

（分かった．それから，この宿題をやってくれないか？）

ここでの焦点は山の位置です．学習者のイントネーションに問題があったら，活動が終わってから，明示的に指導してください.

The focus here is the location of the peak. If learners' intonation is problematical, provide explicit instruction after the activity.

第 20 章
リピート練習をこえて

Going beyond repetition practice

第 1 から第 19 までの各章では，個々の音などの具体的な音声項目を中心にして，発音指導のヒントを提示しましたが，この第 20 章では，一般的な発音指導のワザや戦略について述べたいと思います．発音指導と言うとまずリピート練習を思い浮かべる指導者も多いと思います．リピート練習には一定の効果があるとは思いますが，指導者が意図するほどの学習が起こるという保証はないかもしれません．学習者は練習に集中しないで時間を過ごすこともあり得ます．特に集団で行うリピート練習では，学習者が評価を受ける機会もありません．この最後の章では，リピート練習をこえた発音指導法についてコメントしたいと思います．

We have been looking at specific items from the English sound system and how the instructor can teach them. Here in Chapter 20, I mention more general techniques and strategies for improving learners' pronunciation. Many instructors first think of repetition practice when they hear the term "pronunciation training." While repetition practice is no doubt effective to a certain degree, it may not guarantee as much learning as the instructor wants to make happen: Learners can go through drills without focusing on what they are doing; repetition practice done with a group of learners does not give them a chance to have their pronunciation assessed. In this final chapter, I discuss methods of pronunciation training beyond the all-too-familiar repetition practice.

1. 学習者の発音を真似る (Copying learners' pronunciation)

発音の指導者は，学習者の発音を聞いて舌や唇がどう動いているかを特定する能力，およびその理解に立脚して学習者の発音を真似る能力を持つべきです．自分が口をどう使っているかを学習者自身が認識できることが理想ですが，彼らは，なかなかそのような認識には至らず，たとえ自分の声の録音を聞かされた時でさえもその認識に至らないことがむしろ普通です．この原因として考えられるのが，学習者の音とモデルの音との間に，発音以外の差，すなわち声の差があることです．声が違うと，学習者は発音の違いと声の違いとを峻別できないことが多いのです．この結果，発音の違いが浮き彫りにはなりません．このような場合，指導者が学習者の音と正しい音との両方を同じ声で聞かせれば，両方の音の違いが分かりやすくなります．もちろん，指導者は，学習者の発音を真似るだけでなく，それを瞬時に分析し，学習者に明示的に説明するべきです．こうすることにより，指導者は，学習者に，自分の発音のどこが悪いのかを理解させることができます．

The instructor of pronunciation should be able to listen to learners' pronunciation, figure out how their tongue and lips move and, on the basis of that information, copy their pronunciation. It would be ideal if learners could understand how they are using their mouth when they are saying sounds, but they usually do not have that knowledge, even after listening to a recording of their own voice. One possible cause of this is that, on top of the difference between learners' pronunciation and the target pronunciation, there is a difference between the quality of their voice and that of the voice used in the model presented to them. If there is a difference in voice, learners often cannot separate the difference in pronunciation from the difference in voice. This means that the difference in pronunciation does not stand out in their perception. When such a problem has arisen, the instructor can cope with the situation by letting learners hear their incorrect pronunciation and the target pronunciation using the same voice. Of course, the instructor should not only copy learners' pronunciation but analyze it on the spot and offer an explicit explanation of what problem there is and how to correct it.

2. スローモーション発音 (Slow-motion articulation)

指導者が学習者に対して発音の見本を提示するときに，学習者が発音方法をつかむまでは，スローモーションで発音してみせることをお勧めします．この方法はかなり広範囲に使えます．たとえば第 1 章で取り上げた /r/ と /l/ の指導の場合，rain，lane，right，light などの語のアタマの音を 3 ～ 5 秒かけて発音すれば，学習者は /r/ /l/ の違いをつかみやすくなります．このほか，スローモーションの発音が役立つ項目としては，第 11，13 章で取り上げた /r/ を含む組み合わせ（price，bread，friend，every，cream，great，three，train，dress，Henry の下線部など），第 12 章，第 14 章，第 18 章で取り上げた /l/ を含む組み合わせ（please，blue，close，glad，fly，feel，sleep の下線部など）があります．第 15 章で取り上げた cars と cards の最後の部分の違い，第 16 章で取り上げた finger と singer の -ng- の部分の違い，第 17 章で取り上げた発音に至らない /p/, /t/, /k/, /b/, /d/, /g/ の指導にもスローモーション発音が役立ちます．さらに，音を単純に長く伸ばすことにより学習者に音の響きをよく聞かせることも有効です．この方法で，第 4 章で取り上げた /f/, /v/，第 2 章で取り上げた /θ/, /ð/，第 5 章で取り上げた /s/, /ʃ/ の違いを教えることができます．

I recommend that you use what I would like to call "slow-motion articulation" when you present target pronunciation to learners until they grasp how to move their speech organs. Slow-motion articulation may be used for a wide range of sounds. For example, in teaching /r/ and /l/, discussed in Chapter 1, pronounce the initial consonants in *rain, lane, right,* and *light*, spending three to five seconds to say each one, and learners will understand the difference between /r/ and /l/ more easily than if you said them fast. Other sounds that may be made easier to learn by slow-motion articulation are clusters with /r/, which I took up in Chapters 11 and 13 (the underlined parts of *price, bread, friend, every, cream, great, three, train, dress,* and *Henry*, for example), and combinations including /l/, which I took up in Chapters 12, 14, and 18 (the underlined parts of *please, blue, close, glad, fly, feel*, and *sleep*, for example). Slow-motion articulation is also suitable for teaching the difference between the underlined part of *finger* and that of *singer*, which we discussed in Chapter 16, and the incomplete articulation of /p/, /t/, /k/, /b/, /d/, and /g/, taken up in Chapter 17. Furthermore, just prolonging a sound is also effective. This applies to the articulation of /f/ and /v/, discussed in Chapter 4, the articulation of /θ/ and /ð/, discussed in Chapter 2, and the difference between /s/ and /ʃ/, which was the topic of Chapter 5.

瞬間的な音，たとえば第 17 章で取り上げたラ，リ，ル，レ，ロのアタマの音に似た /t/（たとえば better の下線部）は，一瞬にして終わるので当然スローモーション発音ができません．しかし，スローモーション発音は，指導者が前項で述べた学習者の音(それは瞬間的な音ではないかもしれません)の模倣をするときに役立つことがあります．たとえば，第 17 章で述べた通り，学習者は better の下線部をよく /l/ と混同しますので，学習者の誤った発音（たとえば better と言うべきところで /belɚ/ と言ってしまう）をスローモーションで真似て聞かせることにより，誤った発音がどう誤っているのかを学習者に把握させることができます．このように，スローモーション発音は非常に有効です．

Sounds articulated instantaneously, such as tapped /t/, which resembles the Japanese /r/, as in *better*, are naturally not suitable for instruction with slow-motion articulation. Nevertheless, even when you teach such sounds, slow-motion articulation may turn out to be useful in copying learners' erroneous articulation, which may not be instantaneous. For example, as I mentioned in Chapter 17, learners often use /l/ for the underlined part of *better* and say /belɚ/. In such a case, you can copy learners' pronunciation in slow motion to help them understand in what way their pronunciation is problematical. Slow-motion articulation is thus very useful for pronunciation teaching.

3. 単語の途中で切る (Cutting a word in the middle)

通常の音読やリピートの指導では，センテンスを切るとき，単語の境目で切るのが普通です．しかし，発音指導では，単語を途中で切る方法も有効です．第 6 章で，in your house のリピート練習を取り上げ，アタマの /ɪ/ のない -n your house というフレーズを使う方法を紹介しました．これがその方法です．第 6 章の練習は /n/ の練習でしたが，それ以外の音のつながりに関する目的の練習にもこの方法は役立ちます．

In having learners do repetition practice or oral reading practice, the instructor usually cuts sentences at word boundaries. In pronunciation practice, however, it is sometimes effective to cut a sentence or phrase midword. In Chapter 6, I discussed repetition practice with the phrase *in your house*, and I stated that it is effective to have learners deal at one stage with a string of sounds *-n your house*. This is an example of the method I am mentioning here. It was /n/ that I focused on in Chapter 6, but this method can be used for dealing with other challenges arising from connected speech.

たとえば，第 18 章セクション 4 で，/ð/ や /θ/ の前の音を歯を使って発音する方法を紹介し，that theory というフレーズを例として挙げました．このフレーズを学習者に練習させるときに，that を途中で切って，-t theory (/tθiːəri/) という部分を練習させてからフレーズ全体を言わせると，うまく言えることがあります．すなわち，次のような音の連なりを使います．

For example, in Section 4 of Chapter 18, I took up a dentalized articulation of a sound when it is followed by /ð/ or /θ/ and gave the phrase *that theory* as an example. When you have learners practice saying this phrase, you can cut the word *that* in the middle and have learners say *-t theory* (/tθiːəri/) before having them say the whole phrase. The following is the series of strings of sounds that you should use for this practice.

(1) theory (/θiːəri/)
(2) -t theory (/tθiːəri/)
(3) that theory (/ðætθiːəri/)

よく行われるバックワードビルドアップ練習法では，学習者は theory > that theory と言うのですが，ここでは，単語の境で切るだけでなく，特定の音や音のくずれに焦点が当たりやすいような切り方をするわけです．

In an ordinary backward buildup drill, learners would say *theory* and then *that theory*. The method I am introducing here is not only to cut a phrase at a word boundary but also to cut it in a way in which you can easily focus on a specific sound or a specific case of sound reduction.

4. くずし方を変える (Varying the degree of sound reduction)

指導者が学習者に聞かせる英語のスピードについて，種々の考え方があります．指導者は学習者のレベルに合わせてゆっくり話すべきである，という考えもあれば，自然なスピードや自然な音のくずれに学習者を慣れさせなくてはならないから，指導者はスピードについて手加減すべきではない，と強調する向きもあります．私は，初級であれ上級であれ，学習者はゆっくりした明瞭な発音にも触れるべきであるし，また，速くてくずれの度合いの高い英語にも触れるべきであると思っています．学習者は，多様な話し方の英語に触れることにより，音のくずれに関する知識を吸収することができると思います．

Opinions vary regarding the speed at which the instructor should speak English in class. Some say that the instructor should speak at slow speeds that match learners' levels; others stress the importance for the instructor to avoid slowing down so that learners become accustomed at an early stage to natural speed and natural sound reduction. In my view, learners, beginners and advanced learners alike, should be exposed both to slow, clear pronunciation and to fast speech with a high degree of sound reduction. Learners can absorb knowledge about sound reduction through exposure to a variety of ways of speaking.

このような学習を可能にするひとつの方法として，1 回の授業のなかで，指導者が，意図的に，最初のうちはどちらかと言えばくずれの度合いの低い言い方で英語を言い，授業の終わりのほうでは同じ単語や同じセンテンスをくずれの度合いの高い程度で言う，という方法があります．この方法を使うためには，指導者は，同じ単語やセンテンスをくずれの度合いを変えて言う能力を身につけるべく，発音の自己研鑽をしておく必要があります．

One thing that the instructor can do to make such learning possible for learners is to deliberately say words and sentences with a low degree of sound reduction at the beginning of the class period and say the same words and sentences with a high degree of sound reduction toward the end of the session. If you as the instructor want to do this, it is necessary for you to train yourself so that you acquire an ability to say the same words and sentences with different degrees of sound reduction.

5. 発音チェックリスト (Pronunciation checklists)

自分はどんな音が出せてどんな音が出せないのかを学習者が知ると，学習者は苦手な音に集中しながら練習することができます．この意味で，学習者が発音チェックリストを使い，改善の必要がある音が何かを常に知っておくことは有意義です．ここではチェックリストを 4 点紹介します（リストそのものは付録に掲載しました）．

If learners know what sounds they can say correctly and what sounds they cannot, they can practice pronunciation with a clear focus on the sounds that they have problems with. Learners will thus benefit from using a pronunciation checklist and keeping themselves informed of what sounds they need to improve. I am introducing four examples of pronunciation checklists (the actual lists are given in the appendix).

第一のものは，授業で取り上げる言語材料だけを範囲にしたチェックリストです．たとえば，次のような教材（対話）に対するリストは，その下に掲載したようなものとなります．

The first one is a checklist that covers only the texts used in class. For example, if your teaching material was a dialogue like the following, the checklist would be like the one given below the dialogue.

Dialogue

A: Is the police station far from here?

B: No. It's just around the corner to the left.

発音チェックリスト

キーワード	文中の語		
hit の /ɪ/	□ is　□ it's	she の /ʃ/	□ station
this の /ð/	□ the	fine の /f/	□ far　□ from
like の /l/	□ police　□ left	deer の /ɪɚ/	□ here
see の /iː/	□ police	right の /r/	□ around
		butter の /ɚ/	□ corner

第二のものは，日本語からの連想にもとづくチェックリストです．日本の学習者が間違って発音しやすい英語の音を，その音に近いと学習者が考えがちな日本語の音により分類したものです．同じ音を，音声環境を変えて複数回提示している場合もあります．一方，/m/, /k/ のような，難しくない音は入っていません．リストの最初の項目をご覧に入れると，「ア」に聞こえる音と，その仲間として，次のような項目が並んでいます．

The second list is one where English sounds are grouped by the Japanese sound that they may be associated with. The same sound may be classed as belonging to multiple groups. On the other hand, sounds that are not so difficult for learners, such as /m/ and /k/, are not included. Here are sounds that are listed under the first category, sounds that sound like "a," together with other sounds related to them:

□1.1 /æ/ pat　□1.2 /ɑ/ pot　□1.3 /ə/ appear　□1.4 /ʌ/ cut
□1.5 /ɚː/ bird　□1.6 /aɪ/ kind　□1.7 /aʊ/ sound　□1.8 /aɪɚ/ fire
□1.9 /aʊɚ/ our

日英の音体系の相違のために，分類に無理がある項目もありますが，あくまでも学習者の発音の「健康診断」が目的ですので，分類がきれいであることより，学習者にとって苦手な音をなるべく多く含むことのほうが優先されています．

As the Japanese and English sound systems are different, the grouping is not completely tidy. But, since the purpose of the list is to do a check-up on learners' pronunciation rather than to present a perfect classification, I have given priority to including as many challenging sounds of

English as possible.

このリストは，長いもので，初級の学習者を対象としてこのまま使うことは適当でないでしょう．げんに，本書で取り上げていない音も入っています．リストは，全体としては，むしろ，中級以上の学習者が英語の発音を総合的にチェックしたい場合に使うことができます．しかし，初級の学習者のために，このリストの一部を切り取って使うことができます．たとえば，初級の学習者に対し，アに聞こえる音とその仲間についてだけ発音指導を行うことがあり得ますが，そのようなときに，リストの一部が使えます．

This is a long list, and it would be inappropriate to use it in its entirety with beginning learners. In fact, it includes sounds which are not taken up in this book. The list is useful rather for a checkup on the overall pronunciation of learners at intermediate and advanced levels. But you can also use the list by clipping out part of it for beginning learners. For example, you can teach English sounds that sound like the Japanese "a" vowel by using the relevant part of the list.

第三のものは，英語の音をレベル別[1]に項目立てしたリストです．私は，「英語発音道」なる名前をつけたリストを授業で使っていました．五級から八段まで昇格して行くようになっており，学習者があるレベルの音をマスターしたことが確認された時点で合格のチェック欄にチェックを入れるようになっています．たとえば，最も低い五級には /b/ /k/ などの日本語の音と同じ英語の音が並んでおり，初段には /s/ /ʃ/ の区別があり，最も高い八段には *deadline* にあるような /dl/ の発音が挙げられています．

The third kind of list has items arranged in order of difficulty for learners.[1] I was using a list in my classes in which the levels were likened to the qualifications given in Japan to those practicing sports, calligraphy, abacus, etc. In my list, the lowest level is the 5th "kyu" and the highest is the 8th "dan." Items at the 5th "kyu," the lowest level, include sounds that are the same as sounds in Japanese, such as /b/ and /k/, the 1st "dan" items include the distinction between /s/ and /ʃ/, and, at the highest level, the 8th "dan" items include the articulation of /dl/ as in *deadline*. Learners put a check not for an individual sound but for the level that they have passed.

第四のものは，私が「業務用」と呼んでいるもので，学習者でなく指導者が使うことを想定したものです．英語には，たとえば /t/ の音に何種類かあり，気音（19章の注2参照）を伴う time の /t/，発音が完結しない football の /t/，歯を使う eighth の /t/ などがあります．英語のすべての音のこうした多くの言い方を全部実践でき，かつ指導できれば，プロの発音指導者ということになります．この理想にどれほど近づいているかをチェックするためのリストです（このリストを十分役立てるためには英語音声学の基礎的知識があったほうが望ましいと思います）．

The fourth kind of list is what I call a list for professional use and is for instructors, not learners. It covers various sounds under what ordinary people think is just a single sound, e.g., /t/. In fact, there is /t/ with aspiration (see note 2 to Chapter 19) as in *time*, incomplete /t/ as in *football*, and dentalized /t/ as in *eighth*. If one can say and teach all the various ways of saying each of the sounds of English, one may truly be called a professional instructor of pronunciation, and the checklist is meant to assess how close one is to this ideal (a basic knowledge of English phonetics would be desirable for making full use of this fourth list).

ご紹介したリストには，各項目について学習者ができたかできなかったかを記録するチェック欄がありますが，ひとつの音に対してチェック欄が複数あるチェックリストを使ったこともあります．このリストでは，各項目に次のような複数のチェック欄がありました．

The above lists have tick boxes that learners can use to record whether they have been able to say particular items or have passed a certain level. I have also used checklists where each item has multiple tick boxes for responses such as the following:

□正しい音を単独で出すことができる
(I can articulate the correct sound in isolation.)

□正しい音を使ってその音を含む単語が読める
(I can say words that include this sound.)

□正しい音を使ってゆっくり本文全体が読める

(I can do slow oral reading with a text that includes this sound.)

□正しい音を使って普通のスピードで本文全体が読める

(I can do oral reading at natural speed with a text that includes this sound.)

チェックリストの作り方について正解はありません．指導者が目前の学習者に合わせて独自のリストを作るべきだと思います．

You can write your checklist in any way you like. Be original and make one that fits the learners in front of you.

6. 発音指導におけるアクティビティーの意義

(Significance of activities in pronunciation teaching)

指導者は，しばしば，発音を明示的に教え，学習者に練習をさせ，それ以上のことは特段行わないことがありますが，私は，発音の授業におけるアクティビティーの重要性を強調したいと思います．発音指導の究極の目的は，学習者が，発音を意識しなくとも明瞭な発音で英語を話せるようにすること，すなわち，彼らが発音において「自動化」を達成するのを支援することです．目標となる音の使用を含みながら発音以外のものに焦点を当てた（と少なくとも学習者の目には映る）アクティビティーは，学習者にとり，発音そのものには意識を向けずに明瞭な発音をする訓練になります．

Quite often instructors teach pronunciation explicitly, do some drills with learners, and do little beyond that. I would like to emphasize the importance of activities in pronunciation teaching in class. The ultimate purpose of pronunciation teaching should be to help learners speak English with clear pronunciation without paying attention to pronunciation, that is, help them achieve "automatization" in articulation. Activities that involve the use of certain target sounds and yet focus on something other than pronunciation, at least in the eyes of learners, provide them with opportunities to train themselves in using clear pronunciation without directing attention to pronunciation itself.

発音のレッスンにおけるアクティビティーは，また，学習者の発音を評価するのにも役立ちます．アクティビティーの最中に学習者が明瞭な発音を維持できれば，彼らが発音をマスターしたと考えることができます．しかし，学習者は，時として，意識しているときには—特に問題の音が文脈から取り出された形になっているときには—その音が言えるのに，内容に焦点を当てて自由に話しているときにはその音が言えない，ということがあります．指導者としては，こうした問題の存在に気づいて適切に指導手順を計画できるよう，自由な発話の際の学習者の発音によく注意している必要があります．

Activities in pronunciation lessons serve as a means of *assessing* learners' pronunciation as well. If they can maintain clear pronunciation during activities, we can rest assured that they have reached a level that may be called "mastery." It is sometimes the case that learners can say a sound in their conscious attempt to say it, especially when the sound is in isolation, but cannot say it well when speaking freely, focusing on the content of what they are saying. You need to pay attention to learners' pronunciation when they are speaking freely so that you can notice the presence of such a problem and can plan your instruction procedures accordingly.

7. 最後に (A final word)

発音学習や発音指導の方法については，実に多種多様なものが提案されており，本書に許されたスペースでこれ以上を取り上げることはもとより不可能ですが，最後に，大学時代のふたりの恩師のことばを紹介したいと思います．

A variety of proposals have been made about pronunciation learning and pronunciation teaching, and the space available in this book does not allow me to refer to more of them. But I would like to introduce quotations from two of the professors I had in my own university days.

ひとつのことばは，「速くしゃべれるようになりたければ，ゆっくり話せ．」[2] というものです．英語学習者は，不正確な発音で話していると，結局スピードのある話し方を身につけることは出来ず，それでも無理にスピードを上げると，通じない英語になってしまう[3]ので，急がず正確に話すことを心掛けよ，ということを意味しています．

One of the professors said, "If you want to learn to speak fast, speak slowly."[2] This means that one should try to speak slowly and accurately because, if learners of English acquire the habit of speaking with inaccurate pronunciation, they cannot learn to speak fast and, if they force themselves to speak fast, they will then make their English incomprehensible.[3]

もうひとつのことばは，教員をめざして訓練を受けていたわれわれ学生へのアドバイスで，「ことばを教える教師は，しっかりした言語観を持たなくてはならない．教師の言語観が，その教師の実際の教育ににじみ出るものだから.」[4]というものです．実際，人間はことばを何のために使うのか，外国語指導は何のために行うのか，といったことについて基本的な哲学がなければ，指導者は指針の定まった指導ができませんし，たとえば，発音指導のための規範の選択はできません．

The other quotation is a piece of advice given to those of us who were undergoing training to become teachers: "Language teachers have to have a clear view of what language is all about, for their understanding of language seeps out and affects the way they actually teach."[4] Indeed, without possessing a basic philosophy about what humans use language for and what languages are taught for, language instructors would be working without a sense of direction and would not, for example, be able to choose a norm for pronunciation teaching.

基本を尊重し，かつ，学習者がその基本の上に何を積み上げるべきかについて明確な見通しを持って仕事をすることが，われわれ発音指導者にとって大切だと思います．

Respect for the basics, with a clear view of what learners should build on those basics—that I think is key to the work we are expected to do as pronunciation instructors.

注
Notes

まえがき

1）竹林滋『英語音声学』（研究社，1996）pp. 167–172, 232における教育表記の考察参照．

See the discussion of pedagogical transcription in S. Takebayashi, *Eigo Onseigaku* (Kenkyusha, 1996, in Japanese), pp. 167–172, 232, for example.

本書において言及される小道具など

1） 本書では，歯列弓を含む口の天井の絵を使って舌が触れる範囲を示しているが，こうした画像はパラトグラムと呼ばれ，音声研究で用いられる．パラトグラムを得る方法は，口の天井の形をした板に粉を振って口の中に装着し，舌が触れた場所を調べる古典的な方法（たとえばD. Jones, *An Outline of English Phonetics*, 9th ed. (Heffer; reprint, Maruzen, 1960) にイラストあり），や，そのような板に電極を埋め込んで電気的に接触面を調べる，より新しい方法（たとえばA. Cruttenden, *Gimson's Pronunciation of English*, 8th ed. (Routledge, 2014) にイラストあり）がある．竹内京子・木村琢也『たのしい音声学』（くろしお出版，2019）には抹茶を水と水あめに溶いたものを舌に塗って自分でパラトグラムを得る方法が紹介されている．

Illustrations of the roof of the mouth covering the dental arch and the area inside the arch are given in some chapters of this book to show the area of contact between the tongue and the roof of the mouth. Such illustrations, called palatograms and used for discussion in phonetics, can be obtained through the use of an artificial palate with a powdery substance put on it (illustrations given in Jones, 1960, cited above, for example) or, more recently, through the use of an artificial palate with electrodes (illustrations given in Cruttenden, 2014, cited above, for example). A method of obtaining palatograms by putting green tea powder mixed with water and syrup on the tongue is introduced in K. Takeuchi and T. Kimura, *Tanoshii Onseigaku* (Kurosio

Publishers, 2019, in Japanese).

2）イントネーションの表示の仕方にはいろいろあるが，ここに提示する板書の見本はイギリス系のイントネーション研究の文献によく出て来る方法で，楽譜のような形をしているので分かりやすい．たとえば，J. C. Wells, *English Intonation: An introduction* (Cambridge, 2006) で使われている．

There are different ways of representing intonation. The sample illustrations given in this book follow the visual notation system often used in the British literature on intonation. Used in Wells (2006, cited above), for example, it is easy for learners to understand, as it looks like a musical score.

第 2 章

1）/θ/ は「無声音」と呼ぶべきものだが，平易な「ささやき」という言い方も使った．正確には，ささやくときは声帯がある程度閉じていて，声帯のところを空気が通るノイズが聞こえる．無声音の場合は声帯が開いている．

/θ/ should be called a voiceless sound, but I have also used the everyday word "whispering." Technically, when one whispers, one's glottis is closed to some degree so that noise is created when air goes through it. When a voiceless sound is articulated, on the other hand, the glottis is open.

2）問題の原因について述べると，/θ/ のときには舌をかみすぎないのに /ð/ のときには舌をかみすぎる学習者がいた場合，この学習者は，/θ/ から日本語のサ，シ，ス，セ，ソのアタマの子音を連想し，/ð/ から日本語のダ，デ，ドのアタマの子音を連想していると考えられる．

The cause of this problem may be that learners sometimes associate /θ/ with the initial consonant in "sa," "shi," "su," "se," and "so" in Japanese, which does not require the speaker to stop the flow of air when saying it, whereas they associate /ð/ with the initial consonant in "da," "de," and "do" in Japanese, which does require the speaker to stop the flow of air when saying it.

第 3 章

1）この現象は発音指導上はめったに取り上げられないが以前から存在していた現象で，リスニング訓練をしていると，学習者を困らせる発音として浮上する可能性がある．A. J. Bronstein, *The Pronunciation of American English: An introduction to phonetics* (Prentice-Hall, 1960), pp. 156–157 および J. C. Wells, *Accents of English* (CUP, 1982), pp. 477–479 にこの音が使われやすい音声環境について記述あり．

This phenomenon is rarely mentioned in pronunciation teaching but has existed for a long time. It may surface as the cause of a problem for learners when they are being trained in listening comprehension. Description of the phonetic environments in which it is likely to occur is given in Bronstein (1960, cited above) and Wells (1982, cited above).

第 5 章

1) このトラブルの原因は日本語の音体系である．日本語では，サとシャ，スとシュ，セとシェ，ソとショとを区別する．たとえば，サカ（坂）とシャカ（釈迦），スキ（鋤，好き）とシュキ（手記），セード（制度）とシェード（日よけ），ソリ（雪上の乗り物である「そり」）とショリ（処理）といった単語のペアを言うとき，それぞれのペアにおいてふたつの単語のアタマで別の音を使う．しかし，イという母音があとに続く場合，ふたつの子音の間に意味につながる区別がない．

The cause of this problem is the Japanese sound system. Japanese has the following distinctions:

"sa" and "sha," e.g. "saka" ("slope") and "shaka" ("Buddha")

"su" and "shu," e.g. "suki" ("plow," "like") and "shuki" ("memorandum")

"se" and "she," e.g. "seido" ("system") and "sheedo" ("shade")

"so" and "sho," e.g. "sori" ("sled") and "shori" ("processing")

But there is no distinction between the two consonants that affects meaning when the "i" vowel follows.

第 7 章

1) 多くの日本の学習者にとって /wʊ/ /wu:/ が難しい，という問題の原因をもし ALT などに説明しなくてはならない場合，次のように言うことができる．/wa/ は，本来の日本語の発音のシステムのなかにあり，/wi/ /we/ /wo/ は外来語のなかに現れる．いずれも，表記も発音も可能である．しかし，/wu/ については表記の仕方も発音の仕方も日本語には存在せず，/wʊ/ に始まる英単語から来る外来語はウで始まる（たとえば wood はウッドとなり，woman はウーマンとなる）．以上を表にすると次のようになる．

The cause of this problem is as follows. /wa/ exists in the Japanese sound system, while /wi/, /we/, and /wo/ appear in loanwords. These syllables can be represented in writing and pronounced as such in Japanese. /wu/, on the other hand, cannot be either written or pronounced in Japanese. English words that begin with /wʊ/, such as *wood* or *woman*, are instead pronounced with /u(:)/, without the /w/ sound. See the following table.

日本語 Japanese	外来語になった英単語 English word loaned to Japanese	下線部の日本語としての発音 Pronunciation of the underlined part in Japanese
ワタシ（watashi =“me”）		ワ /wa/
	wax	ワ /wa/
	wig	ウィ /wi/，ウイ /ui/
	wood woman	ウ /u/ ウー /uː/
	wet	ウェ /we/，ウエ /ue/
	watch	ウォ /wo/，ウオ /uo/

2）学習者が直面しやすいもうひとつの発音の問題で，/wʊ/ /wuː/ の問題と同じように五十音表の欠落部分に関連しているものとして，yeast や year の場合のように /j/ のあとに /iː/ や /ɪ/ が来る音の組み合わせの発音がある．これらの組み合わせは，would に出て来る /wʊ/ の組み合わせほど頻度が高くない（would のほうは会話に頻繁に出て来る）ので，本章の本文では取り上げない．/j/ と /ɪ/ の組み合わせを含む単語であって，指導者として発音を教えたい単語があるとすれば，初級の学習者が習う year であろう．この語の発音を教える場合，日本語によるある架空の対話を例にとると有効である場合がある．一方の話し手が何かを指さしてあれは何かと尋ね，もう一方の人が関西方言で「家や」と答えたとすると，「家や」と言うときの舌の高さの変化は英語で year と言うときのそれに酷似している．

One other problem related to the gaps in the table of the Japanese syllabary that learners often face is the pronunciation of /j/ followed by /iː/ or /ɪ/ (as in *yeast* and *year*, for example). I am not covering this topic in the main text of this chapter, as the combination of /j/ and /iː/ or /ɪ/ does not appear so frequently as /wʊ/ (*would* occurs very frequently in oral interaction). One word that has the /j/ and /ɪ/ combination which you may wish to teach is *year*, a word invariably taught to beginning learners of English. If you do decide to teach the pronunciation of this word, you may want to cite as an example a fictitious dialogue in Japanese in which one person points at something and asks what it is and the other person responds with a Kansai accent, "Ie ya" ("It's a house"). The way in which the height of the tongue changes when one says "ie ya" in Japanese closely resembles the way in which it changes when one says *year* in English.

第9章

1) /ɚː/ は /ɝː/ と表記されることもある.

/ɚː/ may be written as /ɝː/.

2) /əː/ は /ɜː/ と表記されることもある.

/əː/ may be written as /ɜː/.

3) /ɑɚ/ ができるようになった学習者にとって, /ɪɚ/ (例 beer), /ɔɚ/ (例 door), /ʊɚ/ (例 tour), /aɪɚ/ (例 fire), /aʊɚ/ (例 hour) の最後の部分は難しくないので, これらの二重, 三重母音は本文では扱わない. これらの音を教える場合は, (a) /ɪ/ は第8章で取り上げたこと, (b) /ɔɚ/ の出だしは日本語のオと同じでよいこと, (c) /aɪɚ/ /aʊɚ/ の第二要素は第一要素ほどはっきり言わなくともよいこと, を覚えておくとよい.

I am not taking up /ɪɚ/ (as in *beer*), /ɔɚ/ (as in *door*), /ʊɚ/ (as in *tour*), /aɪɚ/ (as in *fire*), or /aʊɚ/ (as in *hour*) in the chapters of this book, as learners who have mastered /ɑɚ/ can say them without much difficulty. If you want to teach them, just remember (a) that /ɪ/ is discussed in Chapter 8, (b) that the first element of /ɔɚ/ is the same as the Japanese "o" vowel, and (c) that the second element of /aɪɚ/ and /aʊɚ/ does not have to be pronounced as clearly as the first.

第 10 章

1）caught などに出て来る /ɔː/ を /ɑ/ の母音（cot などに出て来る音）で発音する北米のネイティブスピーカーがいる（J. C. Wells, *Accents of English* (CUP, 1982), pp. 473–475）が，私は両者を別の発音で教えるべきだと考えている．イギリス系発音では区別が存在するし，また，北米系の発音をする人のなかにも区別をする人は多い．さらに，英語を外国語として話す人々を相手に話すとき，区別をしたほうが相手にとって分かりやすい英語になる．区別をしない発音にすでに慣れている帰国生などに無理に区別を強いる必要はないだろうが，区別ができる条件のもとで指導するのであれば区別をしたほうがよい，というのが私の考えである．

There are speakers of English with North American-type pronunciation who use the /ɑ/ vowel (as in *cot*) for /ɔː/ in words like *caught* (Wells, 1982, cited above), but I believe these vowels should be taught as separate sounds. The distinction does exist in British-type pronunciation, and it exists even among many speakers who use North American-type pronunciation. Furthermore, making the distinction makes one's English easy for nonnative speakers of English to follow. If you are teaching learners who have returned from abroad and who are accustomed to pronunciation where the distinction in question does not exist, it may not be necessary to force them to make the distinction. But if you are in a situation in which the distinction can be taught, it is my opinion that you should teach it.

第 12 章

1）イギリス系の発音をする人のなかに，/gl/ と /kl/ とを，それぞれ /dl/, /tl/（これらの音の通常の使い方は第 14 章で取り上げる）とほぼ同じ音で出す人がいる（A. Cruttenden, *Gimson's Pronunciation of English*, 8th ed. (Routledge, 2014), p. 182）．たとえば，glad を /dlæd/ のように，また clean を /tliːn/ のように言う人がいる．ALT のなかにこのような発音をする人がいるかもしれない．リスニングをしていてこの知識が役立つこともある．

Some speakers with British-type pronunciation use /dl/ and /tl/ (ordinary use of these sounds is discussed in Chapter 14) in place of /gl/ and /kl/, respectively (Cruttenden, 2014, cited above). For example, *glad* may be pronounced something like /dlæd/ and *clean* may be pronounced something like /tliːn/.

You may have an English-speaking co-teacher who uses this sort of pronunciation. This information may help learners with their listening comprehension.

第13章

1) この方法がうまく行くかどうかは場合によるが，もしうまく行ったとすれば，その理由は，/dr/ の組み合わせにおける /r/ が普通の /r/ ではなく，「摩擦音」と呼ばれる音の特徴を色濃く持っている，言ってみれば別の音だからである．摩擦音は zoo のアタマの /z/ や usual の途中の /ʒ/ などにその例がある．その特徴は，狭くした息の通り道から息を押し出してノイズを作る，ということである．つまり，/dr/ を教えるのであれば，そこにある /r/ の「摩擦音」的な特徴を利用して，学習者にとって発音しやすい別の摩擦音 /ʒ/ を出発点とすることによりうまく教えられるかもしれないのである．

This method may or may not work, but, if it does, the reason must be that, in a /dr/ combination, the /r/ sound is not an ordinary /r/ but a special kind of /r/ that has the characteristic of a category of sounds called fricative consonants. Fricative consonants are sounds like /z/ (used at the beginning of *zoo*, for example) and /ʒ/ (used in the middle of *usual*, for example). They are sounds such that, in order to articulate them, the speaker pushes air out through a narrow opening, creating noise. Thus, if you want to teach /dr/, you may be able to do so successfully by taking advantage of the fricative aspect of the /r/ in it and using as a starting point another fricative consonant /ʒ/, which happens to be an easy sound for learners to articulate.

第14章

1) 実は，この /l/ も含め，本章と第18章セクション1で扱う /l/ は，「暗いL」と呼ばれ，舌先と上の歯ぐきとの接点が非常に小さい．イギリス系の英語では，このような暗いLと like などにあるような母音の前に出て来る明るいLとの間にははっきりした区別がある．明るいLの場合は，舌と歯ぐきとの接触面が，後ろのほうの歯ぐきも含み，暗いLの場合より大きい．北米系の英語では /l/ は母音の前でも接触面があまり大きくなく，イギリス系のLよりは暗めのLとなる（竹林滋『英語音声学』（研究社，1996）pp. 207–208）．

The /l/ discussed in this chapter and in Section 1 of Chapter 18 is called a dark /l/ and is characterized by a particularly small contact area between the tongue tip and the upper teeth ridge. In British-type pronunciation, there is a clear distinction between dark /l/ and the other sort of /l/ ("clear /l/"), the latter being characterized by a larger area of contact between the tongue and the upper teeth ridge, including parts of the upper teeth ridge further toward the back, than in the case of dark /l/. In North American-type pronunciation, the area of contact in the articulation of /l/ followed by a vowel is not so large, and North American clear /l/ is more "darkish" than the British-type clear /l/ (S. Takebayashi, *Eigo Onseigaku* (Kenkyusha, 1996, in Japanese) pp. 207–208).

第 17 章

1）条件とは次の（a）（b）の少なくとも一方が当てはまる，というものである．これらの条件を明示的に教えることは得策でない．覚えるのが大変であるし，学習者が仮に覚えたとしても，英語を話しているときには，条件を思い起こしている時間などない．条件を習わなくとも，また覚えていなくとも，多くの実例に接した結果正しい条件下で /t/ のこうした発音ができるようになる学習者は大勢いる．/t/ のこうした発音を教えたければ，実例に触れさせて頂きたい．ここでは一応ご参考までに条件を挙げる．

The condition is that /t/ is in one of two phonetic environments. I would not advise you to teach the condition explicitly. It would not be easy for learners to memorize it and, if they had memorized it, they would not have time to recall it when speaking English. Many learners learn to use the reduced /t/ in the correct phonetic environments without being taught or without having memorized the condition. If you wish to teach learners about /t/, expose them to many examples. I am stating the condition below just for your information.

（a） /t/ が母音と母音に挟まれていて，後のほうの母音にアクセントがない場合．たとえば，city，better などがこの例である．city の /t/ については，直前に母音 /ɪ/ があり，直後に母音 /i/ があるから，母音と母音に挟まれている．しかも，直後の /i/ にはアクセントがないから，city の /t/ はこの条件に当てはまる．better の /t/ については，直前に母音 /e/ があり，直後に母音 /ɚ/ があるから，母音と母音に挟まれている．しかも，直後の /ɚ/ にはアクセントがないから，better の /t/ はこの条件に当てはまる．

(a) /t/ is preceded by a vowel and followed by a vowel; the second vowel is not stressed. *City* and *better* are examples of this. In the case of /t/ in *city*, it is preceded by the vowel /ɪ/ and followed by the vowel /i/, which is not stressed. In the case of /t/ in *better*, it is preceded by the vowel /e/ and followed by the vowel /ɚ/, which is not stressed.

(b) /t/ が母音と母音に挟まれていて，/t/ の直後に単語と単語の境目が来る場合．たとえば，that apple (/ðæt æpl/，あのリンゴ)，eight eggs (/eɪt egz/，8 個の卵) などがこの例．that の /t/ については，直前に母音 /æ/ があり，直後に母音 /æ/ があるから，母音と母音に挟まれている．しかも，/t/ は that という単語の最後の音であるから，/t/ の直後には単語と単語の境がある．eight の /t/ については，直前に母音 /eɪ/ があり，直後に母音 /e/ があるから，母音と母音に挟まれている．しかも，/t/ は eight という単語の最後の音であるから，/t/ の直後には単語と単語の境がある．

(b) /t/ is preceded by a vowel and followed by a vowel; there is a word boundary right after /t/. *That apple* (/ðæt æpl/) and *eight eggs* (/eɪt egz/) are examples of this. In the case of /t/ in *that*, it is preceded by the vowel /æ/ and followed also by the vowel /æ/. There is a word boundary after /t/. In the case of /t/ in *eight*, it is preceded by the vowel /eɪ/ and followed by the vowel /e/. There is a word boundary after /t/.

(a) (b) 両方が当てはまる例には，eight o'clock (/eɪt əklɑk/，「8 時」) の /t/，it arrived (/ɪt əraɪvd/，「それは到着した」) の /t/ などを挙げることができる．

/t/ in *eight o'clock* (/eɪt əklɑk/) and /t/ in *it arrived* (/ɪt əraɪvd/) are examples to which both (a) and (b) apply.

第 18 章

1) /l/ のこのくずれは，次のような場合にも起こり得る．ただし，話し方が極端に速いかくだけているかである場合に限る．

(a) /k/, /g/ の前：/lk/，たとえば mil̲k̲；/lg/，たとえば Bul̲g̲aria
(b) /f/, /v/ の前：/lf/，たとえば mysel̲f̲；/lv/，たとえば oursel̲v̲es
(c) /p/, /b/, /m/ の前：/lp/，たとえば hel̲p̲；/lb/，たとえば bul̲b̲；/lm/，たとえば el̲m̲
(d) /j/ の前：/lj/，たとえば tel̲l̲ you
(e) 単語の最後：たとえば bel̲l̲

P. Avery and S. Ehrlich, *Teaching American English Pronunciation* (OUP,

1992）は，dark /l/ の例として feel の /l/ を挙げ，この音のとき舌は歯ぐきにつかなくてもよい（need not touch）とすら述べている．教育的にはこれほど高い許容度に対しては賛否があるだろうが，日本の学習者がルで代用するよりはずっと問題が少ないと思われる．

/l/ reduction may occur in the following environments, if the speaker is speaking extremely fast or speaking in an extremely informal style.

（a） followed by /k/ and /g/, as in *milk* and *Bulgaria*
（b） followed by /f/ and /v/, as in *myself* and *ourselves*
（c） followed by /p/, /b/, and /m/, as in *help*, *bulb*, and *elm*
（d） followed by /j/, as in *tell you*
（e） in a word-final position, as in *bell*

Avery and Ehrlich（1992, cited above）cite /l/ in *feel* as an example of dark /l/ and say that the tongue need not touch the teeth ridge in the articulation of this sound. Teachers' opinions will differ on such a high degree of permissiveness, but this reduced pronunciation will at least be less problematical than the Japanese syllable "ru," which learners in Japan are liable to substitute for the proper dark /l/.

2）/j/ の前の /t/ もかなり高い確率でのどを使った /t/ になる（例：Not yet. の最初の /t/）．ただ，/tj/ の場合は，第 17 章セクション 1 で説明した /tʃ/ にくずれるオプションがあるので，ここでは取り上げないことにする．

/t/ followed by /j/ is highly likely to be reduced to a glottal /t/, too, but I am not including /tj/ in our discussion here, as one may opt to say /tʃ/ for /tj/（see Section 1 of Chapter 17）.

3） 母音の際に舌が口の天井にどのように触れるかは，その母音の質による．ここではこの問題は関係ないので，全く触れない状態のイラストを示した．

How the tongue comes into contact with the roof of the mouth depends on the vowel. As this issue does not concern our discussion here, the illustration given here shows the roof of the mouth when it is not in contact with the tongue at all.

4）この母音を入れる発音は，/sl/ が母音の前に来た場合（sleep，wrestler）には行わないが，そうでない場合（wrestle，wrestled）には実際に行われる．castle，whistle，muscle，wrestle など，語末に /sl/ が来る場合の発音においては，/stl/ の組み合わせを使わない．むしろ，母音を入れて /səl/ と言ったり，/l/ を犠

牲にしてそれを /ʊ/ や /o/ のような母音で代用したりする．つまり，/sl/ の組み合わせの扱い方は，それがどのような場所に来るかで分かれる．

Insertion of the vowel does not take place when /sl/ is followed by a vowel, as in *sleep* and *wrestler*, but does take place otherwise, as in *wrestle*, and *wrestled*. Word-final /sl/, as in *castle*, *whistle, muscle*, and *wrestle*, is not changed to /stl/. At the end of a word, the speaker may say /səl/ or, sacrificing /l/, just say a vowel like /ʊ/ or /o/ after /s/. How /sl/ is treated thus depends on the phonetic environment in which it occurs.

第 19 章

1)「音節」の意味でここでは「拍」ということばを使った．

I am referring to the *syllable* by the word "beat."

2) 英語の強さについては，一部の学習者の間に誤解があるように思われる．すなわち，日本の学習者のなかには，英語とは強く発音しなくてはならない言語である，と思っている人がいるようである．実際には，弱い発音でものを言うクセの英語母語話者もいれば，日ごろ発音が明瞭な人が第三者に聞かれたくない私語を弱い発音ですることもあり得る．英語は強く発音する言語，という誤解があるとすれば，ひとつの原因は，気音の存在かもしれない．英語では，ある種の音がある環境のもとで，気音— /h/ のような息の音—を伴って発音されることがある．たとえば，time（/taɪm/）という単語において，/t/ の直後に気音が入る．この気音を，「発音が強いから出る音」と誤って解釈している学習者がいるかもしれない．実際には気音は単に声を伴わない息にすぎず，その息は別に強いとは限らない．

There seems to be a misunderstanding among some learners about the force with which articulation is made in English: Some learners in Japan seem to think that English is a language that is characterized by forceful articulation as a necessary feature. The fact is that there are English speakers who habitually articulate sounds weakly and that a speaker may be engaged in a private conversation and articulate sounds weakly because he or she does not want to be overheard by a third party. If the misunderstanding that English is a forcefully articulated language does exist, one cause of this may be the existence of aspiration. In English, certain sounds in certain phonetic environments are articulated with aspiration—a /h/-like sound. For example, in the word *time*

(/taɪm/), /t/ is accompanied with aspiration. There may be learners who think that such aspiration is the result of forceful articulation. In fact, aspiration is nothing but voiceless breath, which may not be particularly strong.

3) 第9章のセクション1でイギリス系の発音に登場する /əː/ について述べた．/əː/ がアクセントが置かれる，安定した音であるのに対して，/ə/ はアクセントのない位置に現れる，力を入れずに発音する音であり，力の抜き加減は話す速度や丁寧さに影響されるため，安定した音とは言いがたい．ただ，「アゴを閉じ気味にして出すア」であるという点で両者はほぼ同じであり，導入時の明示的説明としてはどちらの音についてもこの説明で十分であると私は考えている．

There was discussion in Section 1 of Chapter 9 about /əː/, which appears in British-type pronunciation. While /əː/ is a stable sound that appears in stressed syllables, /ə/ appears in unstressed syllables, is articulated without much force, and is unstable in the sense that the force with which it is said depends on the speed and the degree of formality with which the speaker is speaking. But /ə/ and /əː/ are similar in that they are both an /a/-like sound produced without much opening between the jaws, and mention of this general characteristic of the sounds is sufficient in my opinion as explicit description for initially introducing either of these sounds to learners.

4) 弱形は，冠詞，人称代名詞，関係代名詞，不定代名詞，be 動詞，助動詞，前置詞，接続詞などの単音節語に見られ，その他 just, some なども弱形を持つ．

Weak forms are found in certain monosyllabic words such as articles, personal pronouns, relative pronouns, indefinite pronouns, the verb *be*, auxiliaries, prepositions, and conjunctions. Words such as *just* and *some* also have a weak form.

5) 英語ではアクセントのある拍が等間隔に現れる，と言われるが，これは単なる傾向にすぎず，厳密なルールではない．間隔は，アクセントのある拍と拍の間にアクセントのない拍がいくつあるか，アクセントのない拍にある母音は何か，などの要素の影響を受ける．くわしくは，たとえば A. Cruttenden, *Gimson's Pronunciation of English*, 8th ed. (Routledge, 2014) の第 11 章を参照されたい．

A point is sometimes made that stressed syllables appear at regular intervals in English. This is only a tendency and is not a hard-and-fast rule. The distance between stressed syllables depends upon how many unstressed syllables there are between them, what vowels are used in those unstressed syllables, etc. For further information, see Chapter 11 in Cruttenden (2014, cited above).

6) 発音を教えるのではなく，学習を楽しくして学習者のモチベーションを上げる趣旨で，センテンスを速く言わせる指導法が使われることがある．この意義を否定するものではない．

This statement is not meant to deny the significance of rapid oral reading, which is sometimes used as a fun activity intended to raise learners' motivation.

7) デフォルトの型なるものが本当に存在するかどうかは議論が分かれるものの，存在を想定することは少なくとも教育的には有意義であると考えられる．たとえば，J. C. Wells, *English Intonation: An introduction* (CUP, 2006) pp. 91–92 参照．

It is questionable whether default patterns of intonation exist or not, but assuming the existence of such patterns could be meaningful at least from a pedagogical point of view. See Wells (2006, cited above, pp. 91–92).

8) 専門的には「核の配置」として論じられる．前掲書 Wells (2006) pp. 93–186 および A. Cruttenden, *Intonation* (CUP, 1986) pp. 80–95 参照．

Technically referred to as the placement of the nucleus, or, as Wells (2006, cited above) calls it, "tonicity." See Wells (2006, cited above) pp. 93–186 and Cruttenden (1986, cited above), pp. 80–95.

9) センテンスが前掲書 Wells (2006) に言うイントネーションフレーズ 1 個で成り立っている場合．

If the sentence consists of one intonation phrase, as Wells (2006, cited above) calls it.

10) 前掲書 Wells (2006) 第 3 章参照．

See Chapter 3 of Wells (2006, cited above) for further information.

第20章

1）大規模な調査を行い，音を学習者にとっての難度別に並べる方法はあるだろうが，学習者の発達プロセスには個人差が非常に大きいこと（指導を始めればすぐに分かる！），発音できない人の数とその音の難しさとは同じではないこと（習えばすぐできるようになる音なのに，その音についての知識が広まっていないために，その音を発音できる学習者が少ない，という場合もある），などの問題が現実にはあり，統計をもとにして音に一般性の高い難度の序列をつけることは容易ではないと思われる．ここでは，むしろ，指導者が主観的に設定した段階であれ，昇級，昇段のシステムにより学習者がモチベーションをもって学習してくれることが大事，という考え方をとっている．

There will be methods of conducting a large-scale study on learners' pronunciation to arrange sounds in the order of difficulty for them. But it would be difficult to classify sounds into a highly generalizable hierarchy of levels on the basis of statistical data, because learners' pronunciation improves through vastly varied processes of development (as you will find out as soon as you start teaching!) and the percentage of learners who cannot pronounce a certain sound does not necessarily reflect how difficult it is to learn (some sounds are easy to learn but are not correctly pronounced by many learners simply because not many learners know how to articulate them). I am rather inclined to attach importance to the motivation that learners get from the system of promotion, if organized merely on the basis of the instructor's subjective judgment.

2）中尾清秋（1916–2014）・元早稲田大学教授

Professor Nakao Kiyoaki (1916–2014), who taught at Waseda University.

3）第19章注6に述べた通り，発音向上とは別の目的で速く言わせる指導法は行われることがあり，この意義についてコメントするものではない．

This is not a comment on the significance of making learners speak fast for purposes other than improvement in their pronunciation. See note 6 to Chapter 19.

4）五十嵐新次郎（1915–1975）・元早稲田大学教授

Professor Igarashi Shinjiro (1915–1975), who taught at Waseda University.

参考文献
References

I. 本書で言及した本

Avery, P., and Ehrlich, S. 1992. *Teaching American English Pronunciation*. OUP.（第 18 章注 1 で言及）

Bronstein, A. J. 1960. *The Pronunciation of American English: An introduction to phonetics*. Prentice-Hall.（第 3 章注 1 で言及）

Cruttenden, A. 1986. *Intonation*. CUP.（第 19 章注 8 で言及）

Cruttenden, A. 2014. *Gimson's Pronunciation of English*. 8th ed. Routledge.（「本書において言及される小道具など」注 1，第 12 章注 1，および第 19 章注 5 で言及）

Jones, D. 1960. *An Outline of English Phonetics*. 9th ed. Heffer. Reprint, Maruzen.（「本書において言及される小道具など」注 1 で言及）

Wells, J. C. 1982. *Accents of English*. CUP.（第 3 章注 1，第 10 章注 1 で言及）

Wells, J. C. 2006. *English Intonation: An introduction*. CUP.（「本書において言及される小道具など」注 2，第 19 章注 7，8，9，10 で言及）

鈴木渉・西原哲雄編．2019．『小学校英語のためのスキルアップセミナー：理論と実践を往還する』開拓社．（「まえがき」で言及）

竹内京子・木村琢也．2019．『たのしい音声学』くろしお出版．（「本書において言及される小道具など」注 1 で言及）

竹林滋．1996．『英語音声学』研究社．（「まえがき」注 1，第 14 章注 1 で言及）

II. その他，指導者の参考になりそうな本

(a) 英語発音・英語音声学関係の本

神山孝夫．2008．『脱・日本語なまり：英語（+α）実践音声学』大阪大学出版会．

静哲人．2019．『日本語ネイティブが苦手な英語の音とリズムの作り方がいちばんよくわかる発音の教科書』テイエス企画．

竹林滋・清水あつ子・斎藤弘子．2013．『初級英語音声学』改訂新版．大修館書店．

牧野武彦．2005．『日本人のための英語音声学レッスン』大修館書店．

松坂ヒロシ．1986．『英語音声学入門』研究社．

御園和夫編．2009.『英語発音指導マニュアル』北星堂.

Celce-Murcia, M., Brinton, D. M., and Goodwin, J. M. 2010. *Teaching Pronunciation: A course book and reference guide*. 2nd ed. CUP.

Roach, P. 2009. *English Phonetics and Phonology: A practical course.* 4th ed. CUP.

(b) イントネーションに特化した本

Brazil, D. 1997. *The Communicative Value of Intonation in English*. CUP.

O'Connor, J. D., and Arnold, G. F. 1973. *Intonation of Colloquial English*. 2nd ed. Longman.［片山嘉雄・長瀬慶來・長瀬恵美共編訳『イギリス英語のイントネーション』南雲堂，1994］

Wells, J. C.『英語のイントネーション』長瀬慶來監訳，研究社，2009（上記 I に挙げた Wells, 2006 の邦訳）.

付録—チェックリスト見本
Appendix: Pronunciation checklists

チェックリスト見本（1）：教材の範囲をカバーするチェクリスト

Dialogue

A: Is the police station far from here?

B: No. It's just around the corner to the left.

A: How far is it from the corner?

B: About a hundred meters.

発音チェックリスト

キーワード	文中の語
hit の /ɪ/	□ is □ it's
this の /ð/	□ the
like の /l/	□ police □ left
see の /iː/	□ police
she の /ʃ/	□ station
fine の /f/	□ far □ from
deer の /ɪɚ/	□ here
right の /r/	□ around
butter の /ɚ/	□ corner □ meter

チェックリスト見本（2）：日本語からの連想に基づくチェックリスト

1 「ア」（"a"）に聞こえる音と，その仲間

□1.1 /æ/ pat □1.2 /ɑ/ pot □1.3 /ə/ appear □1.4 /ʌ/ cut □1.5 /ɚː/ bird
□1.6 /aɪ/ kind □1.7 /aʊ/ sound □1.8 /aɪɚ/ fire □1.9 /aʊɚ/ our

2 「イ」（"i"）に聞こえる音と，その仲間

□2.1 /iː/ sheep □2.2 /ɪ/ ship □2.3 /ɪɚ/ ear □2.4 /jɪɚ/ year

3 「ウ」（"u"）に聞こえる音と，その仲間

□3.1 /uː/ boot □3.2 /ʊ/ book □3.3 /ʊɚ/ poor □3.4 /wʊ/ would

4 「エ」（"e"）に聞こえる音と，その仲間

□4.1 /e/ bed □4.2 /eɪ/ bake □4.3 /eɚ/ air

5 「オ」（“o”）に聞こえる音と，その仲間

□5.1 /ɔ:/ /ɑ:/ caught □5.2 /oʊ/ coat □5.3 /ɔɪ/ boy □5.4 /ɔɚ/ or

6 ガ行子音 (initial consonant in “ga,” “gi,” “gu,” “ge,” and “go”) に聞こえる音

□6.1 /ŋg/ finger □6.2 /ŋ/ singer

7 サ行子音 (initial consonant in “sa,” “shi,” “su,” “se,” and “so”) に聞こえる音

□7.1 /s/ sank □7.2 /θ/ thank □7.3 /tθ/ eighth

8 「シ」（“shi”）に聞こえる音

□8.1 /s/ sip □8.2 /ʃ/ ship

9 ザ行子音 (initial consonant in “za,” “ji,” “zu,” “ze,” and “zo”) に聞こえる音

□9.1 /ð/ these □9.2 /z/ Z’s（/zi:z/） □9.3 /z/ cars □9.4 /dz/ cards
□9.5 /dθ/ width

10 「ジ」（“ji”）に聞こえる音

□10.1 /dʒ/ e.g.（/i:dʒi:/） □10.2 /z/ easy

11 「ジュ」（“ju”）に聞こえる音

□11.1 /ʒ/ visual □11.2 /dʒ/ individual □11.3 /dr/ drive（*not* derive）

12 タ行子音 (initial consonant in “ta,” “chi,” “tsu,” “te,” and “to”) に聞こえる音

□12.1 /tl/ battle □12.2 /tʃ/ each city □12.3 /tʃ/ each time
□12.4 /tʃ/ each theme

13 ダ行子音（initial consonant in “da,” “de,” “do”）に聞こえる音

□13.1 /ð/ they □13.2 /d/ [ɾ] ladder □13.3 /t/ [ɾ] latter
□13.4 /dθ/ width □13.5 /dl/ saddle

14 「ツ」（“tsu”）に聞こえる音と，その仲間

□14.1 /ts/ cents □14.2 /s/ [(t)s] sense □14.3 /tθ/ eighth
□14.4 /θs/ [ts] months

15 「チャ」「チュ」「チェ」「チョ」（“cha,” “chu,” “che,” and “cho”）に聞こえる音

□15.1 /tʃ/ chain □15.2 /tr/ train（*not* terrain）

16 ナ行子音（initial consonant in "na," "ni," "nu," "ne," and "no"）に聞こえる音

□16.1 /n/ in an hour □16.2 /n/ center (*not* sender) □16.3 /nj/ can you
□16.4 /nw/ can we □16.5 /nr/ Henry □16.6 /nl/ final

17 「ヒ」（"hi"）に聞こえる音と，その仲間

□17.1 /h/ he □17.2 /f/ fee

18 「フ」（"fu"）に聞こえる音

□18.1 /h/ who □18.2 /f/ food

19 バ行子音（initial consonant in "ba," "bi," "bu," "be," and "bo"）に聞こえる音

□19.1 /b/ berry □19.2 /v/ very

20 「ファ」「フィ」「フェ」（"fa," "fi," and "fe"）に聞こえる音

□20.1 /(h)w/ wheat □20.2 /f/ feet

21 ラ行子音（initial consonant in "ra," "ri," "ru," "re," and "ro"）に聞こえる音

□21.1 /r/ right □21.2 /l/ light □21.3 /l/ railing
□21.4 /t/ [ɾ] rating □21.5 /d/ [ɾ] raiding

22 「ン」（"n"）に聞こえる音と，その仲間

□22.1 /n/ ten □22.2 /tn/ eaten

チェックリスト見本 (3)：レベル別の項目立てをしたチェックリスト

発音道五級

レベルの概要：基本的に，日本語の音を使えばよい．

5.1 母音分野　set，say，sign，soy，sound
5.2 破裂音分野　boy，do，go，Spain，stay，sky
5.3 摩擦音分野　hi，say，shine　5.4 破擦音分野　chain，juice
5.5 鼻音分野　nice，hint，send，bunch，change，mouse
5.6 /w/ 分野　wine　5.7 /j/ 分野　yes
5.8 語中の /z/（i 系の前でない）　misery，prosaic　5.9 語中の /z/（i 系の前）

easy

四級への昇級：合格　□

発音道四級

レベルの概要：一通りの説明で十分．発音は非常に易しい．

4.1　子音分野　子音の後に「ウ」のような母音を入れないこと．beep，jet，make，web，Ned，egg

4.2　軟口蓋破裂＋/iː/　keep，geese

4.3 破擦音分野　its，each

4.4 鼻音分野（母音間の n が出来れば合格）an hour

4.5　抑揚分野（声域の最低レベルが使えれば合格．あまり知られていないが，英語らしさの重要要素．）hi，say，dime

三級への昇級：合格　□

発音道三級

レベルの概要：一通りの説明で十分．発音は易しいが，発言中，忘れがち．

3.1 摩擦音分野　/θ/ think　/ð/ this

3.2 鼻音分野　語末の /n/　Come in.　Hi, everyone.

3.3 側音分野　light　3.4 /r/ 分野　right

二級への昇級：合格　□

発音道二級

レベルの概要：一通りの説明で十分．発音の難度は普通．

2.1 鼻音分野　/n/＋母音の繰り返し　an announcer

2.2 側音分野　語中の /l/:　collect　2.3 /r/ 分野　語中の /r/:　correct

一級への昇級：合格　□

発音道一級

レベルの概要：一通りの説明で十分．発音はやや難．

摩擦音分野　1.1 語末の /z/ ease　1.2 /f/ fine

1.3 /v/ very（強調などの目的で，/v/ が持続できること）

破擦音がらみの組み合わせ　1.4 /tst/ It's time.

1.5 /tsr/ That's right.　1.6 /tʃtʃ/ each child

鼻音分野　1.7 in Paris　1.8 ten men　1.9 in Cairo, ten guests

1.10 /r/ 分野　bring　1.11 /l/ 分野　block

初段への昇段：合格　□

発音道初段

レベルの概要：やや分かりにくいが説明可能な事柄.

A-1　歯音化　in this, write this, made this

A-2 摩擦音分野　/ʃiː/ she と /siː/ see の区別

A-3 鼻音分野　dance, answer, can we, can you, infant

二段への昇段：合格　□

発音道二段

レベルの概要：母音の要練習項目：R 音性あり，なし.

母音分野　B-1 sit, B-2 seat, B-3 mast, B-4 must, B-5 socks, B-6 bought, B-7 boat, B-8 book, B-9 boot, B-10 bird, B-11 air, B-12 door, B-13 art, B-14 poor, B-15 beer, B-16 nearer, B-17 mirror

B-18 鼻音分野　/mf/ comfort　　B-19 側音分野　feel

B-20 抑揚分野　JOHN ate that cake after dinner, not ME.

三段への昇段：合格　□

発音道三段

レベルの概要：母音，子音の要練習項目.

破裂音分野　語中無開放　C-1 obtain, C-2 handbook, C-3 rugby, C-4 captain, C-5 football, C-6 blackboard

語末無開放　C-7 cap, C-8 hat, C-9 back, C-10 Bob, C-11 Ned, C-12 dog

Tap　C-13 /t/ [ɾ] it is, Katie, /d/ [ɾ] made it

Glottal stop　C-14 it was, C-15 not you, C-16 Is that right?, C-17 Did we?

破擦音分野　C-18 train（terrain と区別できる），C-19 drive（derive と区別できる），C-20 鼻音分野　Henry

側音分野　C-21 camel, C-22 will you, C-23 fly, C-24 parcel, C-25 nozzle

C-26 /r/ 分野 grow, /r/ /l/ 分野　C-27 lorry, C-28 relate, C-29 peril, C-30 Cyril

四段への昇段：合格　□

発音道四段

レベルの概要：/z/ /ʒ/ /dz/ /dʒ/ 関係の音.

母音分野　D-1 accept, D-2 universe, D-3 ability

破裂音分野（Aspiration）D-4 pine, D-5 time, D-6 kind

摩擦音分野　D-7 /z/（th の前）is the　D-8 語頭の /z/（i 系の前でない）zoo

D-9 /z/（i 系の前）zeal　D-10 /ʒ/ visual（individual と区別できる）measure（major，larger と区別できる）

破擦音分野　D-11 語末の /dʒ/ cage　D-12 語中の /dʒ/ major

五段への昇段：合格　□

発音道五段

レベルの概要：超難.

破裂音分野　E-1 finger（singer と区別できる）E-2 acts（無開放），E-3 lecture（無開放）

摩擦音分野　E-4 he，E-5 who　E-6 /z/ と /dz/ の区別が出来れば合格．cars / cards

鼻音分野　E-7 in his，E-8 king，E-9 singer（finger と区別できる）

側音分野　E-10 climb，E-11 glow，E-12 national，E-13 slow　/r/ 分野 E-14（無声化）pray，cry　E-15 /w/ 分野　would（ooze と区別できる）

六段への昇段：合格　□

発音道六段

レベルの概要：摩擦音，破擦音関係の超超難のアイテム．

（摩擦音と摩擦音の組み合わせ）F-1 /sð/ miss them，F-2 /vz/ lives，F-3 /fθ/ fifth　F-4 /vð/ move them，F-5 /sθ/ sixth

（破擦音と摩擦音の組み合わせ）F-6 /tsð/ That's that.　F-7 /tsθ/ It's thin.

F-8 /tsʃ/ It's chic.　F.9 /tʃz/ each zoo，F.10 /tʃθ/ each theme，

F.11 /tʃs/ each city

七段への昇段：合格　□

発音道七段

レベルの概要：かなりの英語達人のうちにも，出来ない人が多い．

（t, d の nasal plosion ができる）G-1 eaten，G-2 sudden

（Partial devoicing - fricative）G-3 move，G-4 cars

（Partial devoicing - affricate）G-5 judge，G-6 cards

G-7 /kl/ [tl] clear（British），G-8 /gl/ [dl] glass（British）

八段への昇段：合格　□

発音道八段

レベルの概要：超超難.

破裂音分野（nasal plosion）H-1 topmost，H-2 submarine，（lateral plosion）

H-3 might like，H-4 deadline，H-5 little，H-6 saddle
摩擦音分野　H-7 語末の /ʒ/ rouge，H-8 語中の /ʒɪz/ garages，
H-9 語頭の /ʒ/ gigue
/ɚ(:)/＋/l/ 分野　H-10 girl，H-11 Carl，F-12 world
/w/ 分野　H-13 woo　　/j/ 分野　H-14 yield，H-15 year
八段：合格　□

チェックリスト見本（4）：指導者業務用のチェックリスト

音のみのリストです．抑揚などは含まれていません．音素ごとに項目が並んでいます．リストは網羅的ではなく，また，同じ音の項目が異なった焦点のもと複数回登場する場合もあり，分類は必ずしも整ったものではありませんが，発音しにくい項目を数多く並べ，これが全部できれば発音の指導者として困ることはさほどないだろうとの思いで作りました．このリストを使う場合は，まず音声学の基礎を学ばれることをお勧めします．

/p/ ... □ 1. Aspirated (pipe)　□ 2. Unaspirated (speak)
□ 3. Unreleased (captain, cap)　□ 4. Nasal (topmost)
/b/ ... □ 1. Released (boy)　□ 2. Unreleased (obtain, Bob)
□ 3. Nasal (submarine)
/t/ ... □ 1. Aspirated (time)　□ 2. Unaspirated (stay)
□ 3 Unreleased (football, hat)　□ 4. Nasal (eaten)
□ 5. Lateral (battle, might like)　□ 6. Tapped (better, at all)
□ 7. Dental (eighth)　□ 8. Palatoalveolar (won't you)
□ 9. Postalveolar (tree)　□ 10. Glottal (it was, it really, that year)
□ 11. Dropped (twenty)
/d/ ... □ 1. Released (day)　□ 2. Unreleased (handbook, Ned)
□ 3. Nasal (sudden)　□ 4. Lateral (deadline, would like)
□ 5. Tapped (sadder)　□ 6. Dental (add them)
□ 7. Palatoalveolar (would you)　□ 8. Postalveolar (dry)　□ 9. Glottal (did we)
/k/ ... □ 1. Aspirated (cat)　□ 2. Unaspirated (skate)
□ 3. Unreleased (blackboard, back)　□ 4. Nasal ([kŋ] bacon)
□ 5. Lateral (Br.) (/kl/ [tl] clear)
/g/ ... □ 1. Released (go)　□ 2. Unreleased (rugby, dog)
□ 3. Lateral (Br.) (/gl/ [dl] glass)
/f/ ... □ 1. Initial, medial, final (fine, offer, laugh)

□ 2. Followed by /θ/ (fifth) □ 3. Preceded by /m/ (comfort)
/v/ ... □ 1. Initial, medial, final (very, ever, move)
□ 2. Partially devoiced (move) □ 3. Followed by /z/ (lives)
/θ/ ... □ 1. Initial, medial, final (thick, author, myth)
□ 2. Preceded by /p/ (depth) □ 3. Preceded by /f/ (fifth) □ 4. Preceded by /s/ (sixth)
□ 5. Preceded by /m/ (warmth) □ 6. Preceded by /l/ (health)
□ 7. Preceded by /ɚː/ (earth) □ 8. Followed by /r/ (three)
/ð/ ... □ 1. Initial, medial, final (this, father, smooth)
□ 2. Partially devoiced (breathe) □ 3. Preceded by /v/ (move them)
□ 4. Followed by /z/ (clothes, mouths) □ 5. Dropped (clothes)
/s/ ... □ 1. Initial, medial, final (sea, messy, miss)
□ 2. Followed by /θ/ (this thought) □ 3. Followed by /ð/ (miss the)
/z/ ... □ 1. Initial, medial, final (zoo, easy, size)
□ 2. Partially devoiced (cars) □ 3. Followed by /θ/ (as thick)
□ 4. Followed by /ð/ (as that)
/ʃ/ ... □ 1. Initial, medial, final (she, washing, rush)
□ 2. Followed by /(ə)n/ (nation) □ 3. Followed by /θ/ (fresh theory)
□ 4. Followed by /ð/ (wash that)
/ʒ/ ... □ 1. Initial, medial, final (gigue, usual, garage)
□ 2. Partially devoiced (garage)
/h/ ... □ 1. Initial, medial (hat, perhaps) □ 2. Followed by /iː/ (he)
□ 3. Followed by /ɪ/ (hit) □ 4. Followed by /ʊ/ (hook) □ 5. Followed by /uː/ (who)
□ 6. Dropped (drive his car)
/ts/ ... □ 1. Medial, final (Betzy, cats) □ 2. Followed by /t/ (It's time.)
□ 3. Followed by /θ/ (It's thin.) □ 4. Followed by /ð/ (That's that.)
□ 5. Followed by /ʃ/ (It's chic.) □ 6. Followed by /r/ (That's right.)
□ 7. Preceded by /k/ (acts)
/dz/ ... □ 1. Final (cards) □ 2. Partially devoiced (cards)
/tʃ/ ... □ 1. Initial, medial, final (chain, luncheon, each)
□ 2. Followed by /t/ (each time) □ 3. Followed by /θ/ (each theme)
□ 4.Followed by /s/ (each city) □ 5. Followed by /tʃ/ (each child)
□ 6. Preceded by /k/ (lecture)
/dʒ/ ... □ 1. Initial, medial, final (Japan, apology, cage)
□ 2. Partially devoiced (large)
/tr/ ... □ 1. Initial, medial (tree, poetry)
/dr/ ... □ 1. Initial, medial (dry, quadrangle)
/m/ ... □ 1. Followed by /θ/ (something)
□ 2. Followed by /f/ (comfort)

/n/ ... □ 1. Followed by /iː/ (neat) □ 2. Followed by /ɪ/ (knit)
□ 3. Followed by a word boundary and a vowel (in an hour)
□ 4. Followed by /p/ (in Paris) □ 5. Followed by /b/ (sunburn)
□ 6. Followed by /k/ (on cold days) □ 7. Followed by /g/ (ten guests)
□ 8. Followed by /θ / (tenth) □ 9. Followed by /ð/ (in this)
□ 10. Followed by /f/ (infant) □ 11. Followed by /s/ (dance)
□ 12. Followed by /z/ (pansy) □ 13. Followed by /h/ (in his house)
□ 14. Followed by /m/ (ten million) □ 15. Followed by /j/ (can you)
□ 16. Followed by /r/ (unrest) □ 17. Followed by /w/ (can we)
□ 18. Final (Come in.)

/ŋ/ ... □ 1. Medial, final (singer <cf. finger>, going)

/l/ ... □ 1. Initial, medial, final (like, collect, sell)
□ 2. Preceded by /iː/ (feel) □ 3. Preceded by /ɪ/ (fill) □ 4. Preceded by /uː/ (pool)
□ 5. Preceded by /ʊ/ (pull) □ 6. Preceded by /ɚ(ː) / (Carl, girl, world)
□ 7. Preceded by /m(ə)/ (camel) □ 8. Preceded by /n(ə)/ (final)
□ 9. Preceded by /s(ə)/ (parcel) □ 10. Preceded by /z(ə)/ (nozzle)
□ 11. Preceded by /p/, partially devoiced (place) □ 12. Preceded by /b/ (block)
□ 13. Preceded by /t/ (settle) □ 14. Preceded by /d/ (saddle)
□ 15. Preceded by /k/, partially devoiced (class) □ 16. Preceded by /g/ (glass)
□ 17. Preceded by /f/ (fly) □ 18. Preceded by /s/ (slow)
□ 19. Preceded by /rɪ/ (relate, peril, Cyril) □ 20. Followed by /r/ (jewelry)
□ 21. Followed by /j/ (will you)

/w/ ... □ 1. Initial (wine) □ 2. Followed by /ʊ/ (would, woman)
□ 3. Followed by /uː/ (wound)

/r/ ... □ 1. Initial, medial (right, correct)
□ 2. Preceded by /p/, partially devoiced (pray) □ 3. Preceded by /b/ (bring)
□ 4. Preceded by /t/, partially devoiced (tree) □ 5. Preceded by /d/ (dry)
□ 6. Preceded by /k/, partially devoiced (cream) □ 7. Preceded by /g/ (grow)
□ 8. Preceded by /f/, (free) □ 9. Preceded by /θ/ (three)
□ 10. Preceded by /n/ (Henry) □ 11. Followed by /ɚ/ (mirror)

/j/ ... □ 1. Initial (yes) □ 2. Followed by /iː/ (yield)
□ 3. Followed by /ɪɚ/ (year)

/hw/ ... □ 1. Initial (what)

Vowels: /iː/ ... □ 1. (Pete) /ɪ/ ... □ 2. (pit) /e/ ... □ 3. (pet)
/æ/ ... □ 4. (pat) /ɑ/ ... □ 5. (pot) /ɔː/ ... □ 6. (paw) /ʊ/ ... □ 7. (put)
/uː/ ... □ 8. (boot) /ʌ/ ... □ 9. (putt) /ɚː / ... □ 10. (purse) /eɪ/ ... □ 11. (pain)
/aɪ/ ... □ 12. (pine) /ɔɪ/ ... □ 13. (point) /aʊ/ ... □ 14. (pouch)
/oʊ/ ... □ 15. (boat) /ɪɚ/ ... □ 16. (beer) /eɚ/ ... □ 17. (bear)

/ɑɚ/ ... □ 18. (bar) /ɔɚ/ ... □ 19. (bore) /ʊɚ/ ... □ 20. (poor)
/aɪɚ/ ... □ 21. (tire) /aʊɚ/ ... □ 22. (power) /ə/ ... □ 23. Initial (accept, italics)
□ 24. Medial (universe, family, tell them) □ 25. Final (sofa) /ɚ/ ... □ 26. (supper)

索　引
Index

1. まず日本語が五十音順に，次に英語がアルファベット順に並べてあり，最後に主な発音記号のリストがある．
2. 日本語・英語の項目は，用語そのもの，またはトピックである．
3. 発音記号は，連想される文字によりほぼアルファベット順に並べてある．

[あ行]

[か行]

[さ行]

[た行]

[な行]

[は行]

[ま行]

[や行・ら行・わ]

[英語]

[A]

[B]

[C]

[D]

[E/F]

[G]

[H/I]

[V]

[W]

[発音記号]

著者紹介

松坂 ヒロシ（まつさか　ひろし）

MATSUSAKA Hiroshi
Professor Emeritus, Waseda University
Visiting Professor, Shumei University

1948年東京生まれ．早稲田大学教育学部英語英文学科卒，東京外国語大学修士課程（英語学）およびレディング大学修士課程（英語教育学）修了．早稲田大学にて英語教育，英語教員養成に当たり，2019年より早稲田大学名誉教授，秀明大学客員教授．著書『英語音声学入門』（研究社，1986）ほか．共訳書『議論学への招待 ― 建設的なコミュニケーションのために』（著者 van Eemeren, Snoeck Henkemans，共訳者鈴木健，大修館書店，2018）．高校英語教科書 *POLESTAR English Communication*（数研出版）ほか代表著者．もと NHK ラジオ「英語会話」，「英語リスニング入門」，NHK テレビ「英語会話 II」，「ニュースで英会話プラス」講師．

歯型と絵で教える英語発音
―発音をはじめて教える人へ―
(*Teaching English Pronunciation to Learners in Japan: Recipes for using a jaw model and illustrations*)

著作者　松坂ヒロシ
発行者　武 村 哲 司
印刷所　日之出印刷株式会社

2021年9月16日　第1版第1刷発行

発行所　株式会社　開 拓 社
〒112-0013 東京都文京区音羽 1-22-16
電話　(03) 5395-7101　（代表）
振替　00160-8-39587
http://www.kaitakusha.co.jp

ISBN978-4-7589-2355-2　C3082